ANCIENT WISDOM

THIS IS A CARLTON BOOK

Design copyright © 2000 Carlton Books Limited
Text copyright © 2000 Vivianne and Christopher Crowley

This edition published by Carlton Books Limited 2000
20 Mortimer Street
London
W1N 7RD

A CIP catalogue for this book is available from the British Library.

ISBN 1 84222 022 5

Executive Editor: Sarah Larter
Art Direction: Diane Spender
Picture research: Sharon Southren
Production: Janette Davis
Jacket Design: Alison Tutton

ANCIENT WISDOM

EARTH TRADITIONS IN THE TWENTY-FIRST CENTURY
VIVIANNE & CHRISTOPHER CROWLEY

CONTENTS

INTRODUCTION

Ndebele shaman of
South Africa performing
a divination using the
rays of the setting sun.

Long before the great prophets created religions based on sacred text, dogma and creed, people worshipped the spirits of hill, stream, star, wind and tree. They worshipped the forces of nature and venerated the changing seasons. They created myths and legends that told of the hopes, joys, dangers, fears, despairs, and reawakening to hope again of our human lives. They knew the hidden powers of the human mind. Through trance, vision, divination, magical rite and spell, their shamans journeyed into the future to guide their peoples. They learned to use the powers of nature and of the human psyche to protect, to heal and to lead people safely through life's perils. These spiritual traditions are called Pagan, indigenous, primal, traditional or tribal. They have often been in conflict with world religions. They have affirmed the power of ordinary people to take control of their own destiny rather than to have their spiritual life dictated by others. In the twenty-first century, many of these traditions are enjoying a resurgence as people recognize that rites and ceremonies that were once dismissed as mere superstition can transform our lives in powerful and meaningful ways.

From the Americas to the Antipodes, from the Stone Age to the present day, this book explores the rise, development and current resurgence of ancient spiritual belief systems. Their resurgence is all the more remarkable given that most have been at some time marginalized, discredited, driven underground or taken over by the orthodoxy of the day in an attempt to eradicate them altogether. We investigate the philosophy that underpins each belief system – its myths, rituals, magical practices and initiation rites, and explain their relevance to us as we enter the new millennium. We cannot cover all the myriad beliefs and traditions practised on our planet, so we concentrate on those of Europe, North and South America, Africa and Australasia. From these many and varied climates, continents and peoples emerges a picture of difference but also of an underlying similarity in the way that human beings have sought to make sense of their universe. We look at traditions of Europe – Celtic, Scandinavian, Baltic and Slavic. We turn northwards to discover the Inuit and Sami traditions that cover the Arctic Circle, and spread into Russia, Scandinavia and Northern America. We travel down through the American continent, meeting Native American tradition both North and South. In North and South America, we also encounter African-based traditions such as Santeria, Voudon and Umbanda, which thrive among those of African descent and appeal to many others. We turn eastwards across the Atlantic to the home of African traditions and then South and East again to the ancient Australian aboriginal traditions and the newer traditions of New Zealand's Maoris.

Some of these traditions, such as the Australian aboriginal tradition, are practised almost solely in their ancestral homelands. Others have migrated with their peoples to other continents far away. Some of these traditions have been practised openly and continuously throughout the centuries. Others, such as the European pagan traditions, have been savagely suppressed and driven underground. Only now are they undergoing a revival. There are common themes and concerns among these traditions. How best to live in harmony with our planet is a key aim. These traditions tend also to share a view of the cosmos that is different from the conventional Western one. They live in a cosmos that is alive; in which

plants, rocks, crystals and stars have energies that can affect the human psyche. They live in a cosmos in which energy can be psychically used and transformed. In other words, they practise what is often called "magic". They seek to understand the hidden trends and currents of energy that influence our lives and to work with them. Divination through dreams and other special divination systems are common in these traditions. They inhabit societies in which the living are close to the spirits of the dead. The ancestors and their wisdom and knowledge are close at hand and there is a living continuity between past and present.

As we enter the twenty-first century, it is time to acknowledge the wisdom of the past, not in order to turn our backs on all the advantages that our modern societies have to offer, but to come to a greater understanding of ourselves and to see what we may take from the past into the present in order to build a better world in the future to come.

Shaman's curing rattle from the Haida people of Canada's Queen Charlotte Islands, off Canada's Northwest Pacific Islands.

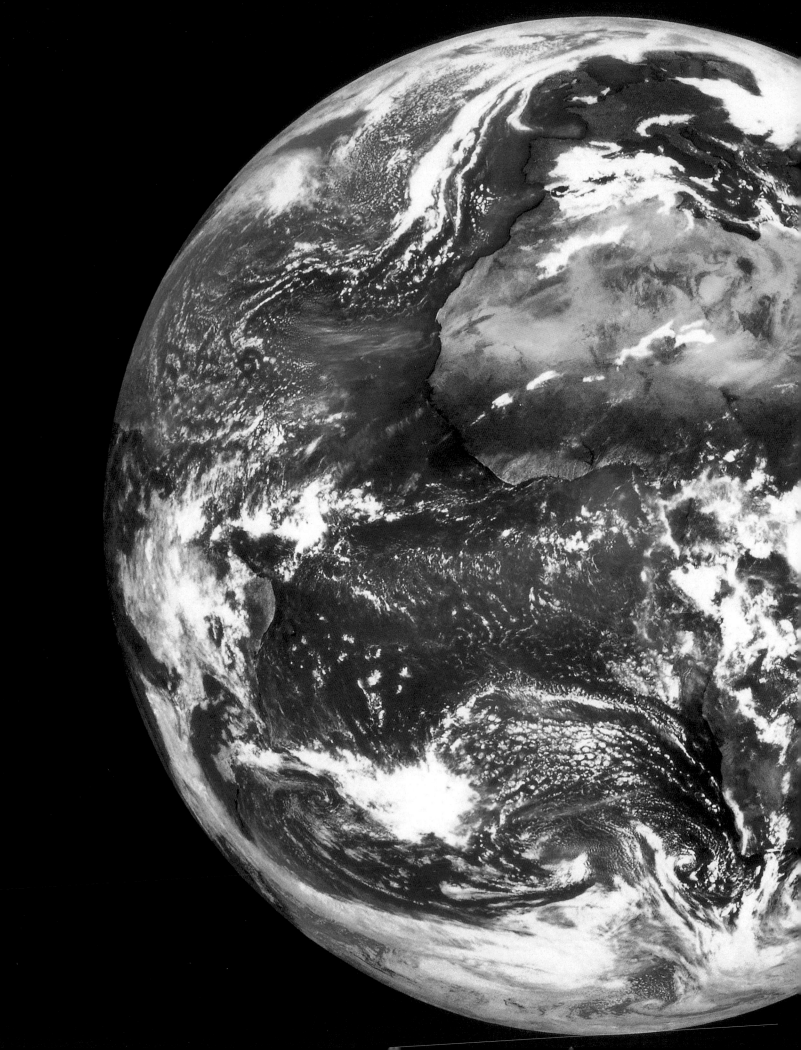

IN THE BEGINNING

In a spiral galaxy of old and new stars called by some the Milky Way, revolving around a five billion-year-old Sun, is a small but beautiful planet, green with vegetation and blue with iridescent oceans. An animal species dominates the planet. Some say they are warlike and destructive. Others point to their great capacity for love and to the beautiful artefacts they can create and say that they are an unusually imaginative species that is destined to evolve and survive. On certain days of the year, fervent prayers and chants might be heard coming from the planet. These are the festival celebrations of the various religious calendars. Some celebrate events in the history of their followers; others commemorate events in the life of a prophet; and others invoke the seasons' change. In their religious celebrations, these humans venerate deities. Some venerate their deity as abstract spirit, others in human or animal form; and others as a force that lies hidden within the wind, sky, Sun, star, Moon, rock, sea, stream and tree. How did these spiritual longings begin?

IN THE BEGINNING

Looking outward from our planet to the starry realms that surround us, we humans tend to take our spiritual longings for granted. We do speculate, however, on how we and this wondrous Universe in which we find ourselves were created. All cultures have myths of origin that represent people's attempts to make sense of the world around them and to understand the place of humankind in cosmic events. To find answers, we looked at the world around us. We knew how young were born – mammals came from the womb, birds hatched from eggs – so we created myths that explained how the Universe was born from the womb of a goddess or hatched by a great cosmic bird. Some myths asked a further question: how were the gods themselves created? The most powerful forces our ancestors knew were the elements – heat and cold, fire and ice, wind and

The world's creation myths often describe human beings as created from earth and clay. Adam comes from the Hebrew, Adamah, meaning "earth".

rain, sea and earth. So our ancient myths told of how natural forces had interacted and from these the gods were born who then brought order to the cosmos. In Norse myth, for instance, the Universe is created from the interaction of fire and ice, but the early Universe is chaotic. It needs the thinking capacity of the gods to order the world and put the stars, planets, seas, sky and earth in their rightful places. The language is that of symbol and poetic image but, in a way, of course, our ancestors were right.

FIRE AND ICE

Myths are not reality. Our early ancestors thought that the Earth was flat. They were wrong. We live on a globe, but the Universe itself is flat, rather like a smooth flat disc expanding into infinity. Modern cosmologists have discovered that our Universe began around 12–20 billion years ago with the "Big Bang", perhaps as part of a chain reaction in which the death of one universe gave rise to many parallel universes. At the instant of the Big Bang, the Universe was both dense and intensely hot. The Big Bang was accompanied by rapid expansion and as the Universe expanded it cooled and underwent what is called a phase transition, just like when water freezes into ice – so the myths that speak of the Universe being born of fire and ice are true. From the Big Bang began matter, energy, space and time. After the cooling, an enormous quantity of energy was released in a process known as symmetry breaking. The Universe began to expand exponentially – and is expanding still. Expansion brought cooling. Rapidly, matter began to form – photons, quarks, neutrinos and electrons, followed by protons and neutrons. The dropping temperature allowed protons and neutrons to join together instead of being torn apart. Nuclei began to form, especially helium, which consists of two protons and two neutrons. Most of the remaining protons became hydrogen. The gases that we know today, and which create the basis for life, were born. These atomic nuclei became the seeds of stars. We could say that this all happened very quickly. Cosmologists talk in terms of nanoseconds and

seconds, but time was not yet meaningful. It was only when the cosmos began to stabilize that we can talk meaningfully about time. Eleven billion years ago, stars and galaxies began to form. The elements on which life depends – carbon, nitrogen, and oxygen – and metals such as iron, copper and gold, were created. Planets formed and began to orbit stars, creating solar systems such as our own. Stars themselves are organized into galaxies, which in turn are bound together in clusters by gravity. Bounded by enormous voids, superclusters of galaxies stretch out like gigantic sheets across hundreds of billions of light years. Our own galaxy, the Milky Way, is a spiral, containing older and younger stars, one of which is our Sun. Orbiting the Sun is Earth, the rotating planet that we call "home".

LIFE BEGINS

Fossil evidence shows that biological life developed on our planet around 3,850 million years ago, less than 700 million years after the Earth's formation. At first life comprised simple single-celled organisms, such as *Archaea*, bacteria of ancient origin that still live in hostile environments such as hot springs. About two billion years ago, eukaryotic cells began to evolve by ingesting other species

The Big Bang was the titanic explosion that created our Universe.

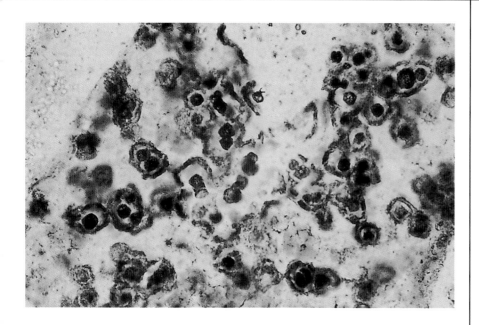

This light micrograph shows fossil remains of two billion-year-old life forms – the earliest yet found.

of cells and incorporating them as permanent, genetically reproducible parts of themselves. Some began to act as "engines", converting solar radiation into chemical energy. This was the basis of biological life. From simple structures we moved to more complex. Some eukaryotic cells combined to form multi-celled organisms and began to diversify dramatically. Around one billion years ago, the higher groupings of life, which scientists call the eukaryote crown groups, appeared. Today, we have five species groups: animals, fungi, green plants, red algae and a more recently discovered group called stramenopiles, most of which look like plants but do not photosynthesize.

HUMANKIND

Most aware and versatile among the animal species are humans. We first began to evolve from apes between five million and seven million years ago. Between one million and four million years ago, the *Australopithecines* evolved in eastern and southern Africa. Recently, a complete *Australopithecine* skeleton, nearly three and a half million years old, was found near Johannesburg in South Africa. About two million years ago, *Homo erectus*, human beings who could walk on two legs, began to evolve from one species of *Australopithicines*. *Homo erectus* were human beings

with intellectual curiosity. They learned to use fire for cooking, though it is not clear whether they could make fire or had to rely on keeping alight fires that occurred spontaneously. They also used fire to harden wooden spears, and made other tools, such as split bone knives and a variety of stone tools. They had effective hunting techniques, which involved co-operation and working together in teams. They could kill and trap whole troops of baboons as well as large animals such as elephants. They led a hunter-gatherer lifestyle, following large herds of animals in their migrations and returning each season to the same encampments. They had memory and knew how to find their way home – co-operative ventures such as large-scale hunting require the ability to plan in advance and to communicate strategies. The parts of the brain that control language developed. Human beings began to communicate with one another using signs and words. The ability to use fire enabled them to make tools and with tools they could skin the animals they killed for food. Skins could serve as clothing, sleeping covers, mats to warm the floors of caves and bundles for transporting tools and food. Fire helped humans use a wider range of foods. Roots and berries that would be poisonous when eaten raw could be nutritious when cooked. Fire, clothing and wider food sources meant that people could leave the warm climate of Africa and migrate into Europe and Asia.

HOMO SAPIENS: PRE-NEANDERTHALS AND NEANDERTHALS

The first *Homo sapiens* (*sapiens* is Latin for "wise") appeared around half a million years ago and are known as transitionals or pre-Neanderthals. Pre-Neanderthals had larger brains than *Homo erectus* and so could think and communicate better. Their skulls evolved to look less ape-like. Pre-Neanderthals human began to think symbolically – one of the first steps toward understanding the abstract and non-material worlds. At Lazaret Cave in France, pre-Neanderthals pitched tents inside and outside the cave placing wolf skulls at the entrances as symbols of power.

Around 125,000 years ago, a new type of human being appeared – the Neanderthals. In Europe, Neanderthal skeletons have been found that are between 75,000–125,000 years old, while in Africa skeletons dating from 35,000–125,000 years ago have been found. The name Neanderthal is derived from one of the first Neanderthal sites, discovered in the Neander Valley in northwest Germany. Neanderthals spread all over Africa, the Middle and Near East, Asia and Europe. There are some who think they also entered North America via the Bering land bridge from Siberia, but that is still unproven.

Neanderthals were similar in appearance to people today, but with thicker bones and shorter limbs. They are likely to have been hairless and, like us, may have had a variety of skin colours depending on how much exposure they had to sunlight. Their brains were slightly larger, but less complex. Their front teeth were worn and rounded, something that develops from chewing hides to soften them for use. They had better tools than earlier humans. They could make hole punches, scrapers, knives and spear points – punching holes in leather allows thongs to be inserted to make more complex clothing. Neanderthals also made jewellery such as pierced

pendants. They were aware of their own and other people's appearance.

Neanderthals would have used language but their neck development meant that they might not have had the vocal range we have today. They could, however, probably chant or sing. A recent archaeological find shows that Neanderthals could make music. At a Neanderthal site near the modern city of Ljubljana, in what is now Slovenia (formerly Yugoslavia), archaeologists have found a segment of a flute made from the femur of a young bear. The flute can make notes in the major western music scale – the do, ray, mi scale. The flute has yet to be dated accurately but is around 43,000–82,000 years old, making it the world's oldest known musical instrument.

Neanderthals had more advanced ideas about non-material reality than their forebears. Burial customs evolved. Bodies were placed in graves in ways that suggest some idea of an afterlife. People were laid in the foetal position with the head facing West and the feet pointing East – the directions of the setting and rising Sun. Bodies were smeared with red ochre, a pigment derived from iron ore and possibly used to symbol-ize the blood of the womb and hence hope of rebirth. Flowers were placed in graves in the same way that we take flowers to funerals today. One grave discovered at Shanidar Cave in northern Iraq features a man lying on a mattress or mat of woven plants. Several species of flower, all with medicinal properties, were placed in the grave, perhaps to heal him in the afterlife or perhaps because he

ABOVE: Fossil skulls discovered in East Turkana, Kenya.

LEFT: Burial rites distinguish us from our animal ancestors and began with the Neanderthals.

was shaman and these were the tools of his trade. Other graves included people's personal property, such as their flint tools. Neanderthals may have had fears of the dead returning to haunt the living. Some bodies were bound before burial and in some cases heavy stones were placed on graves. The latter may have been to prevent them being disturbed by animals, but the practice of placing heavy stones on graves is still found today in many societies. In some cases, such as in Roma (Gypsy) burials, it is to prevent the spirit wandering.

Family ties seemed important. Some Neanderthals were buried in extended family groups. The old and sick were cared for by their families. Burials at Shanidar in Iraq include the grave of an elderly man who could use only one hand and one foot, and at La Chapelle aux Saints in France, graves included people with disabling arthritis. Whereas earlier humans would have left them to die, Neanderthals cared for the sick and frail.

Pre-Neanderthals reverenced animal skulls, but Neanderthals had more advanced rituals, including a bear cult. At several cave sites, bear skulls were collected and put in prominent places in special arrangements. In Switzerland, a number of bear skulls were found stacked in a stone chest, the top of which was covered by a large stone slab. In Regourdou in southern France archaeologists have found a rectangular pit covered by a massive stone slab weighing nearly a ton and containing the remains of at least 20 bears. There may also have been hunting ceremonies. A 50,000-year-old site at a cave in Lebanon revealed a dismembered deer, which had been placed on a bed of stones and sprinkled with red ochre, in the same way as a human body would be prepared for burial.

The development of tools began the evolutionary process that allowed human societies to become more complex.

FROM NEANDERTHALS TO MODERN HUMANS

Where did modern human beings – *Homo sapiens sapiens* – come from? Some scientists believe they evolved from Neanderthals and others that two different species – Neanderthals and *Homo sapiens sapiens* – evolved from *Homo erectus*. One became the Neanderthals, who later became extinct, and the other group became modern humans. A third theory is that *Homo sapiens* and *Homo erectus* evolved separately, with *Homo sapiens* becoming modern humans and *Homo erectus* becoming Neanderthals. In some areas of the world, such as Skhul and Qafzeh in Israel, there are human fossil remains dating from 80,000–100,000 years ago that look much more like modern humans than Neanderthals.

Whatever our earliest origins, we know that modern humans and Neanderthals co-existed for around 50,000–60,000 years, until Neanderthals disappeared approximately 30,000–40,000 years ago. At one point it was believed that Neanderthals and modern humans could not mate, but we now know that they did. In the Near East there is evidence that Neanderthals and modern humans lived together. At the Qafzeh site in Israel, 60,000–90,000-year-old skeletons show a wide range of anatomy that is a mixture of Neanderthals and moderns. This interbred species seemed better adapted to survival than Neanderthals. Skeletons show fewer signs of fractures and stress. DNA tests on skeletons found recently show that some people were hybrids with a mixture of modern human and Neanderthal DNA. The most recent hybrid skeleton find occurred on November 28, 1998, in an area known to be one of the last refuges of the Neanderthals. A chance discovery turned up the 24,500-year-old skeleton of a four-year-old hybrid child at Abrigo do Lagar Velho, Portugal. The child had been buried with a pierced shell ornament and had been wrapped in a cloth sprinkled with red ochre. Over time, the Neanderthals disappeared as a separate species and hybrids were absorbed without trace into the main human population.

MODERN HUMANS

Modern humans probably developed first in central and southern Africa around 60,000–120,000 years ago and then began to spread. Around 50,000 years ago, we migrated East across the Asian rim to Southeast Asia. Modern humans reached Europe around 40,000 years ago, the western Pacific around 32,000 years ago, and the Americas 13,000–30,000 years ago. Migration was assisted by low sea levels. Many areas that are now under water had land bridges. Britain was joined to continental Europe by a land bridge and there was a land bridge where the Bosphorus now separates European Turkey from Asian Turkey. Over centuries, people could easily migrate from Asia to Europe. Rafts assisted human migration. Rafts were developed for fishing offshore but began to be used for longer journeys. Around 35,000 years ago, during a period of low sea level, humans could walk from the Malay Peninsula to what are now the Indonesian islands of Sumatra and Java. They could then travel by rafts to Australia. Once in Australia, people could walk to New Guinea and Tasmania.

At what is now the Bering Strait, another land bridge joined Siberia in northeast Asia to Alaska in North America. Successive waves of Asians crossed the Bering land bridge and fanned out across North and South America. It had been thought that the earliest human inhabitation of South America is a dwelling in Monte Verde that is around 12,500 years old, but claims have been made that another site in Chile is around 30,000 years old. Some dates have yet to be established, but we know that by 10,000 years ago, human beings had moved into most regions of the world except for some islands, the high Arctic and remote areas such as Polynesia, which required good navigational skills to reach. Antarctica, of course, was never inhabited.

THE STONE AGES

Modern humans differ from Neanderthals by being more graceful, with smaller brow ridges, faces and teeth, higher foreheads and small backs of skulls. By the Old Stone Age, the Palaeolithic era, our ancestors looked pretty much like ourselves, though without the flab of modern western human beings, and had the distinguishing feature of modern humans – a gap in the ridge brow or torus between the eyebrows, where the skull goes flat.

About 50,000 years ago, we began to develop artistic appreciation. We began to adorn ourselves, for unlike other animals such as birds we lack bright plumage and other attributes to attract mates. Women made themselves short tunics, and a wider range of jewellery appeared. We learned to beautify essential objects. Carving and making beautiful patterns on domestic objects and weapons could while away the long dark hours of winter. Symbolic figures appear, which suggests that our ideas about religion had evolved. Crude female figurines made from fire-hardened clay have been found which may represent fertility goddesses, and we also began to carve ivory and bone figurines. We began to paint pictures on rock, often of mystical significance and hidden so deep in hard to access caves that there are suggestions that they were used as part of initiatory rites of passage. So vivid and full of artistic talent are these pictures that when the first paintings were re-discovered in 1879 at Altamira in Spain, they were dismissed as a hoax.

Prehistoric rock painting showing a hunter holding a bow.

SPIRIT REALMS

Hunter-gatherer societies, both ancient and those that have survived into modern times, venerate the guardian spirits of each animal species. These guardians could help humankind by releasing animals to the hunters, but in return they must be honoured. They expect the animals that are hunted to be treated with respect and if sacred taboos are violated they will turn their faces from humankind and the hunt will fail. The forces of wind, snow and rain are also honoured, for they can help or hinder the hunt. Sometimes the spirits are favourable; at other times they are silent. Perhaps we have angered them and they have set themselves against us? We need to communicate with the forces that control our lives, but how?

People in all societies notice that in certain states of consciousness we can sense slightly different realities from those of the everyday world. We find that we have dreams that sometimes seem more vivid than life itself. You may remember, especially when you were a child, that when you dreamed something it was not always easy to tell whether the event had occurred in the outer world or in your dream. Maybe, our ancestors wondered, these dream states held clues to how the Universe really worked? Perhaps if we could induce these dreams states, we could communicate with the forces that control the movement of herds, the migration of birds, and even the weather? Our ancestors began to experiment with ways to enter altered states of consciousness. Some plants and fungi produce dreams and visions of extraordinary intensity, which can seem to take us into other parallel spirit worlds. These

became gateways. Drumming can induce a hypnotic trance that has a similar effect. Other methods evolved, such as secreting ourselves in dark quiet places like underground caves. Fasting can open the gateways, as can long vigils in the wild – vision quests. Other gateways into the spirit worlds come through near-death experiences. Common to all cultures are tales of those who have come close to death and have returned to tell of extraordinary journeys. Even today, we find that many people who have been close to dying recover to tell of similar visions – of finding themselves being drawn out of their physical bodies through what seems like a tunnel with light at the end. They emerge to find themselves in a beautiful realm where the normal laws of space and time do not apply. They can fly through the air and there are other beings there. Some see relatives who have died. Others see spirits who know them and know all about their lives. The realm seems incredibly peaceful and beautiful and often people are reluctant to return. However, in the near-death experience people sense that their time on Earth is not yet fin-

ished. They must go back. There are many biological explanations for these experiences. We can talk of endorphin secretion – the natural opiates in the brain that give us "highs", and of the hallucinations caused by loss of oxygen and blood supply to the brain. For those who have had such experiences, however, they are both life-enhancing and seem totally real. For our ancestors, untroubled by rational science, these experiences would seem like gateways to spirit realms.

The experiences that people have of other worlds seem to suggest that there is more than one. We know from contemporary near-death experiences that most people enter beautiful realms and meet beings that are beneficent. From these experiences our ancestors may have woven their myths of the Upper Worlds and of Heaven. A minority of people who have near-death experiences enter a world of terror and of frightening spirits, however, with little love for human beings. In frightening near-death experiences, people often find themselves spontaneously invoking the help of a deity or guardian spirit. These appeals are often successful. The individual experiences something or someone who comes to his or her aid, and so the idea of personal guardian deities or spirits is born.

SHAMANISM

We know from contemporary accounts of near-death experiences that people encounter both dead relatives and deities. Our ancestors believed that by entering the spirit realms, we could communicate with ancestors who might be able to guide us about community problems and with deities that controlled those things on which life depended. Some people were found to be better at entering these parallel realities than others. Their visions were clearer and their guardian spirits appeared stronger. The deities and ancestors spoke more clearly to them than to others. They asked questions of them and came back with useful information. On some occasions, people could undertake the journey into the other realms for themselves, but when it came to dealing with powerful forces, such as spirits whom

Puberty initiation rite, Ghana.

the community might have offended, then perhaps this was a specialist job. The profession of shaman was born.

The word *shaman* first became known in European languages when eighteenth-century German explorers encountered Siberian peoples whose trance practitioners were known as *sama:n*. Soon the word *schaman* appeared in German and later in other languages. Traditional religious belief was largely shamanistic. The role of the shaman was to travel into, and mediate between, the world of everyday reality and the "other worlds". In a shamanistic world view, the cosmos is divided into many layers. The shaman, who is helped or hindered by various spirits, is thought to be able to travel in trance between them and, in so doing, to achieve an integration that is essential both to the health of individuals and to the well-being of the community. Shamanism was humankind's earliest religion. For many indigenous peoples shamanism is still the foundation of their spiritual beliefs and shamanistic ideas are found all over the world. Even within the world religions, our ideas of Heaven and Hell, of guardian angels and of protective deities, are founded on our early ancestors' visions of the other worlds.

RITES OF PASSAGE

Religion serves many purposes. It provides bridges whereby human beings can communicate with the realm of spirit. The rites and ceremonies that religion evolves are also satisfying on other levels. Living in communities is not easy. It creates rivalries and tensions. One of the functions of religion is to bind together disparate groups within society. Rites and ceremonies become a means of creating social cohesion. In the earliest societies, our religious practices are there to help us survive – they help us contact the forces that provide our food. Later, our religious practices also have social purposes. They help us understand our relationships to one another and help to bind communities. Our rites and ceremonies remind us of our shared values and traditions. Sociobiologists maintain that we are biologically programmed to propagate our genes and to survive as a species. Those behaviours that help us survive will develop further through a process of natural selection. Those behaviours that are dysfunctional, such as uncontrolled aggression, are naturally bred out of the human gene pool. Religion helped us live together; our rites and ceremonies helped us survive.

Rites and ceremonies have other social purposes. As societies evolved they devised rites of passage to mark the transition from childhood to adulthood. They marked the time when we had to take on adult responsibilities in our communities and were accompanied by teachings about the myths of our communities and of the relationship between our peoples and their gods. Other rites marked the transition to marriage. They celebrated the creation of a new relationship that would give rise to children who would be the lifeblood of the community and would ensure its survival. There were rites that taught us women's mysteries of menstruation and childbirth and men's mysteries that taught the responsibilities of husbands and fathers. Religion provided rites to rejoice in a new birth, to cope with the sorrow of death, or to rejoice in the making of a leader. These rites of passage are still found in our religious traditions today.

Our first tools, such as this Neolithic grinder, were those that helped us hunt and cook food. Later, we evolved agricultural tools and tools to grind corn.

AGRICULTURE

Shamanism develops in hunter-gatherer societies. With the transition to agriculture, new spiritual visions emerge. Agriculture evolved in the New Stone Age, or Neolithic, era when human knowledge made rapid advances. We began to use sledges and we tamed wild dogs to pull them. We invented new tools such as needles and harpoons. We learned to gather seeds and prepare the ground so that the seeds could grow better, but we had no understanding of how to nurture the soil. We over-used and exhausted the land and then moved on. We found the solution when we domesticated and bred animals to provide meat, milk, transport, leather and wool. We learned to use the manure our farm animals produced to improve soil quality. We also learned when to rest the soil and how to rotate crops. Around 10,000–12,000 years ago, in Asia Minor and in the great river valleys of Iraq and Egypt, human beings began to establish settled farming communities.

With the transition to agriculture, our ancestors had to learn to make a new relationship with the world of nature. From a lifestyle that involved following migrating animal herds or travelling long distances in search of game, many of our ancestors made a transition to being in control of land. With agriculture came the need for settlements. People cleared certain areas of land and put large amounts of work into it. Having done so, they were keen to retain control of that land for themselves and their families. It became necessary to guard that land – by force if necessary. In the new way of life, new deities were needed – deities of the land who could ensure the fertility of the soil, and deities of the elements who could protect harvests from adverse weather and send rain and sun at their appointed seasons. People also needed guardian deities who could help them protect their land and who could

20

make them fierce in battle when strangers came to threaten them. They needed deities and weapons of war.

THE METAL AGES

Around 5,000 years ago in the Nile Valley, Iraq and Syria, humans began casting copper. Later we developed bronze. By 3,500 years ago we were using iron. The use of iron gradually supplanted bronze and copper as, in the never-ending human struggle for territory, those who had not kept up with the new technology were conquered or killed by those that had. As human goods became more complex and specialized, different societies found that their natural resources and skills enabled them to make some things but not others. With the human love for what is new, beautiful and useful, trade developed between different societies in order for everyone to access the widest range of goods possible. From canoes evolved large boats that could be used for long-range trading trips. Until a few years ago, we thought that it was only in recent history that journeys were made from Africa to South America, but there is now increased speculation that many thousands of years ago some South American or Old World traders began to cross the Atlantic Ocean. Some of the first "hard" evidence dates back to 1933, when a Roman head made in black terracotta and dating from around 200 CE was found in Mexico. The archaeological site on which it was found indicates that traders brought it to Mexico before the Spanish conquest.

Trading societies need records – for stock in hand, profit and loss, taxes, ownership shares and property inheritance. To keep records, humans began to create signs and symbols on whatever came to hand – clay tablets, pieces of bark, metal, stone, parchment, wood or paper. At first only these more mundane matters were recorded, but with time humans evolved complex writing with symbols for each sound in the language. Whole sentences could be recorded with all their nuances, and we began to write down myths, poetry, songs, love letters and dreams, as well as our tax records and treasury inventories. With agricul-

ture and trade, communities grew richer. They could feed themselves more easily, leaving time to develop other skills and interests, such as pottery, advanced tool making, writing, philosophy, astronomy, astrology, religion, poetry, painting, sculpture and music. Specialist occupations evolved and just as hunters had their deities, so too did farmers, potters, scribes, poets, priests and astrologers. Our deities began to multiply and religious ideas grew more complex.

TOMBS AND STANDING STONES

As human societies became more complex, so too did burial rites. In Neolithic Europe we began to build elaborate stone tombs that were covered with earth mounds. These formed community burial chambers. Bodies were exposed so that flesh separated from bones before the bones were stored inside the chambers with elaborate care. Tombs that are 7,000 years old have been found in Brittany in France and similar tombs were built elsewhere over a long period – around 3,500 years. Like Neanderthal burials, tombs

This 4,500-year-old clay tablet is a bill of sale for one field and one house. Real estate conveyancing documents and tax records are among some of the earliest writings found.

Poulnabrone Dolmen, a 4,500-year-old Neolithic burial site on The Burren, Country Clare, Ireland.

were built aligned to significant points on the horizon. Many were oriented toward the point where the Sun would rise on Midsummer's Day. In other parts of Europe, such as the Newgrange complex in Ireland, tombs were aligned to Midwinter sunrise. To build these tombs, our ancestors needed to be able to record time. Wooden poles, and later standing stones, were erected to mark points where sunrise occurred at different times of the year.

It was not only the movement of the Sun that interested our ancestors. Our ancestors had no light pollution and had nothing but primitive oil lamps to light the evening darkness. The stars were present and observable in a way that is not true for us today. At the entrances of their huts our ancestors watched the night sky and began to give names to the constellations and planets. Events like

eclipses are frightening when people do not understand how they are caused, but they become less frightening if we can predict when they will happen. Our ancestors observed phenomena like comets and eclipses and found that by placing stones at cardinal points or at sunrise and sunset at different times of the year, it became possible to predict important cosmic events. Those who understood the systems of calculation developed power.

SEASONAL RITES

With agriculture we became ever more dependent on the elements. Agricultural life is dictated by the rhythm of the seasons – when to plough, fertilize, sow, weed, reap and store. We needed to be able to record time and calendars evolved to tell us when the Sun would fade and days lengthen, and when the Sun would come again. Seasonal changes are partly predictable. There are warm seasons and cold seasons and they follow one another in an orderly fashion, but we did not know exactly when it would become warm, or indeed whether it definitely would. Once, shamans entered the spirit realms to ask the guardians to release animals for hunting. Now humans needed to communicate with the agri-

cultural gods to ensure that the land would be fertile, that sun and rain would come at their appointed times, and that the harvest would be good so that people might be fed. There were crucial times in the seasonal calendar: early spring, when the ground must be soft enough for ploughing; spring, the time of sowing; summer, when crops need both sun and rain; harvest, when we need to avert storms that might damage crops; autumn, when we must ensure that winter will not be so long that food supplies will run out; and winter, when we need assurance that days will eventually lengthen and that the Sun will return again. Patterns of seasonal festivals began to emerge, patterns that can be observed all over the world where agriculture is practised. These festival rites involved the whole community, communities which had become large since the development of agriculture. The festivals had to be performed at the appointed time, so the expertise of those who understood the standing stones and other time-recording systems was needed. With agricultural societies, professional priesthoods were born.

PERSONAL RELIGION

Religion also serves personal needs. Sociobiologists believe that religions arose to help us cope with the fears and anxieties of our existence; fears of illness, pain, accident, separation from those to whom we are bonded, and that final and ultimate fear of all humans – death. Our spiritual systems give us explanations for why bad things happen and how we were to prevent them. We devised ceremonies to avert bad luck and special talismans that could hold good magic and protect us from the "things that go bump in the night". Religion evolved to help us control the world around us and to appease, please and propitiate those forces within the Universe that controlled our lives, but which we did not understand. Humans evolved a conscience, an inner voice that told us that some things were in accordance with society's needs and wishes and other things were not. When we fulfil our social duties and the expectations of others, we feel good about ourselves. When we do not live up to the standards that we have learned, we feel guilt. Some aspects of religion involve admission of wrongdoing and rites and ceremonies of purification. They help us to deal with guilt. Religion is also a way for us to express thankfulness for

Native American Sun Dance ceremony.

Our ancestors were instinctive Sun worshippers. Even some higher primates appear to venerate the Sun. The baboon was a sacred animal to the ancient Egyptians, who had observed that at dawn baboons watch the sunrise in silence with paws upraised to greet it. Baboon statues and pictures frequently adorn Egyptian temples.

our survival – for children born in good health, good hunting, favourable weather and bountiful crops. It was natural for us to want to express our thanks to the Universe for its care of us and so ceremonies of rejoicing were developed.

Our earliest ancestors used their spiritual techniques to communicate with the gods for practical purposes but, in altered states of consciousness, we could reach states of ecstasy. These ceremonies were satisfying in themselves, creating outlets for singing, dancing, drumming and bodily adornment, and they drew us into spiritual realms where we could communicate with beings that were wise and loving. For some people, spiritual practice became a mystical end in itself. Personal spirituality was born.

REAWAKENING OUR SPIRITUAL VISION

Our earliest ancestors were animists who venerated the spirits that gave life to the things that surrounded them – trees, the earth, rocks, streams, springs, animal species, the Sun, Moon and stars. Later, people became polytheists. They imagined spirits as human-like beings. They began to form images of them and to depict these in drawing, painting, carving and sculpture. Sometimes, like the ancient Egyptian deities, these figures were part animal and part human to show that they were not of ordinary origin.

As political systems became more complex and nation states and empires began to evolve, societies needed to bind together disparate peoples with different religious backgrounds. We moved from an era of many gods – poly-

theism – to a consolidation of power as the idea of one god became attractive. Life was considerably simpler with only one deity and over the past 2,500 years the idea of monotheism was born. Monotheism has always been in conflict with those of other traditions and has looked down on those who preferred to retain their devotion to many deities. Indigenous spiritual traditions, such as those of Native Americans, Africans and Aborigines, were seen as "primitive" and "superstitious". They were denigrated, as were the indigenous pagan traditions of Europe and disparaged as outdated or even as evil. Other people's deities are problematic for those who believe that their deity is the only "right" way of worshipping the Divine.

The way in which traditional spiritual practitioners are described is symptomatic of a shift in the attitudes of western societies to peoples whose low technology lifestyle is accompanied by different sets of beliefs from our own. Once these peoples would have been described as "primitive" and their spiritual practitioners would have been called "witch doctors". Now we are aware that our technologically-based cultures have a great deal to learn from those societies that have remained living in closer harmony with nature and have held on to a set of values and beliefs that are less materialist, individualistic and ephemeral than western values. It is easy to romanticize the role of the shaman in traditional society. Much of the shamanic world view was useful, which is why it evolved and persisted, but in a world populated by spirits, whom it is important not to offend, life can be an anxiety-provoking business. One of the attractions of Christianity and other monotheistic religions is that there is only one deity to please or offend. The spiritual realm is moved from the everyday and everywhere to special days in a special place – church. For peoples such as the Inuit (Eskimo), who converted to Christianity in the nineteenth century, the new belief enabled them to get rid of many superstitious practices that were unhelpful in a modern society. Unfortunately, the danger of simplifying our spiritual world is that we lose its richness and beauty. Simplicity is attractive but it does not necessarily reflect reality.

Experts on religion divide our different faith traditions into different groups. The group that most people will be familiar with are the "world" religions. These are religions with millions of adherents. Some, like Buddhism, Hinduism, Christianity and Islam, have many nations who follow their teachings. These spiritual paths vary considerably, but they do share some common features. While they are old, in terms of human history they are relatively new. They are all faith traditions that have arisen in the last four thousand years or so. If that seems like a long time, remember that our species, *Homo sapiens sapiens*, is now known to have existed for over 100,000 years, and our earlier human ancestors walked our planet for millions of years before. We have had religious ideas for at least half a million years.

The primal religions are not ancient traditions now long dead. These religious traditions have survived into the present; often in spite of the world religions, which have sought to dominate our spirituality and to claim the human soul for their own. In the chapters that follow, we will look at spiritual traditions whose roots lie in the distant past, but whose beliefs are active and growing in the world today. If we approach these traditions with respect, we find that there is much that we can learn – a respect for our planet and the other species that inhabit it and, importantly for women but also for men, a spiritual vision in which the Divine is worshipped as goddess and not just as male god. We find traditions that have recognized that the human psyche has powers that in modern society we have neglected and left untapped. In reawakening and reclaiming these traditions, we expand our vision and spiritual horizons. We recover and renew the ancient wisdom that took our ancestors on a journey, from ape to humankind.

This Neolithic statuette of a fertility goddess is from Iraq and is around eight thousand years old.

THE CELTIC WORLD

Warriors and poets, dreamers and visionaries, idealists and lovers of righteous causes, the Celts are all these things and more. The Celts are also explorers and travellers, many of them in recent centuries because European economics and politics forced them to seek more hospitable shores. This Celtic diaspora means that many of us today have Celtic blood, even if we do not live in one of the Celtic nations. We know something of the Irish, Scottish, Welsh, Breton, Cornish or Manx versions of Celtic myths, legends and history through tales told us by our parents or our parents' parents. Today, Celtic artwork, with its beautiful patterns, is found everywhere, sometimes in too many places. How many Celtic key rings, mugs and tea towels do we need? Nevertheless, this does not detract from the beauty, power, grace and ability to move the soul, of the Celtic arts in all their forms — music, poetry, visual arts, and even the arts magical.

PREVIOUS PAGE: Modern druids conducting the Midsummer ceremony at Stonehenge Neolithic monument, England. The popularity of the rites led the British government to ban them in the 1980s and 1990s, however, limited access is again being permitted.

WHO ARE THE CELTS?

The ancestors of the Celts are believed to be the proto-Indo European peoples who lived near the Black Sea around 4000 BCE. Some migrated southwest to Thrace and Greece. Others migrated North and West. In Slovakia, there are artefacts dating around 1000 BCE of a proto-Celtic civilization known as Urnfield culture because of the people's distinctive use of urns to inter the remains of their dead. Urnfield culture began to evolve into the peoples we call the Celts around 800 BCE. Over the next six hundred years, this culture spread eastward to Bulgaria and Turkey, South into what are now Spain and Portugal, and westward into Austria, Germany, France, and across the water to the British Isles and Ireland.

The Celts were a tribal people, ruled by a chieftain or king chosen from among the relatives of the previous chief. Chiefs were usually male, but some female rulers emerged – usually the wives of chiefs who had died. In this way, Boudicca became queen of the Iceni tribe in England. Celts enjoyed fighting and inter-tribal warfare was a way of life. To be a warrior hero was a source of great prestige. With the expansion of the Roman Empire, the Celts came under threat from an organized and disciplined military force in the modern style. Roman military might had no interest in the staged heroic battles of individual champions that was the romanticism of Celtic warfare. Rome exploited Celtic inter-tribal rivalries in much the same way as Europeans later exploited the traditional rivalries of African and Native American peoples – and with the same result. Disunited, the tribes were conquered. There was considerable resistance by many Celtic tribes to Rome, but much of Celtic society adopted Roman customs of living in urban environments with some of the facilities that we would now think of as modern – sewage, street lighting and places of public entertainment. Celtic deities fused with Roman ones and customs such as worshipping deities in indoor temples were adopted. Shortly after the Roman invasion of Britain in 43 CE by the army of the Emperor Claudius, the Romans encouraged the building of public baths at Bath, where waters with healing properties emerge from the ground at a temperature of 46°C (115°F) at a rate of over 1 million litres (250,000 gallons) a day. The Celtic Goddess Sulis was merged with the Roman goddess of wisdom, Minerva, as Sulis Minerva, to preside over the healing waters and statues were made of her in the Roman style. In southern Britain, Celtic chieftains built

The Celtic-Roman goddess Sulis Minerva, from the pump room of Roman baths, Bath, England.

themselves Roman villas and cultivated vines. The Celts were being introduced, or maybe seduced, by the pleasures and comforts of an urban way of life.

DRUIDS

Druids are known as a Celtic priesthood, but they may have existed before the coming of the Celts. In any event, by the time of the Roman conquest of Western Europe, they were the most powerful force in Celtic society. Although kings and chieftains had political control, the druids controlled the religious and legal systems within which the leaders had to operate. No king could rule without his druid adviser and Merlin's relationship with King Arthur is but a pale reflection of the power a pre-Christian druid may have had over his king. Most druid advisers seemed to be male. Women were, however, esteemed as seeresses. Those whose advice was good would attract visitors from all over their own kingdoms and beyond. Seeresses were called Veledas or Ueledas among continental Celts and by titles such as Banfhili, female seer, by the Irish.

The high status of druids is obvious from the role they play in myths, but it can also be seen in the legal system. Celtic society was clan based. When an individual committed a wrong, it was the responsibility not only of the individual, but also of his or her extended family or clan. Celts did not favour retribution in the form of "an eye for an eye". The criminal justice system was largely based around fines that it was the clan responsibility to pay. Not surprisingly, there was enormous social pressure on individuals to keep on the right side of the law. Kinship bonds meant that murder was considered a crime that was not only an offence toward the deceased but also to his or her family and clan. The fine or "honour price" that had to be paid varied with the status of the individual attacked. The price demanded for a druid was so high as to make destitute the clan who had to pay the fine. This gave druids a privileged status. They could travel freely and could walk through a battlefield to act as peacemakers and be almost

immune to attack. Worse than being forced to pay large fines was the threat that druids could exclude an offending clan from religious rites. This brought ostracization, shame and the risk of so severely offending the gods that disaster would surely follow.

Merlin was druid adviser to the legendary Celtic king Arthur of Britain. In later texts he is described as a magician.

RELIGION

The word druid may have derived from *drus* or oak tree and prior to the coming of the Romans, the Celts worshipped their deities in sacred groves of trees. The sacred and mysterious seemed to a Celt to be more easily found in nature than in a building made by human hands. The Romans were clever politicians and the occupation of Celtic Europe was designed wherever possible to woo or coerce the Celtic aristocracy into becoming collaborators, good Roman citizens and part of the Roman power structure. Quite rightly, the Romans perceived the druids, with enormous influence over the population, as a dangerous threat to their power. Unlike Celtic rulers, druids were strongly suppressed. The Romans never reached Ireland and considered Scotland too economically non-viable, or its inhabitants too wild and frightening, or a bit of both, to go so far North. A wall was built across Britain to keep the inhabitants of Scotland out, patrolled by bored and disgruntled Roman soldiers who wrote home to their families complaining of primitive conditions, damp and freezing cold.

South of the wall in the first few centuries CE, the destruction of the druids left a spiritual void. This and Romanization created a cultural climate that left the Celts open to the new Roman import of Christianity. Celts adopted Christianity long before it reached more northerly parts of Europe. Christianity took root first in Celtic continental Europe, England and Wales, and was then exported to Ireland. Clever preachers such Patrick who were educated, and willing and ready to do intellectual and, where necessary magical battle, with the druids crossed the Irish Sea and marketed the benefits of the new modern faith being adopted by their cousins across the water. In time, druids either converted to Christianity or were killed. By the seventh century CE, where compatible, druid beliefs and practices were incorporated into Christianity. Other practices and ideas were destroyed or driven underground. Former druid colleges became Christian monastic centres of learning.

The Romans greatly admired the bravery of the Celts. This Celtic warrior is from the frieze of a temple at Civita Alba near Sassoferrato, Italy.

Heads were highly venerated by the Celts, who believed the head was a source of learning and prophesy.

This helped preserve not only Christianity but also pre-Christian Latin and Greek learning during the period of the decline of the Rome Empire that is often known in European history as the Dark Ages. The collapse of the Roman Empire left a power vacuum that was quickly filled by the ruthless and opportunistic. Scandinavian Vikings came to dominate France, and in England invasions of Germanic tribes, such as Angles, Saxons and Danes, pushed the Celtic inhabitants into the Western counties, Wales, or across the sea to northwestern France where Celtic tribes still controlled Armorica, now Brittany, the "Land by the Sea". On Continental Europe the Celts intermingled with other populations; in Britain they moved west. Today, only Ireland, Scotland, Wales, the Isle of

Man, Cornwall in southwest England, Brittany in north-west France, and Galicia in northwest Spain, remain Celtic homelands, but these small territories have provided so many citizens for the United States, Canada, Australia and New Zealand that the influence of Celtic culture is widespread.

DEITIES AND MYTHS

The Celts were not one homogeneous people, but a number of tribes with their own deities. Nearly 400 different deities have been identified from archaeological evidence, some of which appear only once. Identifying them is made more difficult because Celts were reluctant, like many other ancient peoples, to reveal the true names of their deities to strangers. In magical thinking, to know the name of something or someone is to have power over it.

Celts relied on an oral tradition for their sacred legends and lore; so much has been lost to us. Celtic myths are found in Irish material – the *Ulster Cycle*, the *Fenian Cycle*, the *Cycle Of Kings*, and the *Book Of Invasions*, and in the Welsh *Mabinogion*. Unfortunately, monks and other scribes recorded all these texts long after Christianization. It is often unclear whether heroes and heroines were originally deities, and what the religious significance was of the stories described. We know something more about Celtic belief from Roman and Greek writers, but some of what they wrote was for political propaganda purposes and is as accurate as Russian and American propagandists writing about one another at the height of the Cold War. Another source is the manuscripts of the bardic colleges of Wales, Ireland and Scotland, which remained active until the seventeenth century. Later, in the

eighteenth and nineteenth centuries, folklorists recorded folktales and folk practices. All these writings have the common problem of being written long after the events they describe when people's cultural and religious ideas had greatly changed, but together they provide a sketch, if not a full picture, of the Celtic worldview.

OTHERWORLD

Tir na N'Og is the home of gods, of human beings who have died, and also of the fairy folk. Sacred places that seemed full of magical power, such as stone circles, burial chambers or sacred wells, could be entrances to the Otherworld.

It was also possible to reach the Otherworld by sea. In Ireland, the West coast is still referred to as

Three statuettes left as votive offerings to petition for healing or other help at a Celtic-Roman sacred sites at Saint-Germain-sur-Seine, France, the source of the River Seine. The Celts venerated rivers, wells and springs.

"the edge of the Western world" and it seems natural to think of the Otherworld as just beyond the western horizon where silver-grey sea merges into sky and the nearest land lies thousands of miles away in America. Celtic poetry and myth describe the Otherworld as a place where it is eternally early summer–warm, dry, heady with the scent of blossoms and flowers, and filled with the music of bird song and tinkling streams. No one grows old and there is no disease. The Otherworld may not have been a final destination after death, but a resting place. The Roman emperor Julius Caesar wrote that the druids of Gaul (Celtic France) believed in the transmigration of souls. After death, the soul could pass into another human being or into an animal.

FAIRY FOLK

Closely bound up with the notion of the Otherworld was the world of fairy. In Celtic tradition, fairies are not the tiny figures of children's books. They are people-sized, even if they are "little people" somewhat shorter than the Celts. Ireland has its leprechauns, Brittany its korrigans, Cornwall its pixies or piskies, and Scotland its fairy folk and its silkies or seal people. Often these legends seem memories of ancient pre-Celtic peoples accredited with magical powers who inhabited the Celtic parts of Europe before the Celtic invasion and who were now thought to inhabit a parallel Otherworld, which could also be the realm of the dead. There were also other spirits who came from the Otherworld. My father believed firmly in the Banshee, the Irish death spirit, whose cry chills the heart. Anyone hearing it should stay indoors for if you meet with the banshee, you are doomed – and she will throw a bucket of blood in your face for good measure.

IRELAND

We know more about the Celtic deities of Ireland than those of Scotland and Wales, although it seems likely from place names that some of the Irish deities were worshipped in Britain. Irish deities are often divided into three groups:

the "High Gods" of the *Tæatha Dé Danann* or Tribe of Dana, whose worship may have been widely spread, other local deities such as river goddesses and deities of particular tribes, and other perhaps pre-Celtic deities. Ana, also known as Anu and Dana, was widely worshipped as the Mother Goddess of the *Tæatha dé Danann*. Dagda, the Good-God, is the father of the gods. He is wise and knowledgeable. His weapon is a club and he possesses a magical cauldron that can never be emptied. The Dagda has great powers. He can make the Sun stand still and he once stretched a day and a night into nine months in order to mate with a goddess and give her time to bear a son. Like most ancient deities, the Dagda is not monogamous. One of his partners is The Morrigan, a Triple Goddess of the battlefield, whose three names are Morrigan, Badhbh and Nemhain. The Morrigan's symbol is the crow or raven and on the battlefield she feasts on the bodies of the dead. The Morrigan is said to mate with the Dagda every *Samhain* or October 31, which marks the end of summer. She protects those who honour her, but is a terrifying enemy of those who do not. The Ulster hero Cú Chulainn, Hound of Culann, a son of the god Lugh, offends the Morrigan and in time she brings him to his doom. Cú Chulainn's father Lugh mac Ethnenn is a harper, hero, poet, healer and

The megalithic complex of Newgrange and surrounding monuments in County Meath, Ireland, is one of the best preserved in Europe. The photograph shows the Newgrange passage-tomb.

OPPOSITE: The Celts believed in reincarnation, but between incarnations and at the end of incarnations we can enter the beautiful Otherworld. In the legend of the *Wooing Of Etain*, Etain's husband from her previous incarnation, Midir, persuades her to flee the High King's stronghold at Tara and return with him to the Otherworld.

magician. He is given the titles Lugh Lámfad, long-arm, and Lugh Samildánach, multi-talented. His weapon is a spear and he is sometimes known as Lugh the Light-Bearer. He may have been associated with the rays of the Sun. Like deities of many peoples he could mate with humans such as Cú Chulainn's mother, the princess Deichtine, sister of King Conchobor. Deichtine first encounters Lugh in disguise at the *Brug na Bóinde*, a complex of megalithic tombs in County Meath that includes Knowth, Dowth and Newgrange. Often the tombs were thought of as mating places, which seems less surprising if, like many other peoples, the Celts believed in reincarnation. A tomb would be a good place to conceive an illustrious and noble soul.

BRITTANY

Death was often associated with a male deity. Roman sources tell us that among the Celts the god Bil (possible Bel) conveyed people to the world of the dead. In Brittany, the death spirit continued into Christian times to be the Ankhou. He is usually depicted as a skeleton, sometimes in a shroud and sometimes in a long cloak with a hat that hides his face. He may also carry an arrow, spear or sickle.

A wall painting from France depicting the Breton death spirit, the Ankhou.

The word for the death spirit, Ankhou, derives from the Breton word *anken* or sorrow, and *ankoun*, oblivion, which are similar to the name of the Welsh Otherworld – Annwn. Along the coast, the Ankhou comes by the *bag noz* or night boat. Inland, he travels the land at night in a cart with squeaking wheels. The squeaking means death is near and it is important not to open the door and let him in.

Brittany is a land littered with Neolithic burial chambers. These were communal graves where the bones of the dead were interred with other members of their community. Bodies were first allowed to rot so that the flesh parted from the bones and then the bones were placed in the bone chamber of the burial mound for

The Kermario alignments of 4,000–5,000-year-old standing stones at the Neolithic complex of Carnac, Brittany, France.

SCOTLAND

Many ancient Celtic beliefs have endured in Scotland in folklore, ballad and song. Scottish folklore is full of tales of otherworldly beings, such as silkies and fairies, and human encounters with them. The Otherworld of Fairy has its dangers. It is fascinating and alluring and might seem much more attractive than the harsh realities of everyday life. People could be enticed by fairies to wander into the Otherworld. This was not problematic until they tried to return, when they would find that every year they had been away was really seven. Friends and relatives would have aged and died leaving the returnee alone. Sometimes fairies steal people away against their will. Healthy children might be stolen from their cots and replaced with "changelings", sickly fairy children. Sometimes this seems a rationalization for why infants become ill and die. Other stories may reflect practices often found in isolated communities of increasing their gene pool by stealing children from other tribes. Adults might also be taken; again perhaps to replenish an ailing race. Sometimes an otherworldly being becomes fascinated by a human or is captured by one. There are many legends of people who marry mermaids, seal women and mermen, but usually the lure of the sea is too strong. The watery beings return eventually to their own element. Some Scottish noble families are descended from marriages between humans and fairies; here perhaps an ancient memory of marriages between incoming Celts and earlier inhabitants accredited with magical powers. Usually in such marriages all goes well for a while, until the otherworldly spouse misses the Otherworld and returns, or the human spouse transgresses certain taboos and the otherworldly partner flees.

Many stories from Scottish Celtic lore are found in songs and ballads that were originally in Gaelic, but which were translated into English and became well known outside Scotland from the eighteenth century onward. There are a number of stories about humans and fairies including Alice Brand, the Fairy Oak of Corriewater, Tam Lin and Thomas the Rhymer. Thomas of Erceldoune, known as

safekeeping. This had the advantage that if the community had to move, the ancestors could be packed and taken too. In Brittany, the same burial customs continued into the nineteenthth and twentieth centuries. Individual graves were not dug. Instead, bodies were buried under the church floor and then later the bones were displayed in ossuaries, elaborate open-sided stone stores, situated near the church porch. People could say a prayer for their relatives on their way into church. There are some ossuaries, such as that at Lannion, which still contain bones and skulls – a surprising sight for tourists who are unaccustomed to the Celts easy familiarity with the world beyond.

In his play, *A Midsummer Night's Dream*, Shakespeare makes use of the age-old idea that, on special festival nights, humans and fairies can meet.

Thomas the Rhymer, was a famous Scottish seer who foretold many events and great battles of Scottish history and even, according to some, the appearance of the black rain at Aberdeen, the Scottish oil industry. The earliest recorded mention of Thomas the Rhymer is a prediction of his that appears in a thirteenth-century manuscript and he is referred to with other seers in the Scalacronica, a French chronicle of British history begun in 1355. Thomas the Rhymer's story has Christian and Pagan elements, however, and is likely to have sprung from a time before one faith

Thomas seems at this stage to be a rather simple sort. He greets this dazzling lady, who is dressed in a green silk shirt and with tinkling bells on her horse's harness, as "Mary Queen of Heaven". Despite this lapse of judgement, he does have the good sense to fall on one knee before the glamourous queen, which pleases her greatly. She explains that she is not the Queen of Heaven, but the Queen of Fairy, and issues him with a sexual challenge. If he dares to kiss her, then he shall have her. His kissing ability is satisfactory and she takes Thomas up on her horse and rides to a place where there is a triple fork in the road. One road is thorny and leads to Heaven, one is an easy path but goes to Hell, and the third is the green path to the Land of Fairy. Thomas goes with her to Fairy where he lives for seven years, learning the fairy lore in what appears to be a bardic or druidic training. When Thomas comes back to the human world, he has the gift of prophecy, which he speaks in rhyme. Such is his power of seership that he becomes known as "True Thomas" because what he speaks comes true.

The story of Tam Lin is one of the most popular Scottish folk songs and has been recorded in recent times by Steeleye Span, Dave and Toni Arthur, Fairport Convention and the Watersons. Tam Lin is a noble knight who is captured by the Queen of Fairy when he falls from his horse when out hunting. He becomes her consort in the Otherworld. He seems happy with this arrangement until he learns that he can reign for only seven years, at the end of which he is to be sacrificed. It seems that Tam Lin can return temporarily to the everyday world and one day in the woods he encounters Janet, a young noblewoman who is picking flowers. By what seem more like rape than consensual sex, Tam Lin gets Janet pregnant. Determined not to face the shame of being an unmarried mother, Janet decides to rescue Tam Lin to be her husband and a father to his child. On *Samhain* night, when the gates between this world and the Otherworld are open, it is the Fairy Queen's custom to ride into the everyday world. Tam Lin tells Janet that this is the ideal time to rescue him. He

overtook the other. Thomas' adventures begin when as a young man he is relaxing on a riverbank. A beautiful woman rides by on a white horse. This should have been a warning because in Celtic myth beautiful women on white horses often turn out to be goddesses or fairy women.

Llyn Tegid (Lake Bala), Wales, home of the goddess Cerridwen and her husband Tegid Foel.

cannot flee of his own accord, but if Janet is willing to take the risk she must pull him down off his horse and whatever happens she must not let go. Janet hides in the woods and awaits the fairy horses. Tam Lin has told Janet that the fairies honour him by giving him a milk white steed to ride. By this, she can recognize him in the darkness. Janet leaps out and grabs Tam Lin from his horse. The Fairy Queen is furious and unleashes all her magic. In an effort to terrify Janet and make her release Tam Lin, the Fairy Queen changes him into a series of frightening animals, such as a wolf, a bear and an adder, and even, in some versions, into a burning brand that Janet must extinguish by throwing it into a well. In Janet's pregnant state, the lack of a husband is more of a problem than a rival woman's magic. Janet clings on. The queen gives up the battle of wills and allows Janet to keep Tam Lin as her prize. Whether the devious Tam Lin is worth the effort is another matter.

WALES

A famous Welsh myth of magic and shape changing is that of Taliesin and the goddess Cerridwen. There are echoes in this tale of transmigration of souls as described by Julius Caesar. Cerridwen lives on an island in Tegid Llyn, Lake Bala. Tegid with her husband Tegid Foel. They have two children – a beautiful daughter Creirwy and an ugly son Afagddu. To make up for her son's ugliness, Cerridwen decides to give him great magical wisdom. She spends a year preparing a magical brew in her Cauldron of Inspiration, but things go wrong. A young boy, Gwion Bach, is responsible for collecting wood for the fire that heats the cauldron. When the brew is ready and boiling hot, three drops spit out from the cauldron and fall on to his fingers. Instinctively, Gwion thrusts his fingers into his mouth and accidentally tastes the magical drops meant for Afagddu. Cerridwen is furious and chases after Gwion, who runs away. Gwion uses his newfound wisdom to evade her. He turns himself into a hare, but Cerridwen transforms herself into a greyhound. He dives into a river

as a fish, but Cerridwen becomes a fish-hunting otter. Gwion becomes a bird, Cerridwen a hawk. Finally, Gwion becomes a grain of wheat: whereupon Cerridwen turns herself into a hen and promptly eats him. This is not the end of the story. Cerridwen transforms herself back into her own form, but finds she is pregnant with Gwion. She intends killing him, but once he is born he is so beautiful that she decides to leave the decision to the fates. She places him in a leather bag and casts him out to sea. He floats for two days until Beltane, when Elphin, a nephew of the King of North Wales, sees him floating and rescues him. In recognition of his beauty, Elphin gives him the name Taliesin, meaning Shining-Brow. The dead Gwion is now Taliesin.

FESTIVALS

Our knowledge of Celtic festivals derives from folk tradition, historical records and archaeological finds such as the Coligny calendar. This was engraved on a large bronze tablet discovered in France in 1897 at Coligny near Bourgen-Bresse. It is likely that custom and practice changed over time. For instance, Midsummer is widely celebrated in Irish and Breton folk tradition, even though it was not thought originally to be a Celtic festival. It may be a later Viking influence, or adopted from pre-Celtic peoples – or both. Many Neolithic stone circles and burial chambers in Celtic regions are aligned to the rising Sun at Midsummer. Apart from Midsummer, when bonfires were lit to celebrate the Sun, four other festivals were celebrated, though not necessarily by all Celts in all regions.

There were two major divisions in the Celtic year – summer, from April 30 (May Eve) to October 31 (Halloween) and winter, from November Eve to May Eve. In recent years, Halloween has become one of the most popular festivals in North America and Europe, but most people do not know that Halloween is *Samhain*, a Celtic feast to the ancestors. The gates between this world and the Otherworld are open and the dead may converse with the living. Irish Samhain customs include partying, "trick or treating", and ducking for apples in tubs of water. The apple must be captured using only the mouth and this involves much wet hair and carpet. Breton ceremonies also include apples. *Avalon* in Welsh and Breton means Apple Isle and is often described as the home of the dead. In Plougastel-Daoulas in Brittany, in a mixture of Catholic and Pagan custom, there is an auction of a stylized apple tree with apples stuck to it. Prayers are said for the dead, and the bread of the dead, *bara an anaon*, is blessed and distributed in exchange for coins that are used to pay for a mass for the village dead. Lights are important at *Samhain*. A light should be left on the graves of loved ones and candles burned in the window of the rooms where they died.

In Ireland and Scotland, Imbolc on February 1 marked the transition from winter to early spring. It is the time in milder parts of Western Europe when the first bulbs flower and snowdrops appear as a sign of longer and warmer days. Agricultural activity begins in earnest. It is time to plough the soil and prepare it for the next year's crop. There are new food sources to break the monotony of the winter diet. Lambing time approaches, which means not only new lambs but also lactating ewes who can provide milk for cheese. In Ireland, if hedgehogs awoke from hibernation and came out of their burrows, it was a portent of good weather to come. In North America, weather prediction is incorporated into Ground Hog Day. On February 2, if the ground hog can see its shadow, there are more long cold winter days to come.

February 1 was incorporated into the Christian calendar as the festival of St Brigid, "Fiery Arrow", or Bride as she was known in Scotland. Female saints in the Christian era retained much of the veneration given to goddesses in earlier times. Folklorists in the nineteenth century recorded how in the Gaelic-speaking highlands and islands of Scotland young unmarried women made a special doll at Imbolc from some of the previous year's wheat. The doll was dressed and decorated with shells, crystals and any first flowers. The girls then formed a procession and took

Traditionally, hollowed-out turnips were carved into fearsome heads to act as Samhain lanterns. Today, the more convenient North American pumpkin has largely replaced the turnip in European Halloween celebrations.

Bride to every house in the village singing a song to her. Afterwards there was a feast. Young men came to pay Bride homage and then celebrations and dancing continued until dawn when the girls sang the doll a final song. Older women made their own Bride doll and prepared a decorated bed for her in a basket. Bride was brought ceremonially into the house with the words, "Let Bride enter; Bride is welcome". The blessing of Bride on the house was requested for the coming year. The Bride doll was then laid in her bed so that the she could sleep overnight in the house. In Ireland, traditionally Bride's Cross or Star – a woven equal-armed cross of rushes – was hung above the door to protect the house from harm and fire. The oldest daughter might represent the saint and would knock on the door asking to be let in: "Go on your knees, open your eyes, and let Brigid in." To which the correct answer was a communal: "Greetings, greetings to the noble woman."

Beltane marks the beginning of summer when cattle are taken to their summer grazing. In pre-Christian Ireland, all fires were extinguished on Beltane Eve, something not normally done in an era when there were not easy means to light fires. The first fire of the new season was lit on the king's hill in central Ireland at Tara. As the nearest settlements saw the light against the sky, it was a signal to light

Cast bronze head of the goddess Brigid, first-century CE.

their fires for the next settlements to see, until radiating out concentrically from Tara the fires of Ireland were alight again. The custom of making a new fire at Beltane continued into the nineteenth century in the Scottish highlands and islands, as did the custom of making the Sun "dance", an image that often appears in Celtic poetry. A bowl of water is used to reflect the Sun's light and then shaken so that as the water ripples, sunlight dances around the room. To see the dancing of the Sun bestowed great blessings. In the East of Ireland the English custom of Maypole dancing took hold, but western Ireland kept its May bush, which was set up outside by the front door and decorated with flowers and coloured egg shells saved from Easter. Ribbons were added and small candles. The candles were lit and a dance was held in honour of the Virgin Mary.

The god Lugh gives his name to Lughnasadh, the Games of Lugh, on August 1, one of the main Irish festivals. In modern Irish, August is called Lughnasa. Lughnasadh was a time for fairs, horse racing and summer relaxation if the grain harvest had been gathered in safely.

SACRED PLACES

When the Celts became Christian, they retained their devotion to their favourite deities. With a little sleight of hand, ancient cults could be converted to the new faith, deities could become saints, and the saints could be linked to Christ's life, giving the new congregations a direct link to Christianity. Important temples and sacred places, such as that as that to the Celtic Mother Goddess at Chatres in France, became cathedrals. In Ireland, pre-Christian Brigid was a goddess whose chief shrine was in Kildare, where her perpetual vigil fire was tended by a group of unmarried priestesses. Under Christianity she became a saint with nuns to attend her. Sacred springs and wells that had been dedicated to deities were transferred to their new saintly patronage. The same customs and practices – visits to holy wells, pilgrimages to sacred sites, votive offerings, prayers for intercession and help with worldly problems – were carried out under the new dispensation as the old.

Different rivers had their own Goddesses as did springs and wells. Clean water is essential for drinking, but the Celts were keener on washing than some of their neighbouring peoples, so water was important for other reasons. Water was also used for its healing properties. Not all Christian bishops approved. In 658, a Church Council at Nantes condemned the worship of sacred wells, but this made little difference. In Brittany, churches were frequently built right next to the springs and wells, which means that churches are often tucked into hollows with only their spires peering out over the top. With the coming of Christianity, statues were set up at the wells to indicate to the illiterate populace who was now the presiding patron saint, but otherwise veneration of the wells contin-

ued as before. In some cases, the water does have mineral content that can help in healing, but often it is spiritual faith that effects cures. Different wells are associated with cures for particular ailments. In Brittany, dislocated hips were treated at Ploërmel and Gourin, hearing disorders at Saint Mériadec's well in Pontivy, and eye disease at Notre Dame de la Clarté in Chatelaudren. Special rites are associated with the healing waters. In Saint-Guyomard, a rheumatism treatment is to drink the water and then to rub oneself against a large stone in a recess of the chapel. Throwing pins into the water can speed up recovery. As well as healing waters, there are many saints who could help with illness. Brittany has many saints that have their own churches, but who are not officially recognized by the

In order to make ancient sacred sites Christian, Neolithic standing stones were sometimes carved into crosses, such as these from Lampaul-Ploudalmezau in Brittany.

Holy well and rag bush, Fanad, County Donegal, Ireland. The pieces of torn cloth are left by petitioners as votive offerings. Similar customs are found in many other parts of the world.

nine times, "Away, away, away!" For mumps the child was to be wrapped in a blanket, taken to a pigsty and his or her head rubbed on the back of a pig. The theory was that the mumps would leave the child and be passed on to the pig. For red rash, a prayer to Mary and St Columba was recommended. There were also pieces of sympathetic magic with more directly magical aims. Invisibility is often a quality prized in traditional witchcraft. An Irish method of achieving invisibility was to take the heart of a raven, to split it open with a black-handled knife, to make three cuts on the heart and to place a black bean in each. The heart should then be planted and when the beans sprouted, a bean sprout should be placed in one's mouth saying:

"By virtue of Satan's heart,
and by strength of my great art,
I desire to be invisible, and so it will be
as long as the bean is kept in the mouth."

Love charms were also popular, as were spells for sexual potency—the Viagra of an earlier age. An elixir for potency involved seeping two ounces of cochineal, one ounce of gentian root, two pinches of saffron, two pinches of snakeroot, two pinches of salt of wormwood, and the rind of ten oranges in a quart of brandy. If brew did not help, presumably the brandy would be some compensation.

INVOCATIONS AND BLESSINGS

Blessings depend on the ingrained magical belief in the power of the word. By saying something is so, we make it so. By wishing someone "Good Health" or "Good Luck", we have the power to send out positive thoughts that can impact on the lives of others. Drinking toasts remains an important part of Celtic culture, except in Wales and parts of Scotland that embraced austere Protestantism after the Reformation. In Ireland, there are many traditional blessings that reflect the cares and preoccupations of everyday life. Here is a blessing for a good life:

Catholic Church. Many of these are popular healing saints. Saints Roch and Sébastien cure plague, Saint Mamert deals with stomachaches, Saint Yvertin is for headaches, Sainte Appolline for toothaches, and Saint Máen for psychological disorders. There are also veterinarian saints. Saints Cornély and Herbot cure cattle, Saints Hildas, Hervé and Eloi horses, and for poultry there is Saint Ildut.

HEALING AND MAGIC

In addition to healing waters, there is a strong tradition in Celtic countries of herbal medicine. The writer Oscar Wilde's mother Lady Wilde was an Irish nationalist and an avid collector of Irish folklore and tradition. She recorded many traditional remedies that contained both medicinal and magical elements. For weak eyes, an eyewash of boiled down daisies was recommended, but for a sty a gooseberry thorn was to be pointed at the sty while saying

May you be poor in misfortune, rich in blessings,
slow to make enemies, quick to make friends,
but rich or poor, quick or slow,
may you know nothing but happiness,
from this day forward.

In earlier times, travel was a hazardous business not lightly undertaken. Travellers needed many blessings before setting off. Here is a blessing for a traveller:

May the road rise to meet you,
may the wind be always at your back,
the sunshine warm upon your face,
the rain fall soft upon your fields,
and, until we meet again,
may God hold you in the hollow of his hand.

And a prosaic one:

Health and long life to you,
the woman of your choice to you,
a child every year to you,
land without rent to you,
and may you die in Ireland.

Complex invocations were said for special occasions. Here is part of a blessing from the Scottish highlands and islands to a woman on her marriage. Symbolically, the maiden is a young brown swan or cygnet, who is about to become white adult swan. Implicitly the young bride is saluted as an incarnate goddess. On her wedding day she is Mary and Bride, all in one:

I bathe thy palms
in showers of wine,
in the lustral fire,
in the seven elements,
in the juice of rasps,

in the milk of honey,
and I place the nine pure choice graces
in thy fond face:
  the grace of form,
  the grace of voice,
  the grace of fortune,
  the grace of goodness,
  the grace of wisdom,
  the grace of charity,
  the grace of choice maidenliness,
  the grace of whole-souled loveliness,
  the grace of goodly speech.

Dark is yonder town,
dark as those therein,
thou art the brown swan,
going in among them.
Their hearts are under thy control,
their tongues are beneath thy sole,
nor will they ever utter a word
to give thee offence.

A shade thou art in the heat,
a shelter thou in the cold,
eyes art thou to the blind,
a staff art thou to the pilgrim,
an island art thou at sea,
a fortress thou art on land,
a well art thou in the desert,
health art thou to the ailing.

Thine is the skill of the fairy woman,
thine is the virtue of Bride the calm,
thine is the faith of Mary the mild,
tine is the tact of the woman of Greece,
thine is the beauty of Emir the lovely,
thine is the tenderness of Darthula the delightful,
thine is the courage of Maebh the strong,
thine is the charm of the Binne-bheul.

Celtic buckle strap.

Stained glass window in the Chapel of Our Lady and St Non, St David's, Wales, showing Bride as Abbess of Kildare.

Thou art the joy of all joyous things,
thou art the light of the beam of the sun,
thou art the door of the chief of hospitality,
thou art the surpassing star of guidance,
thou art the step of the deer of the hill,
thou art the step of the steed of the plain,
thou art the grace of the swan of swimming,
thou art the loveliness of lovely desires.

The lovely likeness of the Lord is in thy pure face,
the loveliest likeness that was upon the Earth.

DEITIES AND SAINTS AND HEROES

The Celts saw their saints as intermediaries between themselves and a distant God. Just as a peasant could not go straight to his or her king but would need an intermediary, so people felt that the requests of the saints were more likely to be listened to than their own. There are some aspects of life in which people seem to look instinctively for female help. With goddesses banished, the saints had the advantage in the popular mind that many of them were women.

BRIGID

St Brigid is one of the most important saints of Ireland. In Brigid the legends of a pre-Christian goddess have been fused with that of a fifth century saint, until it is hard to discern where history ends and myth begins. The main saint by the name of Brigid is the first Abbess of Kildare (450–525). It is likely that she was the daughter of Dubhthach, an Irish chieftain of Leinster, and his slave Brocca. Saints' lives of the period are full of wondrous events. *The Book Of Lismore* tells us that when Brigid went to take her vows as a nun, a fiery pillar rose from her head to the roof ridge of the church – a sign of her great holiness. Soon afterwards, Brigid founded her own abbey at Kildare, the Church of the Oak. Kildare was the first abbey in Ireland with a com-

munity for women, as well as one for men. In the Celtic world, abbots and abbesses exercised great authority. The Roman Catholic system of bishops' dioceses was unknown. Monasteries and nunneries were the centres of Christianity and Brigid had similar authority to a bishop to appoint priests. Brigid's community was a flourishing centre of learning, as were most of the Celtic monastic foundations. Freed from the cares of family life, men and women could study, write and illustrate beautiful religious and historical books. Until its unfortunate disappearance in the seventeenth century, the *Book Of Kildare* was one of the finest of Irish illuminated manuscripts. Brigid is patron of poets, blacksmiths, healers, dairymaids, cattle, fugitives, Irish nuns, midwives and newborn babies. Scotland linked Brigid or Bride to Christ by creating a legend that she was the Virgin Mary's midwife. Christ was then known as *Dalta Bride bith nam beannachd*, the foster-son of Bride of the Blessings. Bride was invoked to help women in labour.

INVOCATION TO BRIDE

There came to my assistance
Mary fair and Bride.
As Anne bore Mary,
as Mary bore Christ,
as Eile bore John the Baptist,
without flaw in him,
aid thou me in mine unbearing.
Aid me, O Bride!

As Christ was conceived of Mary,
full perfect on every hand,
assist thou me, Foster Mother,
the conception to bring from the bone.
And as thou didst aid the Virgin of joy,
without gold, without corn, without kine,
aid thou me, great is my sickness.
Aid me, O Bride!

In Ireland Brigid is renowned for her love of animals. Wild ducks would land on her shoulders and hands when she called to them. She gave sanctuary to a wild boar that was being chased by hunters and she tamed a fox to give as a pet to the King of Leinster. In her youth, she tended cows and she is often depicted with a cow at her feet. She can be seen as a bridge between the nature-venerating Pagan world and the Christian world. Brigid had many of the miraculous powers of a fertility goddess. In this early Christian era, the ability to perform miracles was essential

for any holy person. Brigid is credited with turning water into milk, producing cows that could be milked three times a day, turning bath water into beer (a novel variation on water into wine), and supplying beer barrels that could quench the thirst of 17 communities. After her death, her relics became important and are distributed in the bizarre fashion that is often the way of saints. Her body is believed to be buried at Downpatrick, along with Saints Columba and Patrick, but not her head, which in 1283 was taken by three knights on a journey to the Holy Land. The unfortunate knights died having in Portugal and Brigid's head is now kept at a chapel in Lumier near Lisbon. Brigid's tunic, a present from Gunhilda, sister of King Harold II, is in Saint Donatian's church in Bruges, Belgium, and a silver and brass shoe set with jewels is at the National Museum of Dublin.

Today, there are churches dedicated to Bridget all over the world, but especially in Ireland, England, Scotland, Portugal, Alsace and Flanders. In England, there are 19 ancient churches dedicated to her, including St Bride's in London's Fleet Street, formerly site of Britain's newspaper industry. The Scottish districts of East and West Kilbride are named after Bride. Recently, nuns of St Brigid's order have rekindled her sacred flame at Kildare and are holding interfaith celebrations for women on her feast day.

Early Christianity often absorbed Pagan deities, transforming them into saints. Carnac, where the main cult centre was dedicated to the cattle god, was placed under the patronage of St Cornelly or Cornelius, patron saint of horned animals. A carved cow is placed next to his image.

CERNUNNOS

Absorbing healing goddesses into Christianity was relatively easy. Deities such as Cernunnos, who is depicted as part stag and part man, might seem more of a challenge, but that would be to doubt the ingenuity of the Celts. At Carnac in Brittany, the cult centre of the cattle god became the cult centre of St Cornelly, in Latin St Cornelius. In mainstream Catholicism Cornelius is a Pope, but in Brittany he is patron saint of horned animals and his statues show him as a bishop with a carved cow beside him. Churches

associated with him continued to have ceremonies in which cows were driven down to the church for blessing until the 1950s. As Bretons tend to maintain their traditional customs enthusiastically, it is traffic, size of herds and European Union cattle movement regulations, that inhibit this custom, rather than lack of interest. Today, worshipped primarily in Wicca, Cernnunos means "Horned One". The most famous image of Cernunnos is on the Gundestrop cauldron, found in a bog where it had

An image of Cernunnos, Lord of the Animals, appears on the Gundestrup Silver Cauldron found in Jutland, Denmark, buried in a bog. It was probably given to the earth as a votive offering.

been placed as an offering. Another image of Cernunnos is on a silver coin excavated in Petersfield, southern England. He is shown as a stag god with a sun-wheel between his antlers. The image of a stag crowned with the Sun appears frequently in dream, poetry and myth across many cultures as an image of positive male energy. Cernunnos is also depicted in Celtic imagery as a dispenser of wealth, an attribute often associated with fertility deities.

SAINT ANNE

The evangelizing monks who came to Brittany found that the most important cult was that of the goddess Ana, also known as Dana, the Great Mother Goddess. Given the similarity in names, it was easy for the monks to say that Ana was really Anne, wife of Joachim and mother of the Virgin Mary. This gave rise to some complex explanations as to why Mary's mother was a Breton. Legend has it that Saint Anne was a Breton widow who travelled to Palestine and re-married, producing a daughter—the Virgin Mary.

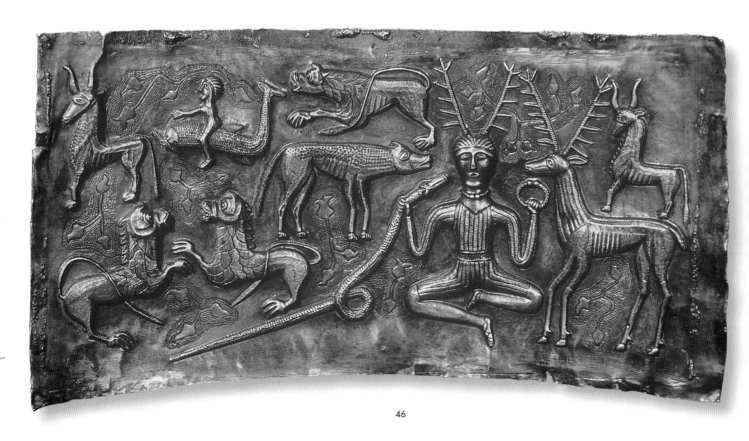

The legend gave Bretons a firm ancestral link to the new Christian belief. It also means that the iconography of Breton churches differs from most Catholic countries. In Brittany the familiar statues of Jesus standing by the knee of Mary are replaced by Mary standing at the knee of Saint Anne who is instructing her from a book. In many churches there is barely any male imagery at all. The veneration of Anne was given further impetus in the sixteenth century when she was officially recognized as a saint throughout Catholicism. In the seventeenth century, Anne appeared in a vision to a peasant, Yves Nicolazic, to reveal that her statue was buried in a field near Auray at what had been the site of a chapel. Some excavation work did reveal a statue, and a large basilica dedicated to Saint Anne was erected on the site. Saints' shrines are visited because their worshippers believe they have magical powers to grant the worshippers' requests. The number of votive offerings left by worshippers indicates the effectiveness of the saint. At the museum of Saint Anne d'Auray, there is a collection of discarded crutches, shrapnel, irons of pardoned prisoners, fragments of wrecked ships, paintings and even the jersey of the world champion cyclist Bernard Hinault, deposited in 1980. These offerings are often carried in procession on the saint's feast day. The pardon or festival of Saint Anne on July 25 and 26 continues to attract pilgrims from all over France. In September 1996, Sainte Anne d'Auray was one of the few places visited by Pope John Paul II on his visit to France.

ARTHUR

It was not only saints who bridged the Celtic and Christian worlds. Celtic myths underwent subtle transition to incorporate Christian elements and play down Pagan ones. King Arthur is an archetypal Celtic hero whose legend still fascinates people today. Arthur's name derives from a Celtic word for bear and he appears originally to have been a Celtic warrior hero who fought in the sixth century against the invading Germanic tribes who were pushing the Celts westward across Britain. Arthur was said to be

the illegitimate son of King Uther Pendragon, King of Britain, and Duchess Igraine of Cornwall. His father was killed shortly after his birth and a noble family fostered Arthur without knowing his royal origins. Fostering one's children with others was considered normal in Celtic society at the time. Links between foster-siblings were as important, or even more important, than those between birth siblings, and fostering created life-long ties of social obligation between people. When Arthur was 16 years old, he attended a tournament where the magician Merlin had arranged for a magical sword, Excalibur, to be fixed into a stone. The challenge was that whoever could draw the sword from the stone would become King of Britain. Much to the surprise of the assembled knights and nobles, the only person who could succeed was the young Arthur. Arthur became king with Merlin as his life long adviser and the Breton knight Lancelot du lac as his greatest friend.

In the early years of his reign, Arthur is too preoccupied with fighting to marry, but during a peaceful lull a marriage is arranged with a suitably royal but young bride, Guinevere the golden-haired, daughter of King Leodegan

Only the pure of heart and mind can find the Holy Grail. This illustration from a thirteenth-century manuscript shows Sir Percival with the Grail.

of Carmelide. Lancelot du lac is sent with an escort to bring Guinevere to Arthur for her marriage, but things take a disastrous turn. Guinevere falls in love with the famous war hero Lancelot.

Peace brings Arthur the problem of what to do with an unemployed warrior band. A solution is found in the form of a spiritual quest to find a sacred treasure. Originally, the treasure was the Cauldron of the goddess Cerridwen, which has magical healing properties, but has been stolen and hidden away in the Underworld. It is retrieved by Arthur and his knights in a series of harrowing adventures. In the Christian era, the treasure was said to be the Holy Grail. There are two separate grail legends. In one the Grail is the chalice used by Christ to consecrate his wine as blood at the Last Supper. Another version has it that the Grail is an emerald bowl, carved from a stone that fell out of Lucifer's crown when he was cast out of Heaven. The bowl was used to catch Christ's blood at his crucifixion. The sacred quest is not enough to keep unity among Arthur's knights. His own son by an incestuous relationship with his sister Morgan rebels against Arthur and fights with the Saxons against him. His wife commits adultery with Lancelot and Arthur is forced to banish them. Finally, Arthur is killed, but he goes neither on the thorny path to Heaven or the smooth path to Hell, but by water to the Otherworld. Mysterious women appear in a boat and take him to the Island of Avalon, there to await rebirth, when a great king shall be needed again. Since then over the centuries the English royal family has given some of its eldest sons and heirs, such as Henry VIII's elder brother, the first name Arthur, but the name seems unlucky. These heirs have not survived to inherit the throne.

The Arthurian myths had an upsurge in popularity in the twelfth century due to a wandering class of troubadour bards who saw the romantic tales as suitable fare to entertain aristocratic ladies. Many ancient Celtic mythical themes were woven into the medieval retelling of the Arthurian legends. These include the quest for the Holy Grail, the story of doomed lovers Tristran and Isolde, Merlin the Magician, the fairy Viviane, Arthur's half-sister Morgan with whom he commits incest, and the knight Sir Lancelot du lac and his disastrous adultery with Guinevere. The legends were also spread for political reasons. King Henry II of England was keen to establish his claims to Brittany, at that point a separate kingdom from France. It was helpful politically if a common ancestry between the Britons of Great Britain, the British Isles, could be established with those of Less Britain, or Brittany. Henry II's court poets were keen to claim that the Grail was in England and that after Christ's death St Joseph of Arimathea had brought it to Glastonbury. Bretons were equally keen to claim that the Grail was in Brittany and there were other rival French claimants. Other legends have it that the Knights Templar were the keepers of the Grail. Despite all the claimants, no Grail was ever found, but the Grail continues to excite the imagination and to feed the plots of films, books and computer games.

CELTIC REVIVAL

Celtic countries have suffered a long history of conquest and impoverishment, from which they are now beginning to emerge. There are European-wide initiatives to stimulate Celtic culture, including the annual Celtic Film Festival, which encourages directors to make films in Celtic languages. In Ireland, Irish is the first language of some and, due to concerted efforts by the education system, most people have some familiarity with their native tongue. Welsh continues to be the first language of large areas of Wales. Education is bilingual. Both languages are used for all official purposes and there are Welsh television and radio channels. In Cornwall people no longer speak Cornish as an everyday language, but poetry is being written and films made in Cornish. There is an active language revival in the highlands and islands of Scotland and some people have Scots Gaelic as their first language. In Brittany, the French government has

King Arthur and his knights from the French fourteenth-century book *Histoire de Merlin*. The Arthurian myths captured the imaginations of all of western Europe.

strongly suppressed the Breton language and a Breton revival is complicated by the fact that there are two main forms of Breton, both with small numbers of speakers. Most road signs and place names in the region are, however, now in Breton as well as French and Breton is taught in some schools.

There are many other changes. The popularity of Irish and Scottish folk music has made people outside the Celtic nations much more aware of their languages and cultural heritage. New technology has brought wealth to areas previously impoverished. Ireland's economy is currently known as the "Celtic Tiger", stimulated by being a European base for multinational information technology corporations and call centres. Ironically, the forced adoption of an alien language – English – and the multinationals' need for the highly educated English-speakers that Ireland can provide, have been keys to this success. In Scotland, new technology links are bringing work to the Gaelic-speaking highlands and islands. These opportunities mean people can find well-paid jobs while remaining in their traditional culture.

CELTIC SPIRITUALITY TODAY

Celtic spirituality has also undergone a revival. Cernunnos is a major deity in Wicca – the Pagan Religion of Witchcraft practised in Europe, North America, Australia and New Zealand. The Celtic nations all have active cultural movements of which druidry is often a part, but surprisingly, the strongest revival of druidry as a spiritual rather than acultural tradition is in England, where there have been a number of active druid orders since the eighteenth century. As a young man, Winston Churchill was a member of one order. The Order of Bards, Ovates and Druids (OBOD) has expanded beyond the United Kingdom and there are groups in many Western European countries, in addition to North America, Australia and New Zealand. The order was originally Christian based but in recent years has become predominantly, though not exclusively, Pagan. OBOD traces its roots to the Ancient Order of Druids (AOD) formed by Henry Hurle in England in 1781 and prior to that to a group founded in England in 1717 by John Toland. The poet and visionary William Blake is reputed to have been a member.

There are two major druid groups founded in the United States. The Reformed Druids of North America (RDNA) started as a student prank at Carleton College in Northfield, Minnesota, in 1963, or possibly earlier. Students were required to attend church, so students unwilling to participate in Christian worship founded their own "church" instead. What started as a joke became a serious study for some and a number of druid groups emerged from it. Isaac Bonewits founded *Ar nDraiocht Fein* (ADF) or "Our Own Druidism". It practises Indo-European Paganism, with elements of Baltic, Celtic, Germanic, Slavic, Greek and Roman beliefs. The Henge of Keltria is a more purely Celtic group which broke away from ADF and focuses purely on ancient Celtic religion.

Interest has also grown in Celtic Christianity. Many Christians from both Catholic and Protestant tradition see Celtic Christianity as a more environmentally aware Christianity that values women. There are now numerous collections of Celtic prayers available that convey a profound spirituality and sense of immanence – that the Divine is present within nature and within each one of us, as well as being transcendent and present in the spiritual realm. There is also much interest in reviving the tradition of the *anamchara*, the soul-friend, who acts as a counsellor and spiritual guide. The *anamchara*'s attraction is obvious in the modern world where people have been encouraged by psychotherapy to be more open about their interior life, but all the major Celtic saints had soul-friend advisers, who could be priests or esteemed lay people. In Ireland, in 1978–9, a series of lectures delivered at the Mater Dei Institute of Religious Education in Dublin awakened Irish Catholic enthusiasm for Celtic Christianity. Tomás O'Fiaich, Archbishop of Armagh and Primate of Ireland from 1977–90, became an active advocate for Celtic Christianity as an expression of Irish culture. Since the

nineteenth century, there has been Protestant enthusiasm in Britain for Celtic Christianity as a truly indigenous church. The Church of Scotland's 1994 edition of its prayer book, the *Book Of Common Order*, has services for morning and evening worship based on the Celtic pattern and a Celtic communion service that uses rhythmic Celtic prayers. Within the evangelical movement, charismatic Christians have begun to take an interest in Celtic Christianity as a tradition hospitable to the miraculous; seeing the missionary wonder-working Celtic saints as early charismatics.

There are many Celtic Christian groups in the United States. Celtic Christianity has also been strongly championed by former Dominican priest Matthew Fox, founder of the Creation Spirituality movement, which aims to honour the Earth and to recognize that the Divine is immanent in nature. Today, Celtic spirituality of all kinds from contemporary Pagan to Christian offers to the Western world a vision of the relationship between humankind, nature and the Divine, that can give meaning to many on the spiritual quest.

Druids of Brittany, northwest france, process to a ceremony of celebration. In Brittany, druidry encourages the revival of the Breton language and Breton dance, music and folksong.

THE
ROMA
TRADITION

The Roma, or Gypsies, are a people who criss-cross
the boundaries of East, West and Northern Europe.
They first appeared in Eastern Europe in the
fourteenth century. Some tribes stayed in Eastern
Europe. Others migrated westward as far as Ireland,
the edge of the western world. Others went North,
and by the sixteenth century had reached Sweden
and Finland. The Swedish kings found the Roma
to be courageous warriors and enrolled them in the
Swedish forces that fought the Thirty Years War,
but their reward was to be exiled to a remote part
of the kingdom – eastern Finland.

The Roma were strange and exotic to the Europeans through whose lands they travelled. Their skins were dark. They spoke an unknown tongue – different dialects of Romany, a language with words derived from Indian languages such as Hindi. Their horse-drawn caravans were painted in exotic colours. Their clothes were different. The women wore bright floral patterned skirts and gold jewellery. The men wore brightly coloured handkerchiefs around their necks. When Europeans first encountered these dark-skinned strangers, they fantasized about them. Where could they have come from? For Medieval Europeans, one of the most exotic countries they could imagine was Egypt. The answer was simple: the dark-skinned strangers must be Egyptians, so Roma became known as "Gyptians" and then "Gypsies".

Like most fantasies, those about the Roma's origins were wrong. They did come from the East, but from further East still. Recent advances in genetics have confirmed that Roma originated in India. Writing in the medical

A group of Roma with a traditional caravan. Today, most Roma have abandoned their nomadic lifestyle.

journal *The Lancet* in August 1987, a team of geneticists at the Boston General Hospital explained that analysis of blood groups, haptoglobin phenotypes and HLA types, established the Roma as a distinct population with origins in the Punjab region of India. A visitor to the northwest Indian state of Rajastan would today notice immediately the connections between Rajastani and Roma culture. Rajastani women's dress still resembles Roma traditional dress, with its brightly coloured floral skirts, its bodices and its head-coverings. Today, we know that the Roma first began migrating from India in the eleventh century CE, driven out by invading Muslim forces. As they journeyed northward, the Roma assimilated new tribal members who merged their own cultural customs with the Roma. The Roma languages have an Indian origin, but also show Persian and Byzantine Greek influences from Roma migrations through these territories many centuries ago. Today, there are three different Roma language groups, each with their own dialects – Domari in the Middle East and Eastern Europe, Lomarvren in Central Europe, and Romani in Western Europe. These languages are spoken by four main Roma tribes and about ten smaller tribes or nations.

DEITIES AND SAINTS

As the Roma fled India in the face of Muslim invaders from the North, they took with them their Hindu beliefs. These included worship of the dark and powerful goddess Kali. Kali's name means "black" and is associated with the Hindu word for "time". Kali devours *kala*, time, and then returns to formlessness until creation arises again. She is usually depicted as dark-skinned and of fearsome appearance with a necklace of skulls or even of severed heads. Her fearsome appearance is, however, a mask behind which lies a loving goddess, who many Hindus worship as the Supreme Mother of All. Over the centuries, the Roma assimilated the belief systems of the *gaji* or *gajikané* (non-Roma). Today, there are Catholic, Protestant, Orthodox Christian and Muslim Roma, but Roma still have their own beliefs.

The Roma recognize the existence of a force of good – a male deity, Del (God), and that he is opposed by a force of evil – Beng, the Devil. Among Catholic Roma, the Virgin Mary and other female saints are greatly venerated. The French pilgrimage to Saintes Maries de la Mer in the Camargue on the Mediterranean coast on May 24–26 attracts Roma from all over Europe. Kali's name still lives among the Roma. Although the town is dedicated to two of Christ's disciples – Mary Jacobé, sometimes described as the sister of the Virgin Mary, and Mary Salomé, the mother of the disciples James and John – the Roma reserve their main veneration not for the Marys, but for Sara-la-Kâli, or Black Sara. It is not clear when the legend of Sara came to be associated with that of the two Marys, but there is an ancient tradition in Provence that the two Marys fled to France in 40 CE to escape persecution. In some versions of the legend, Black Sara is a servant who accompanies them from Palestine. In a Roma version, she is a Roma who assists the two Marys when they are shipwrecked. The first mention of Sara is in an eleventh-century text. The idea that Sara was a Roma appears around the time that the Roma first made their way to France. In some early texts, Sara is described as being an Egyptian servant of the two Marys, and it may be this that led the Roma to link the remnants of their Hindu goddess worship with the veneration of Sara-la-Kâli. The Catholic Church has never formally recognized Sara as a saint, but this does not inhibit the veneration that Catholic Roma feel for her.

For the Roma, the festival at Saintes Maries de la Mer lasts for over a week. In the week before the main festival, Roma come in the evenings to the fortified chapel of Saintes-Maries de la Mer bringing their guitars and violins. There, in the crypt of Sara, each person takes a lighted candle and stands around a larger central candle, while intoning prayers and invocations for the coming year, until the crypt is a blaze of light. Offerings of clothing and jewels are made to Sara and messages for healing and other requests are left for her intervention with the Divine. Sara is a powerful healer and faith in her is reinforced by

the abandoned crutches that lean against the wall in the corner of her crypt. The festival is a time for baptizing children. During the main festival, in a ceremony that would

Statue of the goddess Kali from Katmandu, Nepal.

singing hymns and shouting, "Vive Sainte Sara!"

An important festival for North American Roma is the festival on July 26 of Sainte Anne de Beaupré in the French-speaking Canadian province of Quebec. This is the same former Celtic goddess, now identified with the mother of the Virgin Mary and as a Christian saint, who is venerated at St Anne d'Auray in Brittany. The veneration of Saint Anne came with the earliest French settlers to Canada. A church was dedicated to Saint Anne at Beaupré in 1658 and the saint quickly established herself in popular esteem by the miraculous healing of one of her worshippers, Louis Guimont, of rheumatism of the loins.

HEALING, MAGIC AND DIVINATION

Whatever their nominal religious affiliation, Christian, Muslim or other religious beliefs are grafted on to a Roma world view that includes a strong belief in the supernatural. Many Roma women are thought to have the power to see into the future and practise fortune telling. Fortune tellers are known as *drabardi*. Telling fortunes to outsiders – *gaji* – from door-to-door and at fairgrounds, seaside resorts and, nowadays, from psychic shops or studios, has always been an important source of income for Roma women. Roma do not usually tell fortunes for one another.

The Roma world is full of spirits, called *muló*, who can be spirit beings or human ghosts. It is important to keep on the right side of the spirits. *Baxt* is good fortune and *prikaza* or *bibaxt* is bad luck. Good fortune is strongly associated with good health, *sastimos*, and a common blessing is, "May God give you luck and health". Good luck and good health can be encouraged through the use of charms, amulets and talismans. Women healers, who serve much the same function as the village witch in non-Roma traditional societies, make the charms and talismans. Some Roma carry bread in their pockets as protection against bad luck. Horseshoes are also considered lucky. As well as encouraging good luck, Roma avoid bad luck by maintaining a complex system of ritual purity that affects every area of life through eating, washing, social interaction, sex, childbirth and

Roma pilgrims at the festival of Saintes Maries de la Mer in southern France.

seem familiar to any Hindu, the statues of Sara and the two Marys are processed down to the shore and carried into the sea, while Roma parents raise their children to touch the statues for blessing. The statues are carried by men and are surrounded by an honour guard mounted on horseback. French and Roma pilgrims in their thousands follow the procession to the accompaniment of the Roma

death. Both illness – *naswalemos* – and misfortune can be caused by actions considered contaminating or polluting. When this occurs, the unfortunate individual must return to a state of ritual purity.

Healing is mainly the prerogative of older women. The *drabarni* are "women who know medicine" and have high status in the community. They know about the spirits who might be supernatural causes of illness and also about herbal medicine. *Mamioro* is a female spirit who visits dirty homes bringing disease. Keeping the home clean can keep her away. Interestingly, she is not entirely malevolent. *Johai*, Mamioro's vomit, which is the slime mould *fuligo septica* is a greatly prized ingredient of Roma medicine. As well as herbal medicines, the *drabarni* use healing rituals and chants. Talismans and sympathetic magic are also used. To reduce fever, a young tree can be shaken to encourage the fever to pass from the sick person into the tree. A mole's foot can be carried as a cure for rheumatism and a hedgehog's foot to prevent a toothache. Sympathetic magic may be used to assist in childbirth. One method is to tie knots in a piece of string, which is ritually untied as labour begins. Untying the knots is thought to help the birth and to prevent the umbilical cord becoming tangled.

RITUAL PURITY IN EVERYDAY LIFE

Ritual purity is of overwhelming importance in Roma society in order to avoid bad luck. As with other traditions that emphasize purity, such as Orthodox Judaism, the strict codes of custom help maintain boundaries and separation from mainstream *gaji* society. There are strong distinctions between behaviour that is pure – *vujo* or *wuzho* – and behaviour that is polluted – *marimé*. Roma society has many ritual taboos. If people violate ritual taboos they are said to be *marimé* and can be banished from the community. This is a terrible fate for Roma, whose lives are strongly family-oriented and community-based. Traditionally, banishment was also the main punishment meted out to

criminals. In a nomadic society, there can be no jails.

Ironically, mainstream society tends to stigmatize Roma as dirty, when in reality a preoccupation with ritual cleanliness dominates traditional Roma life. In their turn, Roma consider *gaji* society to be dirty because *gaji* do not follow the strict rules of the Roma.

There are many restrictions around washing. Roma prefer to wash in running water or under a shower. Dishes cannot be rinsed in the same basin as clothing, and hands cannot be washed at a kitchen sink. As women's menstrual and other fluids are considered impure, men's and women's clothing must be washed separately. Some Roma tribes believe that a woman's body below the waist is taboo. Women should not show their legs and their long skirts must not touch any man other than their husband. If a Roma woman is not wearing the traditional long skirt, she must cover her legs with a blanket or coat when sitting. Women usually allow their hair to grow long and, in some tribes, married women cover their hair with a *diklo* or headscarf.

Roma tradition does not have the strict food laws of Hinduism or Judaism, but eating horseflesh is generally considered taboo. Roma were important horse traders and, as in Celtic society, there is much special superstition and lore surrounding horses. Some foods are considered

LEFT: Roma symbol found on jewellery and other decorated items.

Statue of Sainte Anne de Beaupré, Quebec, Canada.

57

health and lucky. Pepper, salt, vinegar, garlic and onions are thought to encourage good health. It is also important that food is pure and clean and there are many taboos surrounding food preparation. Menstruating women, for instance, should not prepare food. Otherwise, when the Roma were nomadic, their food was that of a hunter-gatherer society – game, wild fruit, nuts and root vegetables. Travelling Roma men were skilled hunters and trappers.

A Roma dancer at a camel fair in Rajasthan, India.

Generally, they would hunt small game such as rabbits, pheasant and partridge. In recent years this has been done with guns. Often they would trespass while hunting, which did not make them popular with the authorities. Hunting rabbits with lamps was common. The rabbits become dazzled by the light and are easy prey. Roma are also famous for cooking hedgehogs wrapped in clay, which acts like a tandoori oven. When the clay is chipped off this brings away the skin and spikes. Roma say that baked hedgehog has a rich flavour that is similar to pork.

Ritual purity means that there are taboos surrounding animals in the home. Travelling Roma would normally keep dogs to hunt, as guard dogs and for dog racing, but these were working dogs and not household pets. Both dogs and cats are considered to be dirty and polluted. They are unlikely to be allowed into the home and in particular if a cat comes into a caravan, a purification ceremony may be required. There are also superstitions surrounding cats. Cats are seen by many tribes as harbingers of death, as are owls.

BIRTH

Traditionally, childbirth must take place outside the home because pregnant women are considered ritually unclean and the home would become contaminated. This has meant that, despite their conservatism about modern medicine, Roma women can be attracted to hospital births. Anything that the new mother touches after the birth and before the baby's naming ceremony is considered polluted and must be destroyed. The naming ceremony is a few weeks after the birth. A Roma typically has three names. The first is a name given to the child by its mother when it is born. As in many traditional societies, this name is kept secret so that spirits cannot gain power over the child. A second name is given at the community naming ceremony, and a third may be acquired if the child is baptized in a Christian church or if the birth is registered with the state. This official name if often used only when dealing with people and organizations outside the community.

MARRIAGE

Roma society consisted of small, tightly knit groups. Sexual restraint was seen as essential to avoid sexual jealousies and disruption to family life. Families considered it their duty to see their children safely married as soon as they became physically mature and, traditionally, Roma were married when they reached puberty. Once married, women were expected to be sexually faithful to their husbands for life. Divorce was possible but complicated. The groom's family had to provide the bride's family with a bride price and divorce meant family negotiations about the portion of the bride price to be returned. The marriage ceremony was simple. The couple would join hands in front of a tribal chief or elder and would promise to be true to one another. They would then jump over a broomstick to encourage fertility.

DEATH

As in Hindu society, it is important that Roma die surrounded by family members. If death seems imminent all relatives are sent for and there is a strong obligation to attend to show respect and family solidarity. Like birth, Roma prefer death to take place outside the home and in traditional travelling society an awning would be placed outside the caravan for the dying person. The Roma brought with them into Europe their Hindu belief in reincarnation. They are concerned that the dead person's spirit will not have resentments, as the dead are believed to be able to haunt the living and to reappear as a *muló* or "living dead", which can appear in the form of a wolf. Family members ask forgiveness for any wrongs they have done to the dying person. Sometimes the dead person's nostrils are filled with wax so that evil spirits cannot enter the body.

A bride and groom and their relatives process to church at a Roma wedding in Romania.

Roma society was a nomadic society and the owning of vast numbers of possessions was not encouraged. This did not mean that Roma were never rich, but wealth was kept in portable forms, such as gold jewellery or gold coins called *galbi*. Funerals are elaborate, with processions of grieving relatives and friends. Concern about the dead reappearing means that the dead person's body is touched as little as possible. After death, a dead person's name is rarely mentioned and all trace of his or her possessions would be removed from an encampment. Stones or thorn bushes are sometimes placed around a grave to ensure that the spirit does not return to the everyday world. The aim is for both the bereaved and the spirit to move on.

ROMA IN NORTH AMERICA

Today, there are thought to be around 12 million Roma around the world, but numbers are hard to estimate. Many Roma have been assimilated into mainstream society. The

Roma woman in Transylvania, Romania.

Roma have now spread far beyond the boundaries of Europe. When mass migration began from Europe in the nineteenth and twentieth centuries, many Roma emigrated to the United States. Since the Second World War and, more recently, since the fall of Communism in Eastern Europe, there has been an additional westward migration. There are now estimated to be one million people of Roma descent in North America. Roma were not warmly welcomed into the "land of the free". The first two Roma to head for the New World were forced transportees with Columbus, on his second voyage in 1498. In the sixteenth century, Roma were shipped to the Americas to work in plantations as slaves. In the nineteenth century, Roma came to America fleeing repression in Europe. From 1883, they were the victims of a discriminatory immigration policy that turned them away at Ellis Island, and many states had laws forbidding or restricting the ability of Roma to settle.

A CHANGING LIFESTYLE

Roma life has changed much over the years. They were famed as horse breeders and traders and traded in hand-made goods to supplement their income. Women were economically active, both in selling goods and in practising divination. When Europe was largely dependent on agriculture, the Roma were a useful additional seasonal workforce for grain, hop, apple and vine harvests. The traditional method of travel was, of course, the beautiful hand-painted wooden horse-drawn caravan called the *vardo*. These look much like scaled-down wagons from the wagon trains of the Wild West. It is still possible to hire these types of caravans in Ireland and to travel the quiet roads of the West of Ireland in the same way that Roma did for centuries. Nowadays, among the Roma themselves, picturesque caravans have given way to motorized homes and luxury caravans towed by trucks, and only around five per cent of Roma still live their traditional nomadic lifestyle. Most Roma are now settled in one place. Modern society has little patience with a nomadic lifestyle and government authorities have grown increasing unwilling to allow Roma to park their trailers and camp where they will.

PERSECUTION

The Roma have always led an uneasy existence alongside mainstream society. To conformist societies, the Roma are a threat to the established order. As they were different in lifestyle and language, it was easy for people to project their fears upon the Roma. Nineteenth-century French writer Gustav Flaubert wrote in a perceptive letter to novelist George Sand after he had visited a Gypsy camp at Rouen:

"...they excite the hatred of the bourgeois even though inoffensive as sheep...that hatred is linked to something deep and complex; it is found in all orderly people. It is the hatred that they feel for the

Bedouin, the heretic, the philosopher, the solitary, the poet, and there is
fear in that hatred."

Owing allegiance to no state, the Roma could find themselves without passports and stateless as nations formalized their boundaries. Due to inter-marriage, in western Europe most Roma look white, but this is not the case in eastern Europe, where intolerance and persecution is exacerbated by their dark skins. In many ways, Roma history parallels European reactions to Jews and witches. The Christian persecution of Jews and witches between the fourteenth and seventeenth centuries was also directed against Roma. Rumours were spread that the Roma were descendants of an unholy alliance between a Roma woman and the Devil. Roma depended on horses and therefore had blacksmith skills. Blacksmiths have always been surrounded by myth and folklore from the earliest days when the smelting of iron seemed a secret and magical practice. Roma blacksmiths were subjected to such bizarre accusations as having forged the nails for Christ's crucifixion.

ROMA TODAY

Today, the Roma, a proud people, fight energetically for recognition. Now that the Roma's Indian origins have been proved scientifically, the Indian government has taken an interest in the rights of these long lost citizens. India helped sponsor the First World Romani Congress in Britain in 1971, and has helped the Roma have a representative accredited at the United Nations. The Roma spirit lives on, but persecution is still rampant, particularly in eastern Europe, which has had the largest Roma populations. When the Czechoslovak state was created in 1922, various ethnic minorities were recognized as part of the nation – but only if that minority had a powerful nation state to lobby for their interests. The Roma were not recognized as an ethnic group. Persecution of the Roma in Europe culminated in the Nazi Holocaust of the Second World War, in which Nazis saw the Roma, like Jews, as *Untermenschen*, sub-humans who should be exterminated.

Around 500,000 Roma died and only 5,000 survived the camps. The Roma feel that as a relatively powerless racial group, the sufferings and the horrors done to them in the Second World War have never been fully acknowledged. Unfortunately, in eastern Europe the situation has worsened since the fall of Communism, which has seen a general breakdown in law and order and a rise in racial tensions. Unemployment among Roma is high. They suffer racial discrimination in all aspects of social provision and many bars and restaurants display signs that Roma will not be served. In the city of Usti Nad Labem, the municipal authorities built a wall 65 metres long and two metres high to segregate the Roma from their Czech neighbours. The EU commissioner responsible for EU enlargement described the wall as a violation of human rights and an obstacle to the Czech Republic joining the European Union. In the face of EU political pressure, the wall was demolished in November 1999. In other European countries conditions are better. Finland, for example, amended its constitution in 1995 to guarantee the Roma the right to maintain and develop their own languages and cultures, but Roma still experience problems in getting jobs.

Roma experience considerable hostility. Attempts were made in one Czech city to segregate the Roma from their neighbours by building a wall to separate the two communities.

EASTERN AND BALTIC EUROPE

Eastern Europe has had less political stability than western and northern Europe. The fortunes of history have left some East European nations with a dominant majority and significant ethnic minorities who would prefer to be part of a neighbouring state. Not surprisingly, this is a volatile mix. Another impact of political instability, ethnic tensions and slow economic development has been the preservation of traditional custom, folklore and spiritual beliefs, which can often give fascinating insights into how some of our ancestors may have lived in an earlier age.

Two important groups who inhabit the region are the Slavs and the Balts. Slavs are thought to be descendants of tribes that lived in southern Poland and western Ukraine. There are three sets of Slavs, the largest of which is the East Slavs, made up of Russians, Ukrainians and Belorussians. The West Slavs are Czechs, Poles and Slovaks. South Slavs are Serbs, Croats, Slovenes, Bulgarians, Macedonians and Bosnians. Rather more poetically, Polish legend describes the different groups of Slavic peoples as the descendants of three adventurous brothers – Lech, Czech and Rus – who set off from their mother's home to seek land. They travel for many days and when they reach a mountain range they decide to go their separate ways. Czech goes South to establish the Czech people, Rus goes East to father the Russians, and Lech crosses northward over the Carpathian Mountains to found Poland.

Baltic peoples are found in Lithuania and Latvia and share a common distant ancestry with Celts, Germans and Scandinavians. Balts are the descendants of Indo-Europeans from the Caucasus Mountains between the Black and the Caspian Seas on the borders of northeastern Turkey, northwestern Iran and the Russian Federation republics of Armenia, Azerbaijan, Chechnya and Georgia. They arrived in northeastern Europe between 4000 and 2000 BCE. Nearby are the Estonians, a Finno-Ugric people who were earlier arrivals from Asia and who have common ancestry with Finns and Hungarians. Roma or Romany people, commonly called Gypsies in English, are found in many Eastern European countries and as far North as Finland.

EARLY HISTORY

In order to understand the traditions of these peoples, it is necessary to know something of their turbulent history. After their arrival in Europe, the Balts settled at the eastern end of the Baltic Sea. With their backs to the sea, there was nowhere else for them to go when other peoples began to push northward and westward seeking land. By 200 BCE the southern Baltic tribes were sharing their borders with Germanic tribes known as Goths. Further change came in the first centuries CE when a tribe of fierce horsemen known as the Huns, led by warrior chieftains such as the famous Attila, rode into Europe from the East, terrorizing all in their path. Other tribes moved to escape the Huns. Slavs moved northward into Balt territory. In a population expansion, Scandinavians began making inroads into Balt territory from the West. Swedish Vikings began to build strongholds along the East of the Baltic Sea, but these were mainly short lived, destroyed by the Baltic tribes, so the Scandinavians turned their attention elsewhere. In the ninth century they began establishing trade routes along rivers running into Poland and Russia.

The ninth to eleventh centuries saw the founding of eastern European states. In 966 CE, the Polish nobility under King Mieszko I converted to Christianity and established Greater, or North, Poland. The tribes of southern Poland united to form Little Poland and in 1047 CE, under the rule of Casimir the Restorer, the two Polands were joined. Tradition says that Rurik, a Viking, established the

The Teutonic Knights attack a Turkish stronghold during the Crusades.

first Russian ruling dynasty in Novgorod in 862, but in the thirteenth century Mongol invaders split Russian territory into smaller dukedoms. A new power centre developed in Moscow as a result of the rulers acting as tribute collectors for the Mongols in other Russian cities. Moscow soon became an important administrative and trade centre. In the fifteenth and sixteenth centuries Russia achieved independence from the Mongols and, in the sixteenth century, Ivan the Terrible (1533–84) became first tsar and founded the Russian state.

BETWEEN GERMANS AND RUSSIANS

Since the thirteenth century, expanding populations of Germans in the West and Russians in the East have pressurized the populations of Eastern Europe. The First and Second World Wars of the twentieth century were merely recent chapters in a bloody and violent history. A major upheaval occurred in the thirteenth century, when the Pope initiated a crusade to the Baltic region that evolved into a war that lasted for nearly 100 years. A major part in the war was played by the Order of St Mary's Hospital of the Germans at Jerusalem, which was founded in 1190 in the Holy Land and became known as the Knights of the Teutonic Order. They seized land holdings, became feudal overlords and founded important trading cities. In 1386, Poland merged with Lithuania by royal marriage, as a result of which Lithuania adopted Catholic Christianity. The Polish-Lithuanian state reached the peak of its power between the fourteenth and sixteenth centuries, when the united countries fought successfully against invaders led by the Knights of the Teutonic Order. They also fought against the Ottoman Turks and the Russians, but the power of Russia was growing.

Russia remained medieval until the reign of Peter the Great (1689–1725) who visited Britain, learned shipbuilding techniques and returned to Russia to make extensive reforms. In 1709, Tsar Peter defeated Charles XII of Sweden at the Battle of Poltava and extended Russia's boundaries to the West. Catherine the Great (1762–96)

was another modernizing and expansionist ruler who acquired the Crimea, Ukraine and part of Poland. Alexander I (1801–25) gained further territory, including Finland, and beat off an attempted invasion by Napoleon. Alexander II (1855–81) pushed Russia's borders to the Pacific and into central Asia. Despite modernization the tsars remained despots. Feudal serfdom was abolished in 1861, but did little to satisfy rising demands for democracy. Russia's defeat by Germany in the First World War signalled the inefficiency of the tsarist regime and revolution broke out. Tsar Nicholas II was forced to abdicate on

Eighteenth-century painting of the famous Tsar, Peter the Great, who was keen to modernize Russia.

dence of eastern European satellite countries and former Soviet Republics in the Baltic.

RELIGIOUS TRADITIONS

In the early religion of the Slavs and Balts, worship took place in sacred groves and at impressive natural sites such as the Polish mountains of Mount Slez-Sobotka, which rises out of the fertile plains of Silesia, and Lysaia, or Bare-Mountain. Temples were built about a thousand years ago. King Boleslaw Chrobry, or Boleslaw Wrymouth of Poland, erected a temple in Szczecin sacred to Triglav, a three-faced blindfolded deity, symbolizing dominion over the three worlds – the upper world of sky and heavens, middle earth, and the lower world. Later Christian accounts described the temple as having carvings and sculptures so natural that they seemed alive. The temple was built around an oak tree, probably the original sacred site. With the coming of Christianity, sacred sites were either adapted to Christian worship or destroyed. The sacred groves near Jawór were cut down and their images destroyed by the local bishop in the twelfth century.

In tenth century Russia, Prince Vladimir of Kiev (980–1015), having had many military victories as a follower of the god Perun, decided that his political and trading interests would be best furthered if he converted himself and his people to one of the world religions. A council was summoned to decide between the merits of Orthodox Christianity, Judaism and Islam. The decision went in favour of Orthodox Christianity. Vladimir procured a royal Orthodox Christian bride, the Emperor of Byzantium's sister, in exchange for a supply of mercenaries to help the Emperor in a troublesome civil war. Prince Vladimir returned to Kiev to destroy its pagan temples. Statues of Perun were thrown into rivers or smashed up and Prince Vladimir saw to it that his personal statue to the god suffered the additional indignity of being flogged by 12 strong men before being thrown in the river – such is the gratitude of monarchs. Prince Vladimir arranged for the mass baptism of his people by

The marriage of Prince Vladimir of Kiev to Anna, Princess of Byzantium. Vladimir converted himself and his people to Orthodox Christianity.

March 15, 1917, and he and his family were shot on July 16, 1918. By 1920, the Communists were in control. They continued Russia's expansionist policies and in the Second World War the Baltic and Eastern European countries became the battleground for the war between Russia and Germany. Soviet Communist rule established itself in the region after the Second World War. President Gorbachov's reforms in the 1980s saw a liberalization in the Soviet Union, the fall of the Berlin Wall and the political unrest that led eventually to the freeing and indepen-

the simple expedient of driving them into a baptized river. They went in pagan and came out Christian. For these pious activities, he became known as Vladimir the Saint.

The Duke of Lithuania became Christian when he married into the Polish royal family in 1374. Polish priests were assigned to convert the people to Roman Catholicism, but since they did not speak Lithuanian, this was a slow process. In 1387, however, the altar of the Church of Saint Stanislaw, in the castle at Wilno, was built over the site of an eternal sacred fire. In 1434, the sacred fire that burned on a hill overlooking the Niewiaza River in Samogitia, regarded as the most sacred in the area, was extinguished with water and the ashes thrown into the river to ensure that worshippers would be unable to re-light the sacred flame. Language barriers inhibited the spread of Christianity in other areas controlled by the Teutonic Knights, who appointed German priests to minister to the people. Pre-Christian

traditions continued and were often incorporated into Christian practice.

Russia had chosen the Orthodox Church, but otherwise the area was under the control of the Catholic Church. In the sixteenth century most of the Baltic countries adopted the Lutheran Protestant Reformation. The Catholic Church, with its multiplicity of saints and veneration of the Virgin Mary, adopted pre-Christian customs into its tradition with a freedom that could not be tolerated by austere Protestantism. Protestant Reformation meant destroying as much as possible of any Christian or pre-Christian custom that did not derive from biblical authority. Only Lithuania and large parts of Poland remained Catholic. In rural Catholic and Orthodox regions, pre-Christian traditions continued to flourish into modern times.

A statue of Prince Vladimir with a Christian cross dominates the Dnieper River at Kiev.

The Orthodox cathedral of Saint Sophia, Novgorod, Russia.

The famous ballet *Giselle* is based on legends about female spirits called *wila*.

SLAVIC BELIEFS

The Slavic nations were largely rural communities with conservative agricultural peasants who adhered strongly to traditional beliefs despite equally strong adherence to different branches of Christianity. As in most rural societies, there were aspects of life that were not satisfied by the new faith. The Slavs continued to believe in the spirits of the land, seasonal customs, weather and agricultural magic – to ensure good harvests – and traditional methods of healing. Trees and sacred groves continue to be important in folk tradition and celebration. Slavic beliefs have evolved to give each region of West, East and South Slavs its own colour, but typical of Slavic beliefs are those found in Russia and Poland. In traditional Slavic belief, the number of human souls is fixed. No new souls are born; people are simply reborn into their ancestral line. It is therefore important to venerate the *ród*, the ancestors or clan. Every home had an ancestral shrine where in spring and autumn the dead were honoured. Every aspect of life was under the protection of different spirits. Special female spirits, called *rózanica*

(Polish), presided over birth and the individual's subsequent fate. House and kitchen spirits, similar to those found in such widely spread traditions as Celtic and Chinese cultures, cared for the home. The *domowije* (Polish), or *domovoi* (Russian), are male house spirit responsible for maintaining peace and order in the home, in return for which food should be left out for the domowije at night. Favourite places for the *domowije* to live were under the stove or under the threshold of the front door. When a new house was built, a piece of bread was left out before the stove was installed to attract a *domowije* to the house. The *domowije* will warn the family of threats and death. Important female spirits are *wila* (Polish), who are known as *vily*, *vile*, *samovile*, *samodivi* or *vilevrjaci* in other Slavic languages. In Russia the *vile* are beautiful naked girls. They can be good friends to those who honour them and leave them offerings of flowers, and implacable enemies of those who deceive them, break a promise or disturb their dances. They can lure young men to dance until they die. *Wila* appear in *Giselle*, the famous nine teenth-century ballet written by French poet and writer Théophile Gautier and based on a German version of the legend. Giselle becomes one of the *wila* after dying of shock before her wedding day.

DEITIES, MYTHS AND LEGENDS

Spirits played an important part in people's everyday lives, but there are also many deities whose lives are exciting romances full of love, fighting and magic. Their adventures are reminiscent of those in Hindu and Celtic myth. People's ideas about deities do not remain static but evolve over time. The deities of the Slavs and their Baltic neighbours were originally different, but with population movement and inter-marriage, different cultures adopted one another's deities, in the same way that Christianity was often brought into new lands through royal marriages. Some deity changes were due to new economic activity. As peoples changed from nomadic herding to a more settled agricultural lifestyle, deities of the earth and crop growth became more important. Over time, as social life became more structured, people imagined that their deities led structured lives too. Disparate goddesses and gods were rationalized into family groups, and one deity, usually male, was thought of as the chief of the gods.

LAND AND SEA

The Slavic peoples originally venerated a goddess in the form of bird, bee and snake, but with population movement, the development of agriculture and contact with Indo-European peoples, the Great Mother Goddess, known as Moist Mother Earth – Matka Syra Ziemia in Russian and Polish and Zemyna in Lithuanian or Zemes Mate in Latvian – came to be venerated by the Slavs. The Earth was seen as alive, a goddess who protected people and must be protected in turn. She was honoured at sowing and at harvest. In a mainly rural economy, people felt a deep kinship for the earth that gave them life. A Polish song of the Second World War says:

If I should not return
let my brother sow the seed next spring.
As the moss shrouds my bones,
so will I enrich the earth.
One morning, go into the field
and take a rye-stalk into your hand,
kiss it as you would your beloved.
I will live on in the sheaves of grain.

The sea also had a goddess, who is found in both Slavic and Baltic myth. She is Jurata (Polish) or Jurate (Lithuanian), the queen of the Baltic Sea. Legend says that the queen fell in love with a fisherman and that the thunder god became angry and jealous. He created a great storm, chained the fisherman to the bottom of the sea, and shattered Jurata's amber palace with lightening. Amber is highly valued for jewellery and other precious objects and has been a major trading resource of the region.

Pagan deity statue dominating Kamyana Mohyla Preserve on the Steppes of Ukraine. The area is famous for hot springs, where nymphs are said to bathe in the waters.

The amber found around the Baltic was said to be pieces of Jurata's palace. A more prosaic explanation for its existence is that the Baltic Sea was once a great pine forest. Sap becomes amber after being compressed over millions of years.

TRIPLE GODDESSES

In pre-Christian Europe, goddesses often appear in threes, representing different stages in the life of woman. As in Norse and Greek mythology, there are three female fates in Slavic mythology. These are the Zorya, or Zorza, who guard the Universe. They are the keepers of the Doomsday Hound, which is chained in the constellation Ursa Major. There are also three star goddesses. The Morning Star – Zwezda Dnieca (Polish), Dennitsa in Russian and Auseklis in Latvian – is a maiden and warrior woman who opens the gates of the heavens each day to let the Sun out. She is patroness of horses and is associated with the planet Venus. People prayed to her each morning at sunrise and she was invoked to protect against death in battle. The Spirit of the Evening Star, Zwezda Wieczórniaia, is a mother goddess. Each evening, she closes the gates of the heavens as the Sun returns across the skies. Zwezda Pólnoca is the Night Star, the crone, patron of death and magic.

PERUN

The thunder god is called Perun (Russian), Piórun (Polish), Perkunas (Lithuanian) or Perkons (Latvian). He is an important deity throughout Slavic and Baltic Europe. The Perun statue destroyed in the tenth century by Prince Vladimir of Kiev was said to have a head of silver and a beard of gold. A perpetual fire of oak wood burned at its shrine. As well as thunder, Perun is associated with oak trees and smithcraft. He has many similarities to the Scandinavian god Thor. In Lithuania, where he oversees law and justice, his weapon is an axe. In Russia, he is pictured with a club. In Latvia he brings the rains. Perun lives in shining Iriy, the Russian home of the gods. Perun is son of the goddess Lada, who is sometimes described as the wife of an older god, Svarog, and sometimes as wife of Perun's son Dazhdbog, but this may be another Lada. In Polish myth, Lada is the spirit of harmony, merriment, love, youth and beauty. She is Lady of Flowers. Linden or lime blossom is sacred to her, as is the purple flower loosestrife.

MYTH

A major Slavic myth with a number of versions is that of Dazhdbog (Russian), the son of Perun and Ros, who was a river goddess. As is usual in the world's myths and religious traditions, Slavic myth speaks of cycles of cosmic creation and destruction, rather than creation as a one-off event, as described in the Genesis chapter of the Jewish and Christian bibles. Dazhdbog is a sun god who rides his chariot across the sky, drawn in the Russian version by 12 fire-breathing white horses with golden manes, or in the Polish version by one silver, one gold and one diamond horse. Each day the god is reborn as a beautiful child. Throughout the day he ages, to die in the evening and await rebirth the following day. His image is similar to that of the tarot card of the Sun. Dazhdbog's myth reads like the initiatory journey of the archetypal hero, which can be accomplished only when the hero realizes that he cannot act alone, but must have others to help him. When he realizes the truth of human helplessness in the face of Fate he asks the Universe for assistance and magical women and powerful animals appear to help him.

Dazhdbog, in one version of the legend, marries the three times that are so beloved of magical tale and which match the pattern of three-stage initiation found in many

Those with magical powers – shamans and deities – could change appearance from animal to human. Here, Volga, who is a warrior-shaman, changes himself into a pike, much to the trepidation of the surrounding fish.

The god Perun was widely worshipped in Russia until the tenth century. He was god of thunder and of blacksmiths. He could also bring victory in war.

mystery religions. First Dazhdbog marries the Land, then Death and finally Life. With his third marriage, he is whole and mature. This is his true wife with whom he can create a family. Dazhdbog meets his first wife, Zlatogorka or Golden-Hill, daughter of Vij, Lord of the Underworld, when riding across a field. At first they fight, but this feisty woman is more than a match for him. Zlatogorka captures Dazhdbog and locks him in a crystal casket. Later she decides to marry him. The couple go to Dazhdbog's grandfather, Svarog, and grandmother, Lada, who bless the marriage. Unfortunately, the story has an unhappy ending. When out riding one day, Dazhdbog and Zlatogorka discover an empty tomb (perhaps a stone sarcophagus) and try it for size. As she lies in the tomb, Zlatogorka persuades Dazhdbog to place the lid on top, but he cannot get it off again. She is trapped inside. Her flirtation with death kills her.

By now Dazhdbog should know better than to pursue an adolescent's death fixation, but he does not. His second wife is the goddess of death, winter and magic, Marena Svarogovna (Marzanna in Polish), who is also known as Mara and Marya Morevna. Dazhdbog discovers her palace when he hears music coming from it when he is out walking. He enters the palace and finds Marena sitting on a high throne. He feasts with her but gets cold feet and leaves when she invites him to her bed. When he discovers Dazhdbog's adventure, his father Perun and mother Ros are alarmed for his safety and warn him to keep away from Marena. As with all adolescents, this good parental advice has the opposite effect. He rushes straight back to Marena, where he causes a commotion in her hall. She promptly uses her magical powers and turns him into an ox to teach him better manners. The only way the spell can be lifted is if he agrees to marry her. Preferring the life of a demi-god to that of an ox, he agrees.

Many myths describe a tussle between a dark god and a light god for possession of a goddess. This is often a symbolic struggle between the summer and winter seasons for control over the goddess of the land. In the case of Dazhdbog, Koschcei or Kashchej, the son of Vij, Lord of the Underworld, becomes his opponent. Koschcei is often described as either son or nephew of the witch Baba Yaga. In Christian times, she is portrayed as a demoness who sought children's souls, but her original form may have been as a beneficent deity. Writer Clarissa Pinkola Estes has an interesting retelling of Baba Yaga's story in her best-selling book *Women Who Run With The Wolves*. Koshchei is a powerful magician who has eternal life. Some of his characteristics match those of the Celtic magician Merlin of the Arthurian myths, who was said to begin life as an old man, live for long periods, and get younger each day. Koshchei can travel either on his clairvoyant magical horse or in the form of a whirlwind. He operates according to a strict ethical code and repays all debts threefold. He lives in a palace that lies beyond thrice-nine countries, in the thirtieth kingdom. Here Koshchei imprisons women for his pleasure and is entertained by a magical harp that has the useful characteristic of being able to

play itself. When Koshchei hears about Dazhdbog's marriage to Marena he becomes jealous and determines to kidnap her. Koshchei lures Dazhdbog into a three-day battle with evil spirits, which exhausts him. While he is asleep recovering, Koshchei disappears with Marena. When Dazhdbog wakes up, he discovers what has happened and sets off the find his wife.

There are two version of the kidnapping. In one version, Koshchei's destiny catches up with him when he makes the mistake of kidnapping Marena. Marena is the goddess of death and winter, two things closely associated in the cold Russian climate. She appears dressed in white, a colour anciently associated with death, and carries a broom that sweeps all before it. Like Merlin and Viviane or, in some versions of the Arthurian legends, Merlin and Morgan (whose name has the same roots as Marena), Marena entices from Koshchei the secret of his power. She persuades him to tell her where he has hidden his soul and gives this information to Dazhdbog.

In another version, Marena goes willingly with the wily Koshchei. While Dazhdbog is recovering from his three-day battle with the spirits, Koshchei comes and whispers to Marena that Dazhdbog is unworthy of her – he is only a half-god after all, whereas he, Koshchei, is of much purer birth. Marena is persuaded, turns herself into a bird and flies away with Koshchei. Dazhdbog finds the runaways. He and Koshchei fight, but Koshchei refuses to kill Dazhdbog because Dazhdbog once helped him and he owes a three-fold return of the favour. Eventually, Marena imprisons Dazhdbog by nailing him to the rocks in the Caucasus Mountains. Here, another goddess, Zhiva, or Life, daughter of Svarog, rescues him.

Zhiva is an opposite of the Marena death figure. Zhiva is flying the world as a dove when she spots the imprisoned Dazhdbog and falls in love with him. She frees him and takes him to Irij, the home of the gods, where she heals him. When Dazhdbog recovers he decides to find

Trakai Castle on the Galves Lake in Lithuania was a stronghold in the wars with the Teutonic Knights. Trakai was the ancient capital of Lithuania.

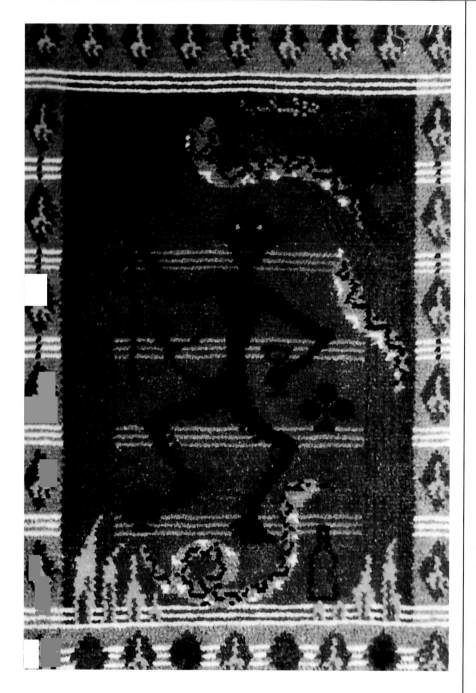

This Lithuanian rug shows the dangers of gambling, symbolized by the emblems of the card suites, and of alcohol.

she reveals Koshchei's secret. Dazhdbog receives magical help from animals, in much the same way as shamans, who traditionally are assisted by animals. A great snake helps Dazhdbog get to the island where Koshchei's death is hidden. The god Perun helps dig up the iron chest, a wolf captures the hare, the eagle Rarog captures the duck, and from the duck the egg containing Koshchei's death is extracted. Death, however, is a dangerous force. When Dazhdbog takes the egg to Koshchei's palace and breaks it, he unleashes a huge destructive fire. The Earth is destroyed, but not Irij, Heaven. Dazhdbog and Zhiva, Sun and Life, marry and begin to create a new world. They plant woods, release fish into the sea and create a new human race. A new cycle begins.

BALTIC BELIEFS

In Lithuania and Latvia, traditional beliefs are conveyed through an oral tradition of poetry and songs known as *dainas*. The *dainas* show that the Balts worshipped a number of gods, and that their religion was based on natural phenomena, such as the Sun's movement in the sky and the changing of the seasons. An important concept in Baltic tradition is *darna*, the ability to live in harmony with the world. The concept is similar to Hindu *dharma* – moral order and principle. The aim of existence is to seek *darna* within our lives, within the home and within the community.

DEITIES

The Baltic peoples were agricultural farming peoples and their deities reflect this. Baltic gods and their mythology and celebrations show an earthy zest for life and a love of the life force. The life of the gods mirrors that on Earth. Deities inhabit farms on sacred hills or celestial mountains. There they work industriously, cultivating gardens and fields.

SUN GODDESS AND MOON GOD

As in most Indo-European religions, the Sun is feminine. In Lithuania, the Sun goddess is called simply Saule, meaning Sun. She is a beautiful woman with golden hair.

Koshchei and kill him. Koshchei is said to be deathless, but this is not strictly true. Koshchei keeps his fiery soul hidden inside an egg, which is hidden in turn in a duck, which is inside a hare, which is inside an iron chest, which is buried under a green oak tree, which is located on the island of Bujan, far out to sea. Dazhdbog goes to the goddess Makosh, or Mokosh. She has control over Fate and

She has silken clothing, a shawl of golden wool, a golden crown and gold rings. She is a beneficent and protective goddess. She is invoked to help human beings who are in need, and to heal the sick. She is also a fertility goddess. She blesses weddings and is goddess of women. During the day, she drives a magnificent chariot across the sky. At night she sinks into the sea. Saule travels the heavens with her former husband, the Moon god Meness. They are now divorced, so they journey at different times so that both can see their elder daughter, the Earth goddess Zemyna. The Moon provides healing to those who pray to him.

EARTH GODDESS

In Lithuanian mythology, Zemyna, or Zemynele, is the creatrix of the world. In Latvian she is called Zemes Mate, meaning Earth Mother. She is the giver and the sustainer of life and brings health and prosperity. She is also the receiver of the dead who transforms death into new life. Worship of the goddess continued into the seventeenth century. Offerings of beer and suckling pig were made and the harvest feast was presided over by a priestess. In spring, Zemyna was honoured as the pregnant mother. Zemyna is also known as Mother of Plants and She-Who-Raises-Flowers. Many rituals to her accompanied the spring planting. In Baltic paganism, all of nature is considered sacred and the Earth is the universal mother. Zemyna, the Earth goddess, is considered holy and must not be joked with or spat upon. The earth was often kissed before starting work or going to bed. She was also invoked when swearing oaths and when seeking justice. Gifts are given to her daily as well as at festivals. Water and fire are considered sacred elements, as they are in Celtic and other Indo-European traditions. Both figure largely in seasonal celebrations.

THE FATES

Like Slavic mythology, the fates in Lithuania and Latvia are a triple goddess. The three aspects are Laima, Dalia and Giltiné. Laima is shown either as a bird or as a beautiful golden-haired woman dressed in fine clothes with silver broaches and flowers in her hair. She determines the life path of the new-born child at birth. Woven braids and woollen threads are offered to her. At weddings, she grants the couple a good life. She also determines the hour of death. People made offerings to Laima on "Chairs of Lamia", rocks that bore the impressions of her feet. Dalia determines health and prosperity and the individual's fate. Giltiné is the goddess of death. She is described as an old woman with a blue face and grey-white hair. Giltiné travels the world unnoticed by anyone except the dying - and dogs, which howl at her presence.

DIEVS

Lithuanian and Latvian mythology also has a sky god who is called Dievs in Latvian and Dievas in Lithuanian, a word similar to the name of the Greek chief god Zeus and to the Latin word for a male god, *deus*. Dievas wears a grey hat and silvery colour coat. Like Greek Zeus and Norse Odin, Dievs visits his people and may help with planting crops. In later Baltic paganism, Dievs is the ultimate creator, who bestows the soul upon a human being at birth and retrieves it after death.

SEASONAL FESTIVALS

Winter

Winter solstice became Christmas in the Christian calendar. In Lithuania and Latvia, preparations for the winter solstice start on the day when bears are first observed to hibernate. This, rather than the solstice, is considered to be the first day of winter. On the first day of winter, a cherry twig is placed in water, so that the twig will sprout roots in time for the winter solstice – symbolizing the hope of new life to come. Winter solstice has two one-day festivals, Kucios and Kaledos. Kucios is a festival for the *vėlės*, or ancestors, who spend spring and summer in the fields where they protect and bless the crops. They come home after the autumn harvest. Traditionally, at Kucios, a grove of wooden and straw birds, and a straw Sun, are made to

European bison in the Bialowieski Forest, Poland. The forest was once the hunting preserve of the Polish kings and has survived almost unchanged as a primeval forest.

decorate the house. Candles are lit and a table prepared for the Vèlès with bread, salt and Kucia bread, containing 13 different vegetarian foods, representing the lunar months. These include grain, peas, beans, seeds, nuts and honey. With the change to the solar calendar, the foods were reduced to twelve. Another table is laid for the living. To prepare for the ceremony, everyone bathes and quarrels are made up. The celebrations begin when the Evening Star appears in the sky. The eldest person present says an invocation to the Earth Mother and breaks the Kucia bread. Beer is then drunk and a libation poured for the Vèlès. There is then a feast of cranberry jelly, hot beet soup, mushroom dumplings, cabbage and fish. No meat or dairy products may be eaten. At the end of the feast, grains are poured into the hearth and a log representing the old year is burned.

Traditional Polish winter solstice/Christmas is similar. Evergreen boughs are cut and brought into the house and decorated with apples, nuts and ornaments of straw or paper such as five- or eight-pointed stars. Sheaves of wheat decorate the corners of the home to ensure a bountiful harvest in the coming year. Fires and lights are allowed to go out. As the day turns to dusk, the youngest child performs the *czuwac*, or star-watch, and stands at the window to watch for the Evening Star to signal the start of the festivities. A Yule log is consecrated and lit, and then a candle is lit first in the *czuwac* window and then at all the windows in the house. From darkness the light is reborn. Instead of Kucia bread, a plate of bread and salt is passed around, followed by 13 meatless dishes, and a flat wafer bread called *oplatki*, the bread of love. The sharing of the *oplatki* bread symbolizes forgiving past wrongs and a new

panied by drumming, banging pots and ringing bells. The revellers would be rewarded by drink, such as mead or honey vodka, and money. In Poland, as in many cultures, the turning of the year is a time for fortune telling. Herbs are thrown on the fire to make smoke patterns and candle wax is dripped into glasses of cold water to make shapes in solidified wax. The patterns and shapes could be interpreted with the help of the village *babci* or grandmother, an elderly wise woman, or *tsarownica*, a witch. The last day of the Yule festivities is reserved to bless the home for the year to come. Consecrated water is sprinkled in each corner with an evergreen branch, and protective symbols and runes chalked over the doors and windows.

Spring

Spring is a time to celebrate the returning life force and celebrations were incorporated into the Christian Easter. Spring festivals frequently have elements of play and people enjoy being able to go outside again after the long cold winter. In Lithuania it was traditional to make *verbas*, which are similar to the bunches of birch twigs used to beat the skin as part of sauna treatment. *Verbas* are made from juniper and willow twigs as well as birch and are interwoven with flowers and coloured paper to symbolize the life force. On spring equinox morning, the aim is to rise earlier than other members of the family. This is thought to bring good health. The Earth is also beaten to awaken the life force from its winter sleep. The winter hearth is extinguished and a new fire is kindled outdoors using a flint. Young people go from house to house playing music and giving out eggs as good luck presents. In Poland, Dyngusy Day is the day after spring equinox. Working on the principles of sympathetic magic, boys and girls try to drench one another in water to bring rains for the spring sowing.

In most of Europe, the egg is a universal symbol of spring in token of birds that lay their eggs at this time. Eggs formed a part of spring celebrations long before they became Easter eggs. In Lithuania, a brightly painted egg

beginning. On farms, any remaining *oplatki* would be taken to the farm animals and people would inform the tree spirits that the new year has begun by knocking three times on the tree trunks.

In Lithuania and Latvia, the second winter solstice festival, Kaledos, celebrates the rebirth of Saule Motule, Mother Sun. Traditionally, people carry images of the Sun through the fields and towns and wish everyone prosperity in the year to come. People would disguise themselves in masks and skins or feathers as goats, bulls, horses or crane birds and process the villages. This guising practice is similar to early English New Year celebrations and similar practices continued in rural areas where groups of mummers would dress up and sing songs door-to-door. A similar custom to bring back the Sun is found in Poland, where the mummers' songs were called *kolêdy* and accom-

RIGHT: In Poland and Russia beautifully painted eggs are made to celebrate the coming of the festival of spring.

called a *margutis* symbolizes the cosmic egg from which the snake Gyvate came to grant life and fertility. This is given as a reward to the spring "whipper in". In Poland and Russia elaborate decorated eggs are made. At spring sowing, the decorated eggs were taken out into the fields with a blessed candle to bring life back to the warming soil. Eggs were buried at the foot of fruit trees to encourage a good crop. The water in which eggs were boiled could be used to mark boundaries against lightening. Traditionally, eggs were decorated only by women and could be passed down the generations. The designs usually include a Sun symbol. Other symbols are circles, solar crosses, stag horns, ram horns, fish, and bear paws. The different symbols bring different qualities such as strength, fertility, bravery or wisdom.

In Lithuania and Latvia, the Earth goddess Zemyna's brother is Zemepathis, the protector of the farm and household. He is patron of the ritual of *Sambariai*, held at the end of May to mark the end of the spring sowing. *Sambariai* is a family rather than a community festival. It is a time for families to gather in their fields with food and drink and to sing sacred songs called *dainas* and rounds called *sutartinés*, and to pour libations of beer on the earth in honour of Zemepatis. The festivities are ended by a procession around the fields where the long *dainas* are sung

by one group and then repeated by another. The songs are to bless the fields, to stimulate growth and also to protect the harvest.

MIDSUMMER

Midsummer is summer solstice, the longest day. In the church calendar, the authorities decided that the traditional Midsummer bonfires to honour the Sun were really bonfires to honour St John, or Jani, and symbolized the fact that he was described in John 5:35 as a "bright and shining light". Midsummer is a solar festival but it begins when the Sun goes into the astrological sign of Cancer, a water sign. In Slavic and Baltic tradition, water symbolism plays an important part in the celebration. In Poland, Midsummer is *Sobótki*, the festival of Kupala, the Water Mother. Kupala comes from the word *kupati*, to bathe. Similarly, in Lithuania and Latvia, Midsummer is the feast of *Rasa*, the dew. The early morning dew of the solstice is believed to possess exceptional healing powers and to wash naked in this would increase one's beauty. At night, the Lithuanian custom is to drag sheets across the fields so that the dew can be absorbed and used for healing. In Poland, the custom on Midsummer's Eve is for people to gather Kupala's dew and anoint themselves with it. Fires are lit and people leapt the fires for purification and fertility. In Poland, women would go into the woods to select a birch tree, which was honoured, cut down, stripped of its lower branches and the upper branches woven to form a crown. The tree is then brought into home, to be set upright and adorned with ribbons. In Lithuania, on Midsummer morning, it is traditional for women to make flower crowns and men to wear oak leaf crowns. The tree, the *kupole*, represents the World-Tree. At the top is a three-

Dancers in traditional costume at a summer festival in Sergiev Posad, near Moscow, Russia.

pronged branch, which in some parts of Lithuania represents the three branches of the World-Tree that gave rise to the Sun, Moon and stars. In southwestern parts of Lithuania, the tree is decorated with flower wreaths and ribbons. Unmarried girls stand with their backs to the pole, throw flower crowns over their heads and try to catch them on the tree's branches. The number of tries before they succeed is taken to be the number of years until they marry. In other parts of the Baltic region, the flower crowns of the women are floated on water with the oak leaf crowns of the men. Where two crowns float together, this is an omen of marriage. In Poland the crowns are made from flowers and nine herbs. Medicinal herbs gathered at this time were thought to have particular healing potency. In the evening, lights are placed on them and they are floated on rivers and streams. Originally, the crowns were to ask the blessing of the water spirits and their protection against storms that could damage the harvest. Later the patterns in which they floated were interpreted to predict how long a young woman would remain unmarried.

At Midsummer in Lithuania the hearth fire is again extinguished and a new fire is lit at the *aukuras* or sacrificial bonfire. Couples jump over the fire and if they do not break grip, this is thought to ensure a successful relationship. Newly wedded couples bring the ashes of the sacrificial fire into their homes to ensure harmony in their married life. Straw dolls, representing everything old, would be burned and burning wheels are rolled downhill to greet the Sun. During the night, there is a vigil to greet the dawn. People walk through the fields to greet the growing crops and then eat a special meal of cheese, eggs and beer laid on a cloth decorated with herbs.

HARVEST

In Slavic areas in August, there was a *dozynki* harvest festival to venerate Mother Earth. Jars of hemp oil were brought to the fields at dawn. Turning toward the East, the peasants would say:

Mother Earth, subdue every evil and unclean being
so that it may not cast a spell on us nor do us any harm.
Turning to the West, they would say:

Mother Earth, engulf the unclean power
in thy boiling pits, in thy burning fires.
Turning to the South:

Mother Earth, calm the winds coming from the South
and all bad weather. Calm the moving sands and whirlwinds.

To the North:

Mother Earth, calm the North winds and the clouds,
subdue the snowstorms and the cold.

Traditional Midsummer ceremony in Russia. Young women throw their flower crowns on to a fire.

Women marching with agricultural implements at a Russian Midsummer festival.

After each invocation oil was poured on the ground, and finally the oil jar was buried.

The autumn harvest festival was sacred to Swigtowid, Strong-Lord, a creating deity with two male and two females faces, representing the four directions and the seasons. His symbol is a white horse. Honey bread was eaten, washed down with wine, and offerings were made to the land.

Autumn

As the nights draw longer, in many cultures it is the time when people commemorate their dead. In Baltic tradition, the dead are invited to return once a year to visit with their descendants at the festival of *Velu laiks* in autumn, where they would be honoured at the household shrine that would have been in the same family for hundreds of years, and where they themselves would have venerated the ancestors in their turn. In the Catholic calendar, these celebrations became the feast of All Saints on November 1 and All Souls on November 2. In Poland, All Souls Day is called *Zaduszki*. *Zaduszki* is a solemn celebration, when the souls of the dead can return to visit their homes. Traditionally, at twilight their families light candles to guide them home and they are invited into the house by the head of the household.

Holy blessed ancestors, we pray you, come!
Fly to us to eat and drink whatever I can offer you.
We bid you welcome to whatever this home can afford.
Blessed ancestors, we pray you, come. Fly to us!

Places are set for dead at the evening meal, vodka is poured in their honour, and they are invited to participate in the breaking of the ritual rye bread. At the end of the meal, their portions are taken to their graves where they can be given to beggars. In some areas candles were floated on rivers to send messages to the dead.

DEATH

In traditional Slavic belief, the Otherworld is merely a staging post before people are reincarnated back into their ancestral line, but ideas evolved. In Baltic tradition, the inhabitants of the Otherworld, the *vèlès* or *velis*, are the shades of all the ancestors, but in the Polish and Russian versions the wila became spirits only of young women who died tragically. In the Christian era, it was necessary to explain how ancestral spirits could exist when Christian teaching was that the soul went to Heaven or Hell. In Baltic folk tradition, in what may have been a later rationalization, instead of reincarnating, humans have a body, a soul, and a velis, a shade or etheric body. After death, the soul returns to the Divine, the body to the Earth, but the etheric body continues to live in the Otherworld, the realm of the *vèlès*, which is closely connected to and interacts with the everyday world. In both Baltic and Slavic regions, ancestral spirits were often thought of as living outside in trees in the summer months, to return home at autumn when the nights grew colder. The autumn festivals were to welcome their return.

BURIAL

The care of the body in life and after death is attributed to the Earth Mother goddess, who appears as Velu Mate or Vala Mate, the Mother of Shadows or Ghosts, and as Velu Valsts when she presides over the etheric bodies of the deceased. In Baltic tradition, funerals last two or three days and have similar wake ceremonies to those found in Celtic societies such as Ireland. The wake is a feast with food, drink and singing in honour of the dead person. The *velis* of the dead person is considered to be present and offerings are

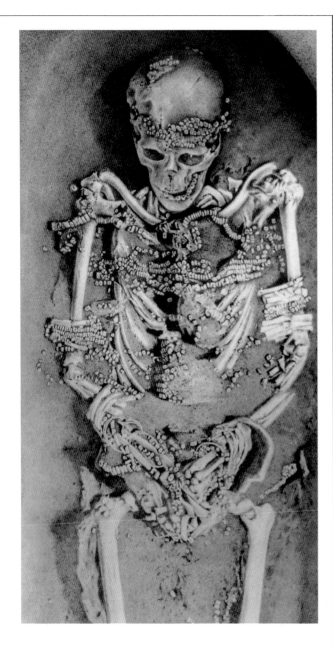

lowed by a ritual dance, which symbolically obliterates the footprints of the deceased in order to let go of grief.

BIRTH

The entry into life is also associated with many ceremonies. In Latvia, there is traditionally a Christian name-giving ceremony, the Krustabas, the "Crossening" or "Cross Ceremony", which incorporates earlier traditions. The name-giving ceremony is on the ninth day after the birth and lasts two days. For a girl, two godmothers and one godfather would be selected, and for a boy two godfathers and one godmother. Godparents should be relatives with good reputations. The name-giving ceremony is performed at a birch grove, which is designated the "church" of the Earth Mother. Before setting off, a meal of white bread, milk, cheese and honey must be offered to the guests. This should be eaten while standing in a circle around the baby. The baby is then taken to the birch grove in search of a name, which is chosen by the godparents. During the name-giving ceremony, the child is first placed in water and the godparents are asked whether they would accept the child and lift it to the Sun, or whether they would leave it in the water of Vala Mate, the Mother of Spirits. The parents do not go with the child to the ceremony and there are suggestions in the *dainas*, that if an infant was sickly or deformed, the godparents would allow it to drown. Before the naming ceremony the infant was called the equivalent of "doll", perhaps to discourage the parents becoming attached to if it was thought that the child would not survive.

LEFT: Stone Age burial near Vladimir, Russia. The head and chest were originally covered by a cloth decorated with ivory beads.

Candles burning on graves at the cemetery at Bialowieza, Poland, on All Saints Day.

made to it. The burial takes place on the second day. From the *dainas* we know that it was usually men who escorted the body for burial. It was important to bury the body in the morning, because Velu Mate, the Mother of Shadows, closes the gates to the Otherworld after noon. In folk tradition, the ancient pagan idea endured that for life in the Otherworld the deceased would need grave goods. Bedding should be burned at the burial site and useful items such as tools and food left on the grave. After the burial is another night-long feast to sing praises to the departed. This is fol-

When the infant returns to its parents with its name, it is a full member of the family.

MARRIAGE

Marriage and betrothal customs vary throughout eastern Europe and the Baltic region, but there are many similarities in that traditionally betrothal and marriage is a many-staged process surrounded by complex ceremonies. Traditionally, as in many rural societies, marriages were arranged through marriage brokers. In Poland, a formal betrothal ceremony was held prior to the marriage and was considered to be binding. The bride hid and had to be found by members of the groom's party, a remnant of earlier customs when young men might kidnap brides from neighbouring clans. Traditionally, in Latvia weddings take place in autumn when there is lull in agricultural activity, and food and beer are plentiful after the autumn harvests. Weddings lasted for three days or more and involved re-enactment of ancient bride stealing ceremonies by the groom's and bride's parties. Inheritance of land was from father to son, so usually women had to leave their homes and perhaps their own villages and make their lives among women of their husband's clan. In Poland, her future father-in-law, as head of the family, would welcome the bride into her new home with lighted candles. A cross was cut on the doorpost before she entered to banish bad luck and the couple exchanged vows and rings in front of the wedding party. A loaf of bread should be broken and offered to the new couple but, to show her sorrow at leaving her new home, the bride eats with reluctance. Her bridal crown of flowers is replaced with the head covering of a married women. She is seated with her husband and a shawl draped around them to show they are now a couple. At night, the couple are escorted to another building, such as a barn, so they can spend their first married night in privacy. Older women sang sexual songs to the couple to encourage their first sexual encounter. Similar customs existed in Lithuania and Latvia, where the *dainas* explain that the songs are necessary to encourage fertility. The

German clergy did try and suppress them, but to no avail.

ANCIENT TRADITIONS TODAY

Slavic and Baltic customs and traditions are spread across a wide area of Europe and beyond. Emigration during the twentieth century has meant that there are over 20 million

people of Slavic and Baltic origin in the United States. Earlier displacement following the Second World War has also created expatriate communities in many western European countries. Slavic and Baltic culture have both undergone an extensive revival since the collapse of the Soviet Union, which often suppressed cultural traditions in case they encouraged nationalist unrest.

Poland preserved much of its folk tradition and custom and between the world wars there was a strong revival of interest in pre-Christian traditions. These became an inspiration for art, including that of Marian Wawrzeniecki, whose works often had pagan imagery. Stanislaw

A bride is prepared for a traditional Russian wedding. In eastern Europe a bride usually went to live with the husband in his parent's home. A wedding was both a celebration and a sorrowful parting for the bride from her parent's home.

Szukalski (1893–1987) was a blacksmith's son from Warta who emigrated to the United States and was then sent back to Poland by his father to study art in Cracow. He was inspired by pre-Christian folk tradition and a group of like-minded artists called "Tribe of Haughty Heart" built up around him. Jan Stachniuk, who was born 1905 in Kowel, founded a pagan magazine and movement called *Zadruga*. Stachniuk believed in the sacred power of intellectual creativity and the ability to harness cosmic energy through strength of will. Neither prayers to a deity or magic would help people achieve want they wanted. They have to do it through effort and manifesting a creative attitude to life. Jan Stachniuk's ideas pre-figure more recent New Age thought on the importance of positive thinking and self-responsibility. In ancient Poland, the *zadruga* was the community – the clan or tribe. The *zadruga* was a patriarchal

institution where decisions were made by male heads of families who gathered after work to discuss social issues under the chairmanship of the village headman. When a tribal decision had to be made, the headman of each village attended a tribal council where he represented his kinsmen under the chairmanship of a tribal chieftain. Some have taken the *zadruga* idea to propagate an ethnocentric nationalism, but much more positive manifestations of Polish interest in ancient tradition lie in the links formed between young environmentalists and cultural revival. The Inter-University Environmental Association in Arturówek, near Lódz, has created a mystery play for the summer solstice. The "Workshop For All Beings", a group of environmentalists from southern Poland, enacts pagan rituals in natural settings. A similar group of anthropology students in Poznań has set up a magazine, *Jantar*, and is creating shamanic-type rituals using masks and drumming.

In nineteenth-century Lithuania there was revival of the traditional festivities for Summer Solstice led by Wilhelm Storosta, a mystic, playwright and philosopher. The popularity of summer festivities grew until the Soviet annexation of the Baltic countries, when any attempts to revive folk tradition were strongly suppressed. Since the 1960s, with gradually changes in the political climate culminating in the fall of the Soviet Union, it has once more been possible for the Baltic nations to celebrate their traditions. Baltic peoples are proud of their pre-Christian heritage and boast of being the last peoples in Europe to accept Christianity. Today, gatherings of organizations reviving Baltic folk traditions and beliefs attract many thousands of people who believe that participating in the rites of their ancestors is an important part of their cultural heritage. Most Lithuanians do not practise the traditions of their ancestors as religion, but as cultural heritage, although there is a strong core of people who are interested in reviving Baltic pre-Christian religion. Baltic spiritual revival is strongly bound up with environmental issues and the Gaia hypothesis of British biochemist James Lovelock that the Earth is a giant living organism, a biosphere of interconnecting and mutually dependent life forms, has been influential. Baltic revival is also strongly bound up with nationalism and a search for ethnic identity after long centuries of foreign repression. Lithuanian pagans have also been influenced by the pioneering work of Lithuanian feminist archaeologist Professor Marija Gimbutas (1921–94), who spent the main part of her career at the University of California, Los Angeles.

The years 1920 to 1939, which saw for a brief period an independent Latvia, marked a resurgence of interest in indigenous culture and tradition. In the 1920s, Ernest Brastins founded a pagan church called Dievturi, dedicated to Dievs, the Supreme Being of Latvian mythology. Ernest Brastins' pagan reconstruction was based on Latvian *dainas*. Christians were opposed to Brastins' church and so too were the Communists. After the conquest of Latvia by the Soviet Union, Dievturi was suppressed and Ernest Brastins was executed in Astrakhan in 1940s. Olgerts Auns, a coordinator of Dievturi for many years, was a lecturer at a clandestine school of Latvian history. As the Soviet grip weakened, he instituted huge folklore festivals that became a focus for Latvian unrest. Following the collapse of the Soviet Union, Professor Janis Tupesis, a member of Dievturi in the United States, returned to Latvia and was elected to the parliament as a representative of the Peasant Party. He later became the Latvian ombudsman. Latvians are also interested in the traditions of the ancient Prussian people. A group called Rasa, or Dew, was founded in 1988 by young musicologist Valdis Muktupavels. Rasa aims to popularize Prussian lan-

guage and culture, preserve Latvian cultural heritage, and bring it into contemporary cultural life. Rasa is also a musical group that aims to become a modern incarnation of Prussia's legendary shamans and singers. Rasa play traditional Baltic musical instruments and sing Lithuanian folk songs translated into Prussian, and Latvian folk songs with Prussian themes. In 1996, after a great deal of opposition from Christian organizations, Dievturi became an officially recognized religion in the Republic of Latvia, with legal powers to baptise and marry its followers. The ancient lives on in the present.

Dressed in traditional costume, a Polish girl celebrates a summer festival.

SCANDINAVIAN AND GERMANIC TRADITION

The influence of the Scandinavians and the Germans on western society has been widespread. Today, Scandinavian and Germanic peoples are found in Austria, Germany, parts of Switzerland, parts of Belgium, the Netherlands, Denmark, Sweden, Norway and Iceland. From the fifth to the twelfth centuries, however, Germanic populations were absorbed into many other countries of Europe and although we think of Ireland as a Celtic country, Viking settlements in the ninth and tenth centuries mean that there is Scandinavian Viking blood in Ireland too. A Germanic tribe, the Franks, gave France its name, while Goths settled many parts of Italy. In Britain, Scandinavians settled on the eastern coast from the Orkney Islands off Scotland, down the Scottish coast and into northern England. Germanic tribes such as Saxons, Angles and Jutes settled further South, in England.

The Scandinavians' boat building skills helped them migrate westward to Britain, Ireland, Iceland, Greenland and, finally, to North America.

SCANDINAVIANS IN NORTH AMERICA

The ninth century was a difficult time for the Scandinavians. There was political unrest. King Harald Fairhair of Norway wished to unify his kingdom and drove out many lesser kings who were forced to flee to Britain, Ireland, Iceland and beyond. The Icelandic sagas described how a group of Scandinavian families left Norway in *knorrs*, large cargo boats, to settle in Iceland. There were already settlements of Irish monks there and the Norwegians may have learned of Iceland through

Vikings settled in Ireland. Scandinavian immigrants flocked to Iceland and by the early tenth century there were estimated to be 30,000 people there. All of the useful land was under cultivation and the more adventurous began to look elsewhere. In the late tenth century, Eric the Red led moves to settle Greenland. With an advertiser's flair, Eric misleadingly called the island Greenland to encourage would-be settlers to the inhospitable terrain. Eric's plan was successful and communities in southwest Greenland soon expanded to around 3,000 people. The Greenland settlements were only around 500 miles (800 kilometres) from the Labrador coast of North America and around 300 miles (less than 500 kilometres), or a little over two days' sailing, from Baffin Island. Scandinavians were excellent seafarers with ships capable of extended ocean voyaging, yet they had only the most primitive methods of navigation and conditions were hard in the open ships. The arrival of Vikings in North America or Vinland, Land of Wine, named because of the grapes they claimed to have found there, is described in the *Grænlendinga Saga* or *Saga Of The Greenlanders*. Ships often survived storms only by running before them for days, which meant going seriously off course. It was a storm-driven ship that first caught sight of North America, though no landings were made. *The Saga Of Erik The Red* tells us that Eric's son, Leifr the Lucky, landed and wintered in Vinland about 15 years later, before returning to Greenland. Vinland is thought to be Newfoundland and two other places described by Leifr the Lucky are thought to be Labrador and Baffin Island. Later sagas describe Icelanders settling in Vinland and trading with small people called Skræling. They are described as using stone knives and weapons of walrus ivory and are likely to have been Inuit. Initial contacts seemed friendly, but relations broke down. There were frequent attacks and the settlement was abandoned after three winters.

While there was a long-standing belief in Scandinavian countries that their ancestors had reached North America, historians were unwilling to accept the saga evidence without

The ancient settlement near L'Anse aux Meadows, Canada.

BELIEFS

Traditional religious beliefs were not recorded until after Scandinavia started to become Christian from the eleventh century onward. The main collections of Scandinavian myths and legends are in two collections of stories, the *Poetic Edda* and the *Prose Edda*. Icelander Snorri Sturluson wrote the *Prose Edda* around 1220. Although he no longer practised his people's traditional religion, he was keen to preserve their cultural heritage. Other sources are the travel writings of the Arab Muslim traveller Ibn Fadlan, the records of the bishop of Hamburg, Adam von Bremen, and medieval Danish historian Saxo Grammaticus.

corroboration. This came in 1960 when Norwegian writer and adventurer Helge Ingstad discovered the remains of what appeared to be an ancient European settlement near the fishing village of L'Anse aux Meadows in Newfoundland. Excavation showed that there had been a Scandinavian settlement of eight buildings, including three large turf-wall houses, two small workshops, a forge and a smithy for smelting bog iron. There was also evidence of boat construction and repair and of women's craft activities. Some members of the settlement were traditional religionists; others were Christians. Jewellery found includes both the hammer of Thor and the Christian cross. The settlement was not long inhabited. No evidence of permanent Scandinavian settlement has been found, although there continued to be trading journeys from Greenland to Labrador for timber, and occasional trade with the Inuit for furs and walrus ivory. Some scholars believe that L'Anse aux Meadows was a transit port for boats journeying further South, but apart from an eleventh-century Norwegian coin found at a Native American settlement in Maine, which is likely to have been brought South through trade with Inuit, there are no traces of early Scandinavians further South. From time to time, artefacts appear, such as the Kensington rune stone, but all appear to be fakes. In 1974, Yale University's Vínland map, a world map supposedly made about 1440 that includes Vínland and Greenland, was revealed to be a modern forgery.

The Kensington Runestone was found in 1898. Thought at first to be evidence of early Scandinavian activity, it has since been shown to be a fake.

From the *eddas*, we know that pre-Christian Scandinavian and German peoples symbolized the Universe as a World-Tree. Why a tree? Trees are evocative for human beings. We fill our gardens with ornamental trees. We like to walk in woods and forests. As children we love to play in tree houses. Environmental campaigns to save or plant trees receive enthusiastic support and we know now that trees are the lungs of our planet. Trees live longer than we do and so represent stability and timelessness. The provide humankind with shade in the heat, wood for fire and, for our earliest ape ancestors, trees were home. The World-Tree in Scandinavian and Germanic mythology is called Yggdrasil. Yggdrasil is an ash tree. Many species of ash, the *fraxinus* family, secrete a sugary substance that the ancient Greeks called *méli*, or honey. Ancient mythologies often speak of a Golden Age when human beings were hunter-gatherers and honey dripped from trees. Poetically, Yggdrasil is said to rain honey on the world and mead, a honey-based drink, flows from its branches. Until the early twentieth century, ash tree secretions were harvested commercially as "manna" and used in medicine.

Yggdrasil means Odin's-Steed, Ygg being one of the names of Odin, chief of the high gods. A sacred cock lives at the top of the Tree, a serpent, Nidhögg, lives at its base, and up and down the trunk runs the squirrel Ratatosk, communicating between the two. Yggdrasil is enormous. Its branches stretch out over Heaven and Earth and it gives rise to nine different worlds, which are divided into Upper, Middle and Lower Worlds, like an evolved form of shamanic universe. Each level has one of Yggdrasil's roots, so Upper, Middle and Lower are only notional terms. Of the three Upper Worlds, Asgard is the home of the Aesir, the high gods. Asgard contains one of the roots of

The Tree of Life, Yggdrasil, showing Midgard – Middle-Earth – the human realm.

Yggdrasil, which is watered by the spring of Urd, the spring of Fate. Vanaheim is the home of the Vanir deities. Alfheim, Elf-Home, sometimes known as Ljössalfheim, Light-Elf-Home, is ruled over by the god Frey, brother of the goddess Freya, and is the realm of the light elves, who are responsible for the growth of vegetation.

One of the four middle worlds is Midgard, Middle-Earth, which will be familiar to readers of J.R.R. Tolkien's *Lord Of The Rings*. This is the human realm. It is connected to Asgard, the realm of the high gods, by a rainbow bridge called Bifrost, which is watched over by the god Heimdall. Jotunheim, Giant-Home, is a hostile realm inhabited by the giants, whose energies when unchecked can bring chaos. Another of Yggdrasil's roots goes to Jotunheim. Nidavellir is the home of the dwarves. Dwarves are useful beings, but they can be greedy, treacherous and unfriendly to humans. They rule the treasures of the inner earth. Svartalfheim, or Black-Elf-Home, is home to the troublesome black elves. There are two contrasting lower worlds. Muspellheim, or Fire-Home, is a world of fire ruled over by the giant Surt. Niflheim, Cloud-Home, is a world of frost and ice ruled by the serpent Nidhögg. The third root of Yggdrasil is in Niflheim, where it takes water from Hvergälmer, the origin of all life-giving waters. Niflheim is the home of the goddess Hel, whose domain is one of many possible destinations for humans after death.

The creation of our world, Middle Earth, is described in the *Völuspá*, the *Seeress' Prophecy*. In the beginning is darkness and silence, called Ginnungagap or Yawning Void. This is the time of Fimbulvetr, Mighty-Winter, a long cold night of non-being that contains the two polarities Fire and Ice – Muspellheim, Fire-Home, and Niflheim, Cloud-Home. Eventually the two interact. The heat of

Muspellheim melts the ice of Niflheim, creating vapour in the Yawning Void. This vapour is Ymer, the frost giant. Ymer commences the process of creation, but giants use raw creative force and the cosmos is disorganized and chaotic.

Sun turned from the South, sister of the Moon,
her right arm rested on the rim of Heaven;
she did not know where her hall was,
or Moon what might he had,
the stars did not know their places.

In the second stage of creation, the high gods step in to create order and rationality.

The high gods gathered in council

in their Hall of Judgement.
They gave names to night and dusk;
they named the morning and midday,
and Midwinter and Midsummer to mark the year.

The Scandinavian and German universe was really a multiverse, inhabited by different beings that perceive reality in different ways. Imagine a bar scene from a *Star Wars* movie and you will begin to get the idea. One legend, the *Allvismál* or *Lay Of Allwise*, illustrates this. The dwarf Allwise wants to marry Thrud, a daughter of the god Thor. Thor tests Allwise on his knowledge of all aspects of creation to see if he lives up to his name. Thor asks him, "What is the Moon that people see in every world?" Allwise answers:

Scandinavian nobles were frequently buried at sea in their own longships, which were ceremonially burned around them, and even graves were made in the shape of boats.

It is "Moon" to humans, to gods "The Ball",
"Turning Wheel" in the house of Hel;
giants say, "Hastener", dwarfs call him "Shine",
elves they name him "Tally of Time".

Thor then asks, "What is Night, Daughter of Dark, named in each world?" Allwise answers:

Humans call her "Night", gods say "Dark",
the Aesir say "Disguiser";
giants say "Unlight", elves "Joy-of-Sleep",
dwarfs call her "Dream-Spinner".

In a multiverse, death is not the end, but a transition to a new world. There is some evidence that Scandinavian and Germanic peoples believed in reincarnation, particularly rebirth back into their own ancestral line. The *Flateyjarbok*, the *Book Of Flatey* from the Irish monastery of that name, tells us that when the Christian king Olaf the Holy was born, there was great anxiety because his mother was in such long labour. Olaf was not born until a sword and a ring were brought from the burial mound of his ancestor, Olaf of Geistad. In adult life, Olaf was believed to be the reincarnation of Olaf of Geistad. In common with other traditions that believe in reincarnation, the Scandinavian and Germanic traditions did not believe that the creation of the cosmos was a one-off event. Rather there were ever-renewing cycles and spirals of evolution and becoming. The World-Tree is not eternal. That which has been created is slowly being destroyed.

RIGHT: Gold necklace made in Alleborg, Sweden, in the sixth century. Tiny carved figures separate the three rings of filigree.

BELOW: This silver charm is in the form of Thor's hammer and was made in Uppland, Sweden, in the tenth century.

The serpent Nidhögg is undermining Yggdrasil by gnawing through one of Yggdrasil's roots, four stags are nibbling at the leaves, and two goats eat the bark. Another concept common to many ancient traditions is that the deities are not all-powerful. They have command over certain spheres of existence, but there are cycles of change that are more powerful than the deities. In the *Vaftrudnismál*, or *Lay Of Illusion*, Odin disguised as Gagnrád, Gainful-Counsel, questions the giant Vaftrudnir about the end of the world. Interestingly, the giant, one of the forces of chaos, is seen as knowing more about this than the chief of the high gods. Vaftrudnir tells Odin that the world as he knows it will eventually be destroyed, but that is not the end. Our present Sun will be swallowed up by the Fenris-Wolf, but first the Sun will bear a daughter, whom Vaftrudnir calls Radiant Mane. A new Sun will replace the old and while most of the high gods will be destroyed, some of their children will survive to create a new Divine dynasty. Humans will also survive. A man and a woman, Lif and Lifthrasir, or Life and Survivor, will hide in the leaves of Yggdrasil and when the destructive phase ends, they will descend to Midgard to create a race of human beings. In an era when we are surrounded by ecological threat, we can find hope in these ancient myths.

DEITIES

Scandinavian and German tradition is polytheistic, with different deities responsible for different aspects of life and the natural world. Many scholars believe that the Vanir were Bronze Age deities of early inhabitants of Northern Europe whose followers were invaded by Iron Age Indo-Europeans with warrior Aesir gods. The Aesir, the high gods, are deities of order, civil institutions, skills and crafts. The Vanir are deities of fertility, peace and plenty.

The giants may originally have been deities too, the deities of the Stone Age inhabitants of this part of Europe. The myths describe a war between the Aesir and Vanir which comes to an end when the two sides devise a peace treaty whereby they will exchange hostages to ensure that neither side breaks it. This was a common practice among Scandinavian, German and Celtic tribes. Relatives of the royal family and important nobles would be sent to live with the opposing side. If the peace was broken, the hostages would be slain. As part of the peace treaty between the gods, the Vanir goddess Freya and her father Njörd are sent to live in Asgard. In return, the Aesir send the giant brothers Mimir and Hoenir to the Vanir. The Aesir are wily in comparison with the Vanir, however, who find themselves less than satisfied with their part of the bargain. In Asgard, Mimir had been keeper of a sacred spring of knowledge at the root of the World-Tree. He is useful to the Vanir and can give good counsel, but his brother, the stupid Hoenir, can do nothing unless advised by Mimir. The outraged Vanir cut off Mimir's head and return it to Asgard, where the ever-resourceful Odin finds that the head has retained Mimir's wisdom and uses it as an oracle of prophecy.

ODIN

Odin is chief god of the Aesir. In Anglo-Saxon his name is Woden, and he gives his name to Wednesday. He is Alfadhir, All-Father, and a god of wisdom, knowledge and communication. He is depicted wearing a cloak and with a wide-brimmed hat pulled down over his face. This is to disguise a missing eye. Such is Odin's desire for knowledge that before Mimir's ill-fated departure to the Vanir, Odin sacrifices one of his own eyes to the giant in exchange for a drink from Mimir's well of wisdom. As well as Mimir's head, Odin has two ravens – Hugin (Thought) and Munin (Memory) – which bring him news of what is happening in the world. Ravens were considered a good omen for Odin's followers who fought in battle under raven banners. At the Tower of London, which traditionally houses Britain's

crown jewels, ravens whose wings have been clipped to prevent them flying away are still kept to bring good fortune to the realm. Odin also has a magical ring that creates eight more like itself every ninth night. This was the inspiration for the rings in J.R.R. Tolkien's *Lord Of The Rings*.

Odin has many of the characteristics of a mythical shaman. He can change shape and appear in different guises. He has great knowledge and can travel into different worlds on his eight-legged magical horse, called Sleipnir. Eight-legged horses are known further East in Siberia as the horses on which shamans ride between the worlds. Wisdom in ancient myth is not easily gained and often involves initiatory ordeals. In order to discover the secret of the runes, Odin undertakes a nine-day fast that involves hanging upside down from Yggdrasil. If you are familiar with the tarot, the image of the Hanged Man may spring to mind. The story is found

Relief from the tombstone of a Saxon horseman dating from the seventh century CE. The knotwork below the rider shows two intertwined snakes.

A nineteenth-century painting of a Valkyrie battle maiden.

in the *eddas* in the *Hávamál*, the high one's (Odin's) words.

I know I hung
on the wind swept Tree
through nine days and nights.

I was struck with a spear
and given to Odin,
myself to myself.
They helped me neither
by meat nor drink.
I peered downward.
I took up the runes,
with piercing cry I took them,
then fell to the ground.

OPPOSITE PAGE:
The goddess Freya obtained a magical necklace by having sex with each of the four dwarves who made it. Freya is closely associated with amber, which was said to be formed from the tears she cried when her husband went missing.

Each of the major deities has a feasting hall and pious followers of the deities might be welcomed into these after death. Odin's hall is Valhalla. Originally, it was thought of as a home for warriors who died in battle. Each day was occupied in the joys of fighting, but unlike on Earth this was a risk-free activity. Anyone killed would be resurrected in time for the nightly feast, where the warriors satiated themselves on pork and mead. The mead flowed from the udders of the goat Heidrun and was served in drinking horns by Valkyrie battle-maidens. In the *Lodbrok*, the *Death Song Of Ragnar*, Lord Ragnar speaks of Valhalla.

It gladdens me to know that Baldur's father (Odin)
makes ready the benches for banquet.
Soon we shall be drinking ale from the curved horns.
The champion who comes into Odin's dwelling
does not lament his death.
I shall not enter his hall with words of fear on my lips:
the Aesir will welcome me.
Death comes without lamenting…
Eager am I to depart…
The days of my life are ended.
I laugh as I die.

Later, providing they observed the rites of cremation, Valhalla was thought to be the destination of all followers of Odin, male or female, not just those slain in battle. Viking burials, where ships were sent out to sea and burned, were designed to take their dead passengers straight to Odin.

FRIGGA

Frigga is the mother of the Aesir deities, wife of Odin, and goddess of the sky. She can see into the future and knows the ultimate fate of every being, but she rarely reveals it. She blesses marriages and her health is toasted at wedding feasts. She is invoked by women in labour. In her hall, Fensalir, Frigga spins golden threads and the constellation

of Orion's Belt is sometimes named Frigga's Spinning Wheel. A twelfth-century picture of Frigga, naked and riding a distaff that looks like a broomstick, can be found on the wall of Schleswig cathedral in North Germany. Frigga's hall is for faithful loving couples, and she is associated with sexuality. Her name was used to create the slang word "frigging", another word for having sex.

FREYA

Freya is the best known of the Vanir deities. She is a goddess of love, beauty and fertility, but unlike Frigga she is not sexually faithful. She has many lovers as well as a husband and her chariot is drawn by tomcats. If she is not sexually constant, however, she does at least love her husband, Odur. When he goes missing, Freya rides in search of him. Along the way, she weeps tears that turn into droplets of golden amber – to the Scandinavians amber was Freya's tears. Freya is also a deity for warriors. After a battle she rides the battlefield with the warrior maidens, the Valkyrie. Half of the slain go to Freya's feasting hall and half to Odin's. Freya is also a patroness of magic.

THOR

Odin may not have been the original chief of the Aesir. Snorri Sturluson tells us in his prologue to the *eddas* that Thor was the first of the gods and that Odin was one of Thor's sons. Later, Odin seems to have come to supremacy, but there are few place names in Northern Europe associated with him, a possible sign

Small bronze statue from Iceland of the god Thor, dating from around 1000 CE. The Scandinavians colonized Iceland in the ninth century.

The three witches from Shakespeare's play *Macbeth* are a folk memory of the three Scandinavian fates, who are also known as the Wyrd Sisters.

that he was not widely worshipped, or was primarily a god of kings and nobles. Thor rules over Midgard, our human world, and was one of the most venerated of the gods. He gives his name to Thursday. When Saxons converted to Christianity, Thor was one of the three deities they were specifically required to renounce. Thor is a "people's god" and a friend of farmers and workers. He is larger than life with a red beard. He can out-drink and out-eat anyone. He is renowned for his strength and has a hammer, Mjolnir, which he uses to slay giants and to shatter rocks. He is the god of lightning and throws thunderbolts at those who upset the gods. His vehicle is a chariot drawn by goats. The sign of Thor's hammer was used to mark boundary stones. It was also used in rites of passage. The hammer sign was made over new-born infants to protect them. It was also carved on memorial stones for the dead. Today, modern followers of Scandinavian and Germanic spirituality often wear a small Thor's hammer around their necks.

NORNS, THE WYRD SISTERS

Three sister goddesses, called the three Norns or Wyrd Sisters, preside over fate. Shakespeare's three witches in *Macbeth* are based on the three Norns. The chief Norn is Urd, or Origin, who rules the past. She is the cause of present and future. The second sister, Verdandi, or Becoming, represents the present. Together the two sisters create Skuld, or Debt, who represents the future and is the result of the actions of the past and present. The Norns determine the fate of every individual, including the moment of death. Skuld cuts the thread of life when it is time for us to die. She wears a veil indicating that the past and present are known, but the future has yet to be revealed. Together the Wyrd Sisters spin the web of destiny of gods and men. It is by the well of the goddess Urd in Asgard that the gods hold daily council.

MAGICAL PRACTICES

To know the future requires the ability to be able to interpret an individual's wyrd or destiny. Magic is about changing that destiny. Magical and divinatory powers were generally the work of women. Healers too were women, and healing was under the patronage of the goddess Eir. *Volvas* or *seidkonas*, who practise *seithr* or trance magic were also mainly female. A description of a volva is found in the saga *Erik The Red*. She has a cloak with a hood lined with cat fur and cat-fur gloves. On her belt she has a pouch, which contains items to help her with her magic. The cat fur links the volva to the goddess Freya, whose chariot is drawn by cats and who is patroness of *seithr*. Although *seithr* was primarily a female art, in his quest for knowledge, Odin persuades Freya to teach him. To practise *seithr*, it is necessary to enter a trance. Traditionally, volvas sit on a platform surrounded by priestesses who chant to help induce the trance. *Seithr* was used to contact beings in the other worlds of the World-Tree for advice, and to give advice on matters of concern to the community, such as disease, war, farming and unsolved crime. The words of the *volvas* were greatly respected. *Volvas* often travelled to different communities to practise their art and their role seems connected with the rites of travelling deities. The Roman historian Tacitus describes how a goddess visited settlements in her sacred ox-drawn wagon, driven by a priest. The priest knew the goddess was ready to set off

when the wagon became heavy. It is likely that at these ceremonies, a *volva* priestess represented the goddess. The wagon became heavy once the priestess had secreted herself inside. The goddess' arrival was welcomed with great ceremony. Tribal wars ceased and weapons were put away. There were also travelling gods. The *Flateyjarbok* describes how King Eric of Sweden led the wagon of the god Frey, Freya's brother, to a certain place and waited until it became heavy. This was the sign that the god was present. The wagon was then brought into King Eric's hall, where he greeted the god, drank a horn in his honour and put questions to him.

Another form of divination was the runes. The runic alphabet is called the FUThARK, after its first six letters. Together the letters can be used to form words, but like Hebrew, the individual letters also have meanings. The runes have been used for many centuries. Tacitus, writing in 98 CE, describes rune casting. A branch is cut from a nut-bearing tree. It is sliced into strips and these are marked with signs. The strips are thrown on to a white cloth. Three wooden strips are drawn and a divination performed based on the combined meanings of the drawn runes. Today, runes may be inscribed on wooden strips,

A copper locket from Grotland, Sweden, containing a small snake. The locket would be worn to give magical protection.

ABOVE: Carved stone in Skanse Park, Stockholm, Sweden, with runes around the edge.

OPPOSITE PAGE: Young girl representing St Lucia.

*"Help" is it named, for help can it give
in sadness, sorrow and sickness.*

*A fourth I know, if my foes
have bound me hand and foot.
I chant the spell that breaks the chains
so they fly from hands and feet.*

In the *Sigdrifumal* there is a verse that explains how to deal with a difficult birth:

*Help-runes you should know,
to help bring forth,
a woman of her child:
mark them on your hands,
take hold of her wrists,
and invoke the Disirs' aid.*

The *Disir* are female guardian spirits.

SEASONAL FESTIVALS

We know less about how the Scandinavians and Germans celebrated the seasons' change than we do about some other traditions, but we do know that Midsummer and Midwinter, which are still celebrated in various forms today, were of major importance. Midwinter celebrations have been incorporated into our Christmas festivities. Although the festival is a Christian one, its trappings – Christmas trees, holly, mistletoe and great feasting – are all relics of earlier pagan traditions that celebrated the lengthening of days after the longest night of Midwinter. To northern Europeans, the Winter Solstice is of great importance. In northern countries where winter means little daylight or even none at all, the point of transition when people know that the Sun will grow stronger again is a huge psychological relief and a cause of celebration. In pre-Christian tradition, Winter Solstice was celebrated for

but more often small rune stones are used.

Runes can also be used more actively as spells. One method is to intone the names of a combination of runes, which together represent a particular intention. The chanting of an experienced practitioner is an eerie experience. Combinations of runes may also be written on pieces of paper in complex talismans and spells. These are mentioned in the *Hávamál*:

*A spell unknown to queens I know,
or any of humankind:*

A German festival to give thanks for the harvest. In the background women are garlanding the trees for the celebration.

12 days, hence the carol *The Twelve Days Of Christmas*. The 12-day period began with the longest night of the year, December 20–21 and ended on December 31–January 1. With the coming of Christianity, December 25 became the first of the 12 days and Twelfth Night became January 6. Like most parts of the western world, Christmas in Scandinavia is a major celebration. In Sweden, for instance, the main meal and present giving are on Christmas Eve, with a tree and a great spread of food. The Swedish Santa Claus is the Jultomten. Before this is St Lucia's Day on December 13. This was originally a pagan festival dedicated to Lusse, a spirit who wanders abroad at Winter Solstice to snatch unwary revellers and imprison them in the underworld. In time, Lusse merged with the Christian St Lucia and the festival moved to earlier in the month and became a celebration of the triumph of light rather than the danger of darkness. A young woman, usually the oldest daughter of the family, is chosen to be Lucia. On the morning of St Lucia's Day, and while wearing the traditional white robe and a crown of lighted candles, she wakes her family with coffee and a tray of saffron buns, called *lussekattor*. St Lucia's Day is primarily a Swedish festival, but in the twentieth century it became more widespread across Scandinavia. In the 1950s, it was introduced into Finland by the Swedish-speaking minority, where it is used mainly for charity fundraising. Girls chosen to represent Lucia visit hospitals and schools.

The other major festival is Midsummer celebrated in Scandinavia takes place around June 21. In the northern parts of Scandinavia at this time of year, it may be light nearly all night. This is a major excuse for a wild party. Everyone who has a summer cottage decamps to the countryside. Huge bonfires are lit to celebrate the Sun. In some regions, Midsummer, probably through German influence, has many of the features of May Day in warmer countries further South. Tall phallic poles are erected and are decorated with green leaves and flowers. There are circle dances around the poles and much feasting, drinking and general jollity. So enthusiastic are Swedes about their traditional celebrations that the government has moved the festival to the nearest Friday to Midsummer, so that people have the weekend to recover.

SCANDINAVIAN AND GERMANIC TRADITIONS IN THE TWENTY-FIRST CENTURY

Since the nineteenth century, there has been a revival in northern European traditional religion. Often this has been associated with reclaiming national heritage. Education in Scandinavia and Germany in the nineteenth century was dominated by the study of Latin and Greek, and by study of Roman and Greek cultures. These were considered to be the epitome of civilization and people knew more about the myths of Roma and Greece than those of their own people. This began to change in the nineteenth century when folklorists, alarmed at the population movements and social disruption caused by the Industrial Revolution, realized that old traditions were in danger of disappearing. Folklorists began to visit rural areas to record the wisdom of their ancestors. Among traditional songs and stories, they found many old spiritual practices still carried out in rural areas, though often under a thin veneer of Christianity. Scandinavian religion began to revive and, in the nineteenth century, Danish scholars devised a new word to describe it – Asetro. Today, Asetro is more often known by the Icelandic version of the name, which is Ásatrú. Ásatrú means belief in or loyalty to the Aesir, the high gods. It can also be referred to as *Forn Si_r*, meaning "Ancient Way", *Forn sed*, meaning "Old custom", *Nordisk sed*, meaning "Nordic custom" or *Hedensk sed* meaning "heathen or pagan custom". In the nineteenth-century revival of Ásatrú, there was an emphasis on Odin and some Ásatrú call themselves "Odinists".

In North America, interest in Ásatrú was stimulated by the 1960s archaeological finds of an early Scandinavian settlement and has grown since the 1970s, mainly among people of Scandinavian or Germanic descent. The Ring of Troth, the Arizona Kindred, the Ásatrú Free Assembly and other groups have sprung up to bring people together for veneration of the old gods and to learn more about the tradition. There has been a similar growth of interest in Europe. In 1972, Icelandic poet Sveinbjorn Beinteinsson persuaded the Icelandic government to recognize Ásatrú as the traditional religion of Iceland with equal rights to Christianity. Ásatrú believers can have marriages and other religious rites of passage solemnized by their own community leaders. There are two main Odinist organizations in Britain: the Odinshof and the Odinic Rite. The Odinic Rite has branches in France and other European countries and there are similar organizations in Germany. The Ásatrú revival was largely male led, but in recent years women have become more prominent. Freya Aswynn, writer of a beautiful and original book about the runes, is well known in the European community, and Dr Jenny Blain of Mount Saint Vincent University in Canada has conducted research within the North American Ásatrú community that has encouraged serious study of Ásatrú.

At the end of January, the British Shetland Islanders celebrate the Viking fire festival.

FINLAND AND LAPLAND

*To the East of Norway and Sweden and bordering
Russia lies Finland, a beautiful land of lakes, rivers,
marsh and pine forests where the trees outnumber
the people. Across northern Norway, Sweden,
Finland and the Kola Peninsula of Russia, in the
Arctic Circle region and beyond, is the Sami, or
Lapp, territory of Lapland, which is not an
independent nation but which is attempting to obtain
some autonomy. Finns and Sami people have a
different origin from their Nordic neighbours, the
Swedes and Norwegians. Both peoples descended from
Finno-Ugric tribes who came westward out of Asia
from an area between the River Volga and the
Ural mountains. They appeared in Finland around
four to five thousand years ago, leaving evidence in
the form of prehistoric skis and around
1,500 rock drawings.*

Finland did not become Christian until the twelfth century, when the Swedish king known as Eric the Good and one of his bishops – the English-born Bishop Henry of Uppsala, who later became Finland's patron saint – declared Finland to be a province of Sweden. Sweden lost

the eastern Finnish province of Karelia to Russia in 1240, but retained control of the rest of Finland until 1809, when the Russians invaded the remainder of Finland. Karelia came under the control of the Orthodox Church, but the rest of Finland was Catholic until the seventeenth century, when the Scandinavian countries accepted the Protestant Reformation. The Finns were obliged to change their religion in line with their Swedish overloads.

There were other changes, particularly for the Sami. From the sixteenth century onward, the Sami found themselves pushed northward into Lapland (*Sapmi* in Sami) by agricultural settlers who took control of the coastal regions, disturbing the Sami hunting and fishing lifestyle. The process did not stop there. Colonizers from the major powers in the region – Denmark, which had political control of Norway, Sweden, Swedish-controlled Finland, and Russia – began to settle further North in Lapland, competing to claim Lapland's territory for their own. For the reindeer herding Sami, whose reindeer herds' migration patterns criss-crossed the new national boundaries, the political problems were endless. Some Sami found themselves paying taxes to three different states.

Christianity reached the Sami peoples later than most European peoples. The Catholic Church had little interest in them and it was not until 1532 that the Orthodox priest Saint Trifon began to convert Sami living on the Finnish-Russian border. The majority of Sami retained their traditional beliefs, however, and it was only when Sweden became Protestant in the seventeenth century that Sami living farther to the West were subjected to Lutheran missionary influence. This was unfortunate for the Sami. Sami belief was condemned as idolatrous magic and their shamanistic beliefs and practices were violently suppressed. Sami shamans, or *noaidi*, suffered the same fate as Jews, witches and others who did not subscribe to the dominant beliefs of their day. In the spring of 1693, Lars Nilsson, a Sami *noaidi* was burned to death in the square at Arjeplog. Traditional beliefs did not die, however, and shamans continued to practise their skills.

FINNISH TRADITION

Finnish and Sami traditions evolved from common origins in a shamanic culture. Under the Catholic and Orthodox Churches, this culture was allowed to survive. With an illiterate population who attended services conducted in another language, the churches were not minded to enquire too closely what the Finnish populace thought as long as they turned up for church services, and the Sami were largely left to their own traditions. The Lutheran Church had other ideas. Pastors forbade the singing of the traditional songs that told the myths and the persecution of shamans began. In rural areas, however, the songs continued to be handed down through families and in the nineteenth century attitudes began to change. A serious effort began to collect the songs, poetry and myths of the ancient culture, although the impetus was less spiritual than political. Finland was beginning to struggle for independence and, like other European independence movements, reviving the national culture and language was an important part of awakening the desire for freedom. The "hero" of Finnish folklore revival is Elias Löhnrot. Löhnrot began travelling the eastern province of Karelia where, unlike Protestant Finland, the Orthodox Church had allowed the indigenous traditions to continue to flourish. He published two compilations – an epic, the *Kalevala*, and a collection of poetry, the *Kanteletar*.

As an awakener of national consciousness, the *Kalevala* was a resounding success. Finns realized that they were the inheritors of an ancient and important mythological and cultural tradition. The singing of the *Kalevala* and its focus on fundamental questions of human existence inspired the famous Finnish composer Jean Sibelius (1865–1957). He began to base works on the *Kalevala*, such as the *Swan Of Tuonela*, written in 1893, and a suite of four orchestral works based on the Lemminkäinen legends. In 1899, Sibelius' *First Symphony* and his famous *Finlandia* suite were performed. *Finlandia* was so patriotically stirring that it was promptly banned by the Russian occupation. Later, postage stamps were issued in Sibelius' honour, and February 28, the date of the preface of the first edition of the *Kalevala*, became a Finnish national holiday.

THE KALEVALA

The *Kalevala* is orated or sung by pairs of orators, often sitting opposite each other and holding hands. As they sing, they rock to and fro to create a hypnotic effect on the audience. The singers performed prodigious feats of memory. Larin Paraske (1834–1904), a famous singer known by Sibelius, had 11,000 lines in her repertoire. Like other oral traditions, there are a number of repeated or echo lines to help the singers make smooth transitions from one to another and to jog one another's memories. Memory is also helped by the rhythm. The songs have an unusual, archaic trochaic tetrameter, consisting of four long-short pairs of syllables, that has been part of the oral culture in the Baltic and Finnish region for two thousand years. The *dainos* songs of Lithuania and Latvia have a similar rhythm. More recently the *Kalevala* stimulated the poet Longfellow to use the rhythm in his epic poem *The Song Of Hiawatha* (1855).

By the Shining Big Sea Water
stood the tent of Hiawatha…

Kalevala means "home of Kaleva", a mythical giant who was considered to be an early ancestor of humankind. It consists of a number of story cycles centring on three main characters. Väinämöinen is a mighty singer and shaman, who journeys to the Otherworld to seek knowledge. Another cycle tells how Väinämöinen competes with the smith Ilmarinen for the hand of a goddess figure, the Maid of the North. Later, the hero, Lemminkäinen-Of-The-Many-Names deserts his wife to woo the goddess. Another

An example of
Elias Löhnrot's poetry.

Lemminkäinen's mother mourns her son in Tuonela, the land of the dead.

cycle tells of the search for a mysterious magical treasure, the *Sampo*, which is made from the tip of a swan's feather, a barren cow's milk, a grain of barley and the wool of a summer ewe.

BELIEFS AND COSMOLOGY

Finnish pre-Christian religion has roots in shamanism and the cosmology is that of a shamanic world with an Upperworld, a Lowerworld, *Tuonela* or *Manala*, the home of the dead and the world of everyday consciousness,

Middle Earth. Four pillars at the four corners of the world hold up the sky. In the centre is the Pole Star, from which the canopy of the heavens is hung. The concept of a World-Tree, similar to the Scandinavian Yggdrasil, is also found in Finnish tradition. The souls of babies yet unborn live in the boughs of the World-Tree and our destinies are written on its leaves. When a leaf falls, a person dies. In rituals, shamans would ascend the tree until they entered the Upperworld in a state of ecstasy.

In Finnish myth, the world is created by a goddess –

Ilmater, or Air-Daughter. At first there is no land, only air and water. The goddess is a virgin and for many aeons she floats alone in the empty airy wastes above the surface of the waters. As the centuries pass, Ilmater becomes lonely. She decides to descend on to the surface of the waters beneath her. As she does so, the wind whips up foaming waves that make her pregnant – Air-Daughter is now Water-Mother. Ilmater's pregnancy lasts for 700 years, but eventually labour begins. The labour is difficult and, despite Ilmater's efforts, the child does not come until she prays to Ukko, god of the sky, for help. Ukko sends a primeval duck that mistakes Ilmater's knee for a green hilltop, lands, builds a nest and lays seven eggs. The nest begins to irritate Ilmater and she jerks her knee. The eggs fall into the water and break. Six eggs are of gold and from these she uses a half shell to create the Lowerworld and another half for the Upperworld. A yolk becomes the Sun and the white the Moon. Other parts of the eggs become stars and clouds. The seventh egg is made of iron and Ilmater uses the iron shell to create our world. After another nine years, Ilmater begins to create order. She raises her hand and arranges the headlands. She makes hills, islands, underwater caves, rocks and reefs. She sets the sky on its pillars. After another 30 summers, Ilmater's child begins to fight his way out of the womb. Earth has been created and the conditions necessary for his survival exist. The child of Ilmater is Väinämöinen, the first shaman.

Väinämöinen, like other mythological Divine heroes, is already old before his birth and is full of wisdom. He is an accomplished bard and shaman who accompanies his songs on a five-stringed *kantele*, a folk instrument like a zither. Väinämöinen completes his mother's work of creation by instructing the young god Sampsa Pellervoinen, Strong-Field, to sow the world with trees – birch, juniper, alder, cherry, rowan, willow, oak, pine and spruce. Vegetation now begins. Other verses of the *Kalevala* tell of how copper comes to Finland. Axes are made and trees are felled to thin out forests to encourage bushes and berries to grow at ground level. Forests are slashed and burned to create agricultural land, in the same way that ancient forests such as the Amazon are being cleared today. Väinämöinen discovers barley seeds washed up on the shore and begins ploughing and sowing to create agricultural production. He asks for divine assistance. From the Earth goddess, "Lady of the soil" and "Mistress of the Earth", he requests the power of fertility, and from the sky god he asks for rains to make the seeds grow. The *Kalevala* also has an environmental message. The birds commend Väinämöinen's work. He has not felled all the trees, but has left birches for the birds to sit on. Väinämöinen asks the cuckoo to sing at evenings, mornings and midday, so that:

My weather may be fair,
My forests pleasant,
My shores prosperous,
My belly full of grain.

The *Kalevala* ends on a sad note. The last story cycle is that of the maid Marjatta, or the Virgin Mary. Here, the Christian tale is retold by Karelian Orthodox Finns. Around the sixteenth century, they combined their ancient legends with the new story of the Christ child. In this version the child is born miraculously without a human father when Marjatta swallows a berry. The child goes missing but is found in the swamp, the place where illegitimate children were abandoned. He is taken to the god of oats,

Petroglyph from North Cape, Lapland, of two men in a boat with fish traps. Around 1,500 rock paintings have been found, made by the ancestors of the Sami.

Virokannas, whose festival was at Midsummer, and who was later merged with St John the Baptist in Finland. The child is baptised by Virokannas. The old order acknowledges the new and the child is named King of Karelia and Guardian of all Power. Väinämöinen is angry. He knows that for the present his time is over – but not forever. One day the people will need him again to create a new magical treasure. His era will return:

> *Years will pass, new aeon dawning,*
> *you will need me, longing that I,*
> *make new Sampo, make new music,*
> *send new Moon and free new Sun,*
> *when Earth lies in joyless darkness.*

As in the Scandinavian and Hindu traditions, eras come and go, the cosmos changes and the old gods are reborn.

OTHER DEITIES

Karelia has different deities from those found in West Finland, but they are similar in that they are the deities of northern peoples reliant partly on agriculture but also on hunting. The first record of names of Finnish deities was made by Bishop Mikael Agricola in the sixteenth century, rather surprisingly on the pages of his psalter. Other deity names are found in the *Kalevala*. Ukko is god of sky and thunder, the Upperworld. His wife is Rauni, goddess of lightning, winds and the Earth. She lives in the Middleworld. The god Tuoni is lord of the Lowerworld and lord of the dead. His home, Tuonela, is encircled by the black Tuoni River, on which glides the Swan of Tuonela.

The forests of Finland are populated with wild animals and deities of the forest. Two of the best known are Mielikki and Tapio. The English writer J.R.R. Tolkien was familiar with the *Kalevala* and, in his fantasy cycle *Lord Of The Rings*, his descriptions of Goldberry and Tom Bombadil are similar to Mielikki and Tapio. Mielikki is known as the Golden Goddess and is Mistress of the Forest. She has clear skin and is beautiful to look at. She appears dressed in a blue cloak and with golden earrings, headband, and necklace. The name Mielikki comes from the Finnish word *mieli*, meaning mind. *Sinipiikat*, blue maidens, assist her in her care of the forest. *Sinipiikat* are tree spirits and each species has its own guardian. Pihlajatar, for instance, is the *Sinipiikat* of the rowan. Mielikki opens "Tapio's larder" to send animals to hunters who invoke her and make the correct offerings. Her preferred offerings were milk or honey, which would be left in special stones with hollowed out centres. Tapio wears a cloak of lichen and a hat of fir twigs or pine needles. He has golden ornaments on his breast. His titles are Old Man of the Forest, Golden Forest King, Old Forest Greybeard, Lord of the Mound, Old Man Hill, Giver of Gifts and Strong God. He has the power to help hunters. If hunters invoke him correctly, he will release to them the animals he wears around his belt. He will make sure that the hunter's aim is true and give advice on where to find game. His daughter, Tuulikki, will drive game toward the hunters.

SEASONAL FESTIVALS

Until the twentieth century, most Finns were farmers and their festivals were a mixture of traditional agricultural festivals and Christian holidays. Wintertide festivities are now an important part of the Finnish year. Prior to Christmas, evening parties called *pikkujoulu*, or "Little Christmas", are held with seasonal food, drink and music. Christmas is a family holiday with Christmas Eve being more important than Christmas Day. At noon, there is a ceremony dating from the Middle Ages whereby the peace of Christmas is proclaimed from Turku, the former capital. This marks the beginning of the Christmas feast. The Finns have always had a reputation for cleanliness and Christianity did not suppress an easy acceptance of the human body. Communal nudity is commonplace and

Nineteenth-century print of a traditional Finnish sauna.

Finns do not consider a home to be complete unless it includes a sauna. On Christmas Eve, cleansing saunas are part of the preparations.

Relatives who have passed away are remembered on this family festival. At sunset, families go to the churchyard, where a service is held and candles placed on family graves. Thousands of candles flicker in the snow to remind the living of their ancestors. Those who have died for Finland's freedom are also remembered. Former soldiers visit the graves of the fallen and army officers mount a guard of honour at the tomb of Finnish hero Marshal Mannerheim. In the evening, children dress as Father Christmas' helpers in red tights, a long red cap and a grey cotton suit decorated

with red to await a visit from a relative or neighbour dressed as Joulupukki, the Finnish Father Christmas, who comes laden with a basket of presents. Father Christmas always asks the same question, "Are there any good children here?" His "helpers" give a resounding "Yes". Children then sing to Father Christmas, who tells them he has come a long way, all the way from Korvatunturi in Lapland.

Spring is another festival time. On the morning of Palm Sunday, children dress as witches and visit local homes. They carry a basket decorated with brightly coloured feathers and containing willow twigs. The children wave the willow twigs in front of the house and recite spells over them before giving them to the house as a blessing. Like the Irish *Beltane* and *Samhain* festivities, the visiting children expect sweets or money in return. Spring comes late to Finland and the ground is frozen. Then, with the long spring days of these northern latitudes, suddenly everything comes to life again. Streams melt and start to flow. Leaves appear on the trees and birds migrate back to their summer breeding grounds.

April 4 was a major feast of the traditional Finnish seasonal cycle, the agricultural festival of Ukon Vakat, or Ukko's Day, which celebrated the end of spring ploughing. The legend of the bringing of barley to Finland was sung and, as is typical of European spring festivals, there would be feasting, beer drinking and courting. Similar songs are still sung at Ritvala in Finland, but at Whitsun rather than earlier in the year. Another spring festival is May Day, Vappu, which celebrates the coming of summer, a welcome event in this northern land. Every high school graduate receives a white cap and Vappu is a day when people wear their white caps and crown certain statues with white caps.

Midsummer is an important festival. In the North of the country, it is the time of the Midnight Sun and endless day. Most Finnish families have second homes by country lakes and Midsummer is very much a country festival. The highlight of the festival is the lighting of the Midsummer bonfire. Birch wood is traditionally included and at Midsummer even buses and trains may be decorated with birch.

On Palm Sunday morning children dressed as witches visit local homes to bless the home and occupants. The children are given sweets or money in return.

Sami couple in traditional dress with reindeer. Reindeer herding was traditionally a principle occupation of the Sami and continues to be important.

Väinämöinen, he the ancient,
he, the great primeval shaman,
hurried then unto the alder,
cut the sticks, put them in order,
and began the lots to shuffle.

Other sources indicate that the alder sticks would have had signs marked upon them. Here is a spell for casting the runes:

I will cast my alder rune sticks,
Ancient Kavé, Nature Goddess,
Golden Kavé, Lovely Lady,
come to us, set out the rune sticks,
with your hands, shuffle the bundle,
turn the rune sticks with your own hands.

Some of the earliest folklore chants collected in the seventeenth century were for assistance with, and protection during, hunting. Hunters would pursue large animals that could be savage in defence of themselves and their young. Bear hunting in particular was a dangerous occupation and surrounded by many taboos. The bear was so fearsome that it was considered unlucky to give it its true name. Terms such as "apple of the forest", "honey paw" and "beastie" were used to make the fierce bear seem less threatening. The hunters had also to deal with the bitter cold and the hazards of unexpected snow. A small amount of snow could help the hunt. On frozen ground, animals leave no tracks. Hunters would call on the sky god Ukko for a short snowfall, so that tracks might be found in the new soft snow. Ukko is also called on to help with healing.

Autumn was the time of the important harvest festival of *Kekri*, which marked the beginning of New Year. Like most New Year festivals, it was a time to foretell the future for the year to come. The Finnish method is to melt tin and to pour the molten metal into cold water. The tin cools into shapes that are held up to the wall to form shadows. The shapes of the shadows are omens for the year to come. During the twentieth century, *Kekri* declined in importance and the old *Kekri* divination traditions were transferred to Christmas and New Year.

MAGICAL PRACTICES

Like the Scandinavians, the Finns also had rune divination. The *Kalevala* describes how Väinämöinen, the first shaman, uses alder wood to make runes:

HEALING

Shamanic healing practices were found among the Finns into the twentieth century. Those who lived outside towns depended heavily on the traditional healer and shaman –

the *tietäjä*, one-who-knows. The *tietäjä* was responsible for knowing about the world of the spirits and knowing how to keep at bay the spirits that caused sickness. Sickness is the shamanic world view always has a cause. Spirits can cause illness, but not necessarily of their own volition. They might be sent by ill-wishing neighbours or others that the sick person has offended. The *tietäjä* could be called upon to help with any community or individual problem that seemed to require remedies beyond the scope of everyday knowledge. The *tietäjä* would also divine the future, identify criminals and give children names. One sign that someone might be a *tietäjä* was being born with a tooth. In other families, the tradition was hereditary. Juha Kellokoski was a mid-nineteenth century *tietäjä* who was interviewed by folklorists and persuaded to part with his precious "Black Book" of spells and cures. The book has black pages, the writing is in red ink and it contains the types of useful spell that would be needed by his clientele, such as spells for getting rid of nightmares. Juha Kellokoski had a familiar spirit who helped him and he liked to perform most of his spells at the rapids where his familiar spirit lived.

A *tietäjä* would teach others and one tradition, found elsewhere in Europe, is that a *tietäjä* must pass on his or her power to another before dying. It was a rule in Finnish tradition that the knowledge must only be passed to someone younger than oneself. In the case of the famous Finnish *tietäjä* couple Hetastiina and Heikki Hurstinen, there was an age gap of 22 years. Hetastiina and Heikki lived in Vilppula in central Finland. Hetastiina was already 42 year of age and a famous healer when she met the 20-year-old Heikki in around 1906. Hetastiina recognized in Heikki a rare magical talent and, in 1916, despite the age gap they married. Hetastiina divined the causes of sickness and the appropriate cure by entering a trance and writing down her visions. To assist her work, she had a "Black Bible", a translation of the sixth and seventh books of Moses, an obscure ritual magic text, which she kept in a locked and darkened room. Hetastiina died in 1936, but Heikki Hurstinen sur-

vived her to 1972, becoming more famous after his wife's death. He was particularly popular during the 1940s and 1950s and on one occasion a queue of 36 people was waiting outside his door for a consultation. Like his wife, Heikki Hurstinen used trances to help in his work. His specialisms were dowsing for wells – an important agricultural occupation in the era before piped water supplies – and locating the bodies of victims of drowning, a common fate in a land of sea, lakes and wild winds. Like Juha Kellokoski, Heikki Hurstinen consulted his familiar spirits outside, in this case at a sacred grove near his home. He is buried with his wife in Vilppula cemetery.

SAMI TRADITION

In recent years, Lapland has been promoted in tourist brochures as a land of Santa Claus, reindeer-drawn sleighs and the Midnight Sun, but life is more rugged than these picture postcard images. Lapland is a place of cruel wind that tears trees from the ground and whips up lake surfaces into furious cascades of water that drown unwary fishermen. High up in the mountains, birch trees grow almost horizontally, permanently bent before the wind. Yet, the barren landscape is not uninhabitable. Even in the darkest days of winter, thousands of animal tracks criss-cross the snow providing game for hunters. Originally, Sami people lived a semi-nomadic life hunting and fishing, and keeping some domesticated reindeer. A change came in the sixteenth century when the Sami in the tundra regions began to domesticate large reindeer herds and a nomadic herding way of life developed to meet the herds' grazing needs. Today, few Sami are nomads, but reindeer herding remains an important occupation. About ten per cent of Samis are involved in herding and most Sami have relatives who are herders. Contemporary Sami reindeer herders supplement their income with fishing, hunting and traditional arts and crafts. The importance of reindeer is conveyed by Sami language. There are about 400 names for reindeer, which distinguish reindeer by their characteristics, such as sex, age and colour.

SAMI SPIRITUALITY

Sami think of "religion" as meaning Christianity and see their traditional belief system as a way of life rather than a "religion". Their world view is that of a shamanic culture. There is an Otherworld that exists alongside the material world, where everything is more perfect than in the everyday world. The Otherworld is the home of the dead. Sami spirituality is animist. Every object has a soul and must be respected. This includes the forest. People were expected to move through it quietly, causing as little disturbance as possible. Sami tradition has many deities or spirits with control over different aspects of nature. Interpreting the will of the spirits was the responsibility of the community shaman. People could not choose to become a *noaidi* or shaman. The spirit world chose those through whom it would speak, so to be a shaman was a "vocation", a calling. Like their counterparts in other cultures, Sami shamans enter the Otherworld through rhythmic drumming that induces trance and out-of-body experiences. The Sami were famed for their proficiency at trance and when Scandinavians invaded the region, women seeresses turned to Sami shamans to help them perfect the trance art of *seithr*.

Sami *noaide* or shamans used their trances to provide advice to the community about hunting and to mediate with the deities of the animals to ensure a successful and safe hunt. Other deities of the Sami people were deities of the elements, a major influence on Sami survival. The wind god, Bieggaålmaj, could send warming or chilling winds. Raudna was the goddess of lightning and of the Earth. Important places had their own guardian deity. Evocative rock formations and trees that resembled human form, either through natural growth or because they had been specially shaped, might be thought to have their own guardian spirit. These were known as *sieidde* (*seitas* in Finnish) and offerings were left for them.

SEASONAL CYCLE

The traditional Sami year is divided into eight seasons that relate to different phases of the reindeer-herding cycle. Reindeer roam large areas and a reindeer-herding district can range from 1,000 to 5,000 square kilometres. The year alternates between movement to different grazing sites and rest. In early spring, herds follow pregnant females from the forests to the mountains.

In spring, the females give birth to their young in the mountain foothills. In early summer, the herds graze on new spring growth. In summer, Lapland enjoys endless day. For over two months, there is little darkness. During the long hours of daylight, the reindeer herders mark the ears of new-born calves to indicate their owners. Ruska, early autumn, begins at the end of August. The green leaves of summer changed to reds and yellows. Bull reindeer fattened by summer grazing are sorted. A few are kept through the winter for breeding and the remainder are killed for meat and hides.

Kaamos is autumn and the time of the first new snowfalls. The snow cover starts to build up in September. Light disappears, not to be seen again for days or weeks on end. Autumn is the reindeer's mating season. Reindeer herders fish while the remaining bull reindeer mate with the cows. In early winter, the herds move down from the frost-covered mountain slopes to the marshlands, where grazing is still available. As snow thickens with the onset of winter proper, the reindeer herds are broken down into smaller groups and taken into the forest, where they can graze on lichen and have more protection from snow and

RIGHT: "Snow boats" from the Lapp Museum, at Inari, in Finland.

OPPOSITE PAGE: The Aurora Borealis or Northern Lights appear as a spectacular phenomenon against the star-filled skies of the Arctic winter.

A sami herder protesting with the flag of his people. The flag is based on the symbol of the drum, an important instrument for the Sami shamans.

orally through *yoik*, which are rhythmic sung poems that may be some of the oldest forms of music in Europe. *Yoik* varies between different regions of Lapland. Some yoik sounds melodious, but other yoik sound more like bird song and can seem odd to the untrained western ear, though not to contemporary minimalist composers.

A *yoik* is not just a song; to sing it is a magical act that reaches to the essence of that which is sung. In traditional Sami culture, every person must have a yoik, just as he or she must have a name. A *yoik* expresses the individuality of the person and helps give that person being. There are *yoiks* for people, animals and the land. A *yoik* is not linear and does not have beginning, middle and end. Singer, song and subject matter are part of a unified world view. Singing *yoik* is a creative act that sings into being that which is sung. It may also send someone into trance. In the *Kalevala*, the young Sami singer Joukahainen hears of the famous shaman Väinämöinen and wants to go South to the lands of the Finns to see if he can out-sing him. His parents warn his against this rash endeavour:

You'll be sung and chanted face into the snow,
head into drifts, fists into cold hard air,
until your hands cannot turn,
until your feet cannot move.

bad weather. At Midwinter at the Arctic Circle, the Sun disappears for a week, but further North it will be dark for six weeks. Only the Moon, stars and the brilliant spectacle of the *Aurora Borealis*, the Northern Lights, break the dark night sky.

DRUMMING AND YOIK

Singing and drumming are an important part of Sami culture. Drumming is essential for shamanic trance journeying and drums are made into objects of beauty. They are painted with animals and other phenomena from nature, which over the centuries have evolved into symbolic images. In eastern Finland, Sami drums have three segments representing the Upperworld, Middle Earth and the Lowerworld. Southern Sami have drums based on solar symbolism. Sami myths and legends are transmitted

Joukahainen's parents are convinced that their son will be overcome by the trance-inducing power of the magical singing of the older shaman but, like many a foolish young man before and after him, Joukahainen knows better than his parents. Off he goes in his horse-drawn sleigh across the snows, only to be out-sung and thoroughly humiliated by the wilier Väinämöinen.

Yoik was strongly suppressed by the Lutheran Church and in some parts of Finland it was illegal to sing it. Today, however, traditional Sami folk song is being revived and becoming better known. Nils-Aslak Valkeapää sang *yoik* in the opening ceremonies of the Lillehammer Winter Olympics and Sami singer Mari Boine Persen from Norway has a growing international reputation among world-music fans.

FINNISH AND SAMI TRADITION TODAY

There is strong interest in Finland it traditional culture and in the *Kalevala*, which inspires modern artists and craftspeople, but the spiritual tradition of Finland is only a minority interest. There is, however, some revival of interest in traditional shamanic practices and folk witchcraft. Across the water in neighbouring Estonia, a Pagan Heritage Protection Club has been formed at the University of Tartu to revive Estonian tradition, which is similar to that of their cousins the Finns. The Pagan Heritage Protection Club performs rituals led by a shaman and publishes a journal, Hiis, or Sacred Wood.

The Sami traditional lifestyle has undergone dramatic changes in the last decades. Reindeer herding has changed, as technology brings in helicopters and snowmobiles instead of skis and sleighs. Some older Sami regret that their healthier lifestyle is gone. Environmental problems impinge more and more on the Sami. Tourism can bring wealth, but there is concern about the environmental cost and tourist operators' trivialization of Sami cultural heritage. The Sami do not appreciate being Santa's window-dressing. Commercial logging is also a serious problem. Clear felling of forests deprives animals of food and shelter and forestry companies' bulldozers destroy the ground lichen that provides reindeer with winter food. Even where there is replanting, this does not replace the other main source of winter reindeer food – hanging black lichen, which is found only on old trees. Summer brings other problems. The lakeside second homes that add to the quality of life for boat-loving Norwegians, Swedes and Finns, can impact badly on the Sami. Building development can disrupt reindeer territories and prevent the reindeer's access to lakesides for drinking water. The Sami have also been affected by twentieth-century environmental disasters. The accident at the Soviet Chernobyl nuclear power plant in 1985 spread radiation that damaged some reindeer herds and polluted the lichen on which they feed.

Like other indigenous peoples, the Sami have struggled to establish their rights. Samis in Norway, Sweden and Finland have each set up parliaments with representatives elected by Sami voters. The parliaments have a joint Nordic/Sami Council that liaises between the Norwegian, Swedish and Finnish Sami, and Russian Sami are now represented. The Sami now have their own flag based on a drum symbol with a circle of a red sun, a blue moon, and green and yellow bands, all colours featured in traditional clothing.

Through the Nordic/Sami Council, the Sami participate in the World Council of Indigenous Peoples (WCIP), which engages governments on issues such as land rights. Mineral rights are another important issue for the Sami, as for other indigenous peoples, but there has been little progress in discussions with the governments involved. Often the areas into which indigenous peoples were pushed by invaders were those perceived as having little value when economies were dependent on agriculture. Of course, with industrialization, these areas often proved to have considerable mineral wealth, a wealth that the indigenous peoples would like naturally to claim as their own.

A Kobdas drum with beater. The drum is used by shamans to induce trance. The skin is reindeer.

THE FAR NORTH & THE INUIT

The Arctic was the last region of our planet to be inhabited by humankind. It takes its name from the Greek word "arktos", meaning bear, for from the perspective of those to the South, the Arctic is the home of the constellation Ursa Major, the Great Bear. From Greenland around to Alaska, the indigenous inhabitants of the northern Arctic region are the Inuit. When new peoples encounter one another, the names they give each other often represent what seem to be the distinguishing and not always attractive characteristics of the other. Cree Indians told European traders that the Inuit were called "Eskimos", a Cree term meaning "eaters of raw meat". This is not a name the Inuit use for themselves and in 1977, the Inuit Circumpolar Conference at Barrow, Alaska, adopted Inuit as the official name for their peoples.

PREVIOUS PAGE: Inuits in traditional dress. Behind them is a prefabricated house. Houses have largely replaced traditional winter igloos and summer tents.

The Inuit developed skilled methods to produce beautiful carvings in soapstone and other materials. This is a nineteenth-century carving of polar bears wrestling.

The ancestors of the Inuit crossed the Bering land bridge from Siberia into Alaska around 5,000 to 10,000 years ago. The first group, who spoke Na-Dene, moved inland and southward. They became the ancestors of the Athabascan-speaking peoples of Alaska, northern Canada, British Columbia, and California, as well as of the Apache and Navajo of the southwestern United States. A second group arrived between 6,000 and 7,000 years ago. By 4,000 years ago, this group had separated into the southern Alaskan Aleut and the Inuit, who developed a highly adaptable culture based largely on sea and land mammal hunting, and salt and freshwater fishing. Today, Inuit is spoken along the northern polar region and is sub-divided into two major languages, Inupiaq and Yup'ik. Yup'ik is spoken by the Yuit (singular, Yuk) as far North as the mouth of the Yukon River, which is named after them. Mutually comprehensible dialects of Inupiaq are spoken from Point Barrow on the northern Alaskan coast to as far East as Greenland, although people at the extreme eastern end of the swathe of Inuit settlements might have difficulty understanding far westerners. Inuit and Aleut languages show strong similarities to their Asian cousins, the Chukchi-speaking peoples of far northeast Siberia, and there are similarities with the Mongol tribes.

Early Inuit encounters with other races are described in their myths and legends. The legend of the origin of the mountains describes the Inuit's ancestors as coming into North America on the trail of migrating caribou. Two types of people already lived in the new land. The happy-go-lucky little people could be seen only out of the corner of the eye and if caught in the hand could be made to sing. Like Irish leprechauns, it is not clear if they are a smaller race or supernatural beings. The other inhabitants are the giant Tunit, who are fierce and warlike. They are enemies of the Inuit and try to capture them to cook them and eat them. Although the giants have superior strength, the Inuit defeat them through superior cunning and advanced technology – the bow and arrow. In this instance the Inuit could be describing Neanderthal peoples, but we have no evidence yet of Neanderthals in North America.

We know something of the history of the early Inuit from archaeological evidence. In other parts of the world, archaeological artefacts are quickly covered by soil and vegetation, but in the barren Arctic landscape they are found close to the surface, which makes archaeologists' work easier. Like other cultures, graves have been found. Here they are piled up cairns of stones. Most other artefacts are associated with hunting – tools of antler, ivory and bone, rock traps for fox and *nanuk* – polar bear – the Inuit's most feared enemy, and *inuksuit*, rock cairn decoys for caribou hunting.

The Inuit were not isolated in the northern vastness. Once the Bering land bridge had disappeared, the Yup'ik Inuit of Alaska continued to cross back and forth between the Asian and North American sides of the Bering Strait by skin boat, particularly to barter for iron from the Old World, which was traded right across North America, as far as Hudson's Bay on Canada's East coast. From around 1000 CE, the Inuit had trading contacts with a tall, pale people with thick beards who came from the East in large wooden boats that had fierce animals painted on their high prows. These were Scandinavians, such as Eric the Red's son, Lief the Lucky. The Europeans established settlements and traded iron implements for products of seal and ivory, but the settlements died out and trading declined. Martin Frobisher made exploratory voyages to Baffin Island in the 1570s and there was sporadic contact following these visits, but the impact was minimal. The Inuit were left to manage their own affairs.

INUIT LIFE

Inuit society was based on family bands rather than the larger tribes of Native American peoples below the tree line. Small groups can survive better in extreme climates than large communities. Families would sometimes come together for periods to hunt or for festivities, but they did not form large permanent groupings. This meant that many of the social structures of more complex societies were not needed. Inuit camps did not have chiefs. Samuel Hearne, an eighteenth-century trader and explorer, commented on how the Inuit lived in "a state of perfect freedom; no one apparently claiming the superiority over, or acknowledging the least subordination to another, except what is due from children to their parents, or such of their kin as take care of them when they are young and incapable of providing for themselves". Parents taught their children the skills needed for survival, and knowledge was passed through the family group, which comprised the parents, close relatives and relations by marriage. Marriage was important for physical survival and involved a strict division of labour, with husband and wife owning their own tools, household goods and personal possessions. House building, hunting and fishing were male responsibilities. Cooking, dressing animal skins, making clothing and, in some cases, boat building were female responsibilities. Marriages were usually by choice rather than arranged and monogamy was the norm, although polygamy occurred for both men and women. Sexual sharing occurred with co-marriages, where couples would meet and exchange partners on a temporary basis and the head of a household might honour a guest by offering him the opportunity of sleeping with his wife. These customs created bonds of obligation between families and were biologically helpful in increasing the gene pool in small communities and preventing in-breeding.

There were strong obligations to support kin. Those who did not fulfil their obligations were shamed and could be forced out of the community. Like other earlier soci-

The Inuit developed clothing from furs that enabled humans to survive the hostile climate. This parka from West Greenland is large enough for a woman to cover a mother and baby.

eties, people were responsible for the actions of their kin. To harm someone could create a feud between families, not just individuals, so provocative behaviour or displays of anger were strongly frowned upon. Some groups devised outlets for aggression through wrestling matches and song duels, in which the aggrieved parties had to use their wits to shame their opponent by extemporizing insulting songs. A loser might be so humiliated as to have to leave the community. There was no traditional word for law. Social norms were conveyed through unwritten social custom. All family members – with the exception of babies – had duties and responsibilities. Previous experience of dealing with difficult situations was important for survival. Elders were respected information providers and looked to for knowledge and guidance.

Inuit life is built on shared values. In a paper presented to the 1998 General Assembly of the Inuit Circumpolar Conference at Nuuk, Greenland, Finn Lynge described these as: *nunamut ataqqinninneq* – pride and respect in knowing the land, and its whales, caribou, plains and mountains, light and dark, hardness and beauty; *akisussaassuseq* – responsibility toward the land and its species; tukkussuseq – generosity and hospitality; and *inuk nammineq* – personal independence and individual strength. These are values that create the basis for survival in the Arctic.

Inuit traditional life is dominated by the extreme Arctic climate. Inuit have learned to accept that human beings cannot always control events. A hunter would say, "I'll try and catch that game," rather than, "I will catch that game". Accidents and hardships happen and the attitude must be one of *ajurnarmat*, meaning "it can't be helped". Tragedy had to be accepted and life allowed to move on. Many concepts and ideas that are vital to Inuit survival are meaningless to those of us who live in more urban environments. It is often said that the Inuit have a hundred words for snow. This is not strictly true. There is only one word for snow – *aput* – but there are many words to distinguish different conditions of snow. Knowing snow conditions is essential in a climate where people seek game across long distances and

must communicate about hunting conditions to others. Here are some words for snow conditions:

anamana	space between drifts and obstruction
anniu	falling snow
api	ground snow
kaioglaq	sharply etched, wind-eroded surface
kalutoganiq	arrow-shaped snow drift
kimoaqtruk	snow drift
mapsuk	overhanging drift
natatgonaq	rough surface of large particles
pukak	bottom snow layer (depth hoar)
qali	snow on the boughs of trees
qamaniq	bowl-like depression under tree
quinzhee	snow shelter
salumaroaq	smooth surface of fine particles
siqoq	smoky (drifting snow)
siqoqtoaq	sun crust
tumarinyiq	ripple-type drift
upsik	wind-beaten snow

BELIEFS

Inuit spirituality was originally shamanistic and resembled other shamanistic traditions, such as those of the Sami, Finns, Siberians and other northern peoples. Beliefs about life after death reflect the cosmology of a shamanic society with an Upperworld, a Middleworld of everyday reality and a Lowerworld. Dying was viewed stoically and the Inuit had a strong belief in life after death. For many Inuit peoples, the Northern Lights were the spirits of the dead. More is known about the afterlife beliefs of the Netsilingmiut Inuit people than others, because they maintained their traditional lifestyle for longest. Their *angakkoq*, or shamans, travelled into three different Otherworlds, all of which could be final destinations after death. Agniriartarfik is an Upperworld in the sky where the

OPPOSITE PAGE: An igloo made from cut blocks of ice. Igloos are winter dwellings. Tents would be used in summer.

Inuit grave effigy made of wood with a walrus ivory inlay.

dead live forever at the age at which they die. There is eternal happiness, games and excellent hunting. Aglirmiut is a Lowerworld located deep under the tundra but otherwise similar to Agniriartarfik. Noqumiut is a Lowerworld just under the tundra crust for those who have failed in their social obligations. Lazy hunters or women who are afraid to be tattooed might go here. To be sent to Noqumiut was to suffer something the Inuit feared most, a life of useless bored idleness. The Otherworlds seemed only to be thought of as resting places. There are also beliefs in reincarnation or the transmigration of souls. New-born babies were named after those who had passed away and were treated as if the deceased person's spirit occupied the child. A girl named after an elderly man's mother would be treated by him with the same respect that he would show his mother. This created bonds between different families.

ANGAKKUT

The Inuit universe was an animistic one, populated by spirits. Among some Inuit peoples, particularly the Nattilikmiut, there is a supreme being called Naarjuk, who made land and water, and cares for the dead. Tatqeq is a male spirit of the Moon who is responsible for fertility, rebirth and weather. Sila is the spirit of sky and air.

Each animal species has a spirit that cares for it. One of the most important is Nuliajuk, the Mother of the Sea, a female spirit who controls sea mammals, especially seals. She is half woman and half fish and has a fin. Many Inuit are named after spirits such as Nuliajuk, who is also known as Sedna or Takanaluk. Like Tapio of the Finns, Nuliajuk watches whether people obey the hunting taboos. If they do, she releases her animals to the hunters. If seal hunts were unsuccessful it was because Nuliajuk was angry. It was the shaman's job to find out why and to appease her. Shaman can enter a trance to visit Sedna's underwater kingdom. Rules of

An inuit sled handle carved in the form of a polar bear.

politeness governed all such encounters. When they meet Sedna, etiquette demands that they comb the algae from her hair because she cannot hold the comb for herself.

Some spirits are benevolent, but there were also thought to be malevolent spirits, which represent people's attempts to make sense of the frightening aspects of life, such as sickness, bad weather and accidents. To have contact with, or control of, the spirits was the function of the *angakkoq* (pl. *angakkut*). *Angakkut* are the shamans of the Inuit. In traditional Inuit society, the angakkoq was both doctor and solver of community problems. Shamans could be male or female. People could not choose to be shamans. They were chosen by the spiritual world to act as mouthpieces for the spirits. A potential *angakkoq* would be recognized by his or her light and warmth – the aura. This would attract a spirit who would ask to dwell in the person's aura. In return, the spirit would give the *angakkoq* powers. The greater the *angakkoq's* aura, the more spirits he or she would attract. In many cultures, there is an archetypal shaman who is said to have been the most powerful of all. Väinämöinen is the first and archetypal shaman of the Finns. Kiviok is the archetypal shaman of the Inuit. The lack of trees in the Arctic is explained by saying that Kiviok chopped them all down and their chippings fell into the water to create different species of fish.

Shamans would have one spirit guide, the shaman's personal *tuunngaq*, who was his or her chief helper and divining spirit, but other specialist spirits would be called upon for particular tasks. Some would be in animal form and others might be dead relatives. Illness was the work of malevolent spirits and it was the shaman's job to banish them. First the shaman needed to locate where in the patient's body the spirit was residing. The shaman's spirit guide assisted in divination rites. The shaman would lift the patient's head, or the patient would lift his or her own leg, and the spirit guide would be asked if there was a good spirit present or a bad one. If the head or limb became heavy, this indicated the presence of a bad spirit. The shaman could also divine using a rock tied to a sealskin rope. When the rock became heavy, this indicated the presence of a bad spirit. Shamans also sang special songs, *sakaubiit*, to identify bad spirits and where they were located. Songs could also be used to identify people who had caused illness, bad weather or lack of game by breaking taboos or by deliberately cursing someone. Once the bad spirit had been identified, it was ordered away.

Shamans were also consulted about fertility problems. The Moon spirit was responsible for fertility, so the shaman would make a journey to the Moon, to ask him to make the woman pregnant. Once he had completed the spirit journey, the shaman has the right to sleep with the woman. This social custom ensured that, regardless of the Moon god's intervention, women with infertile husbands would not remain barren.

Divination and other shamanic tasks were often performed in a state of trance. Trance was induced by drumming, singing and chanting to help the *angakkoq* leave his or her body to travel great distances to determine the causes of sickness and other community problems. Masks were used to assist the shaman to enter a trance state and to speak with the voice of a spirit in a way that would impress the shaman's audience. The shaman would grip animal teeth between his or her own to enhance the mask's realism. Tubes, similar to those in other shamanic cultures, could be used to suck out spirits that were causing illness in a patient's body. Other equipment included antler wands with carved faces representing spirit beings and carved wooden human figures with detachable arms and legs, which may have been used in sympathetic healing magic.

HUNTING MAGIC

Animals were of enormous significance in Inuit life since there were few vegetable food sources. It was essential for

All parts of the walrus can be used by the Inuit, providing meat, oil, skins and ivory for tools, jewels and carvings.

Inuit travelling by dog sleigh. Long winter journeys in search of food were opportunities for parents to teach their children about navigation, the weather and other features of the environment.

the continued survival of the Inuit that they maintained a balanced relationship with the animal kingdom, ensuring that their own numbers and hunting style did not decimate food stocks. Animal lives could not be taken without following a complex system of taboos that were designed to maintain the goodwill of the species by showing it respect and ensuring that animals were not killed unnecessarily. Inuit depended for their livelihood on an intimate knowledge of the species around them, their migrating and mating habits and their behaviour when hunted. It was important to maintain animal numbers. When fishing, small fish were thrown back. Hunters took older animals, leaving the pregnant and the young, so it was important to know the signs of pregnancy in each species.

Once animals had been killed, there were strong taboos about playing with food or joking about a dead animal. Inuit belief is that *anua* or *inua* (personalities or souls) exist in all people and animals. When an animal dies, its *inua* is not destroyed. It transmigrates to inhabit another animal. Many rituals and ceremonies were performed before and after hunting expeditions to ensure hunting success. Certain rites had to be observed in order to appease the animal's *inua*. When, for instance, the Netsilingmiut people killed a seal, they would leave a small piece of freshwater ice for the dead seal's *inua*. Seals are believed to be always thirsty because they swim in salt water, so the freshwater is a welcome offering.

Magic was used to improve the chances of a successful

of great significance. Stars foretell the seasons' change. Weather can be predicted from phenomena of the Moon and so too can tides, animal movements and women's menstrual flows, which tend to coincide in natural environments with either the new or full Moon. The Inuit can use the stars to navigate across the whiteness of the ice and snows in the same way that mariners used the stars to guide them across the seas. Traditional ways of travel, such as the dog sledge, allowed time to star gaze and to learn the sky maps that could take a hunter safely home. Nowadays, motorized snowmobiles mean that the stars rush by in the same way as landscape rushes by in a blur when we travel by fast car. A more regulated way of life, with school semesters to worry about and jobs with fixed hours, means that families rarely have the opportunity to travel together and for star lore to be passed down the generations during the winter months when the stars are most visible.

Their celestial paths and patterns made some stars much more important than others. The star *Aagjuuk* in the constellation known as Aquila, which appears in the sky at Winter Solstice is a herald of daylight. It appears on the northeast horizon during *tauvikjuaq*, meaning winter or "the great darkness", and was used to mark the time of day. *Tukturjuit*, the Plough or Ursa Major, is another timekeeper, but other stars that seem significant further South are of little importance. The Pole Star, *Nuutuittuq* or Never-Moves, is of little help as a navigation star and of no use at all above the Arctic Circle.

The Sun assumes overwhelming importance in far northern latitudes when it is absent from around early December to mid-January. The Moon provides light for hunters everywhere, but it is particularly important in the Arctic winter as a major source of light, especially when in some years it remains above the horizon for extended periods of time. All around the North Pole is the Arctic legend of sister Sun, Siqiniq, and brother Moon, Tatqeq. The Sun and the Moon start off as human sister and brother, but the Moon breaks the incest taboo, which may have been a much more common social pressure in isolated family

hunt. Sympathetic magic seems to have been important. Carvings discovered near Cape Dorset, Baffin Island, from what is known as Dorset culture, frequently show polar bear and falcon, the consummate hunters of the Arctic. These carvings are designed to be worn and may have acted as personal amulets to give strength and skill in the hunt. Sometimes animal symbols are combined to give the hunter the qualities of both, such as a talisman that shows a falcon with the head of a bear.

MYTHS AND COSMOLOGY

Many Inuit myths relate to natural phenomena and are designed to provide oral teaching about the planets, stars, weather and animals. In the vast Arctic wastes, the sky is

units. Moon desires his sister so comes to her igloo at night, extinguishes the soapstone lamp so she cannot tell who it is and has sex with her. Eventually, Sun thinks of a ruse. She covers her fingers with smoke soot from her lamp and rubs her fingers on the nose of her visitor. When he returns to the communal house, all can see what has happened. Sun lights some moss and runs outside with it round the communal house. Moon does the same and follows her. They run and run. Moon's flame soon goes out, but Sun's gets brighter, but still he pursues her until they ascend into the sky, where, to this day, the Moon still pursues the Sun. Solar eclipses occur when the Moon catches up with the Sun and embraces her again.

The first day of the Sun's reappearance was a cause for rejoicing and special ceremony. The coldest weather had yet to come, but there was a promise of renewed light. The kindling of new fire to mark a time of transition has been an important rite in societies far away from the Inuit, such as the Celts and the Balts. In traditional Inuit belief, all the lamps must be extinguished, often by children or sometimes by two men – one of whom is dressed as a woman. The old lamp wicks were replaced with new ones and a new flame was kindled using flint and dried moss or other plant material. This new flame is used to re-light all the lamps.

There were many spiritual practices regarding the Sun. Mourners circled once sunwise (clockwise) around graves after burial, and among polar Inuit it was important to repeat this for the five days after a relative's burial. Burials were oriented toward the Sun, with children being oriented toward the East, adolescents to the southeast, adults to the South and elders to the West. Like other traditional peoples such as the Roma, women did not give birth in the main dwelling but went to a house especially set aside. On the first occasion when the mother emerged again, she walked sunwise around the house.

SEASONAL CYCLE

Life has always been a precarious balance for the Inuit. They have inhabited for centuries parts of the world that most of us could not even dream of surviving in. To those of us used to softer climates, the Arctic seems a place of extremes, with endless summer sunlight followed by unbroken winter darkness, when even the sea freezes over. We cannot imagine how people can live in such a barren and inhospitable place, but the Arctic contains an abundance of bird, animal and fish life. There are large numbers of caribou, musk oxen, seals and walrus, which gather in dense seasonal concentrations, making them easy to find and hunt. In the summer, migrating birds come North to the summer tundra, taking advantage of the lack of predators and the food supplies stimulated by 24 hours of sunlight. Rivers and lakes teem with char, trout and whitefish.

Traditionally, Inuit life involves following food sources as the seasons change. Spring was the time to travel to rivers

An eskimo with a fish he has caught
through a snow hole.

Inuit children gazing at the sky at Midsummer, the season of the midnight Sun.

along the coast to fish for Arctic char and to hunt migrating birds. Fish and fowl were a welcome change after the winter diet of caribou meat. At first holes must be cut in the ice for fishing then, as the ice melted, natural holes would form. Birds were snared as they nested. Seals could be caught as they gathered to feed on the fish coming down the river. This required patience as it meant waiting for seals to come up from the ice holes. Seal meat fed people and dogs and also provided oil fat for the *qulliq*, a soapstone oil lamp in the shape of a half-moon with a carved out hollow for fat and wick. As the weather grew warmer, people travelled up river by canoe to caribou crossings to hunt them with bow and arrow. The places were chosen carefully and surveyed to ensure a good hunt. *Inuksuit* were used to help steer caribou toward the hunters. Missionaries frequently mistook *inuksuit* for sacred sites, but they are stone cairn decoys made with a similar silhouette to human beings. The caribou would flee the decoys and find themselves in range of where the real hunters were hiding. Inuksuit were used over long periods of time but have fallen into disuse since the Inuit acquired long-range rifles. *Inuksuit* still, however, function as landmarks and markers for food caches.

Around May to July is *Nipisuiqtuq* – Sun-never-sets – the time of the Midnight Sun. In June and July, the last snow melts under the almost perpetual daylight. Fish swim upstream through the melted waters and birds nest inland. June is *Manniit*, meaning egg-month, and a good time to find birds' eggs. Fish can be caught and dried for winter food. Late summer and early autumn were for picking berries to store for winter. Autumn brings cold weather again and a retreat to the coast for sea fishing and caribou hunting. Rites could be used to help with hunting. Caribou hoof prints can be cut out of the snow and turned round to bring the caribou back to the hunters. Late autumn is seal hunting time. Seal blubber can be used for heat and cooking fuel and can also be stored for when food is scarce.

Autumn was the opening of the ceremonial season when families would gather in the communal house, the *qargi* or *kaggik*, for games, story-telling, dancing, gambling, making string figures – a type of Cat's Cradle game – and rituals. Dancing was popular. Some male dances enacted important events, such as polar bear hunts. Women's dances involved rhythmical movements of hands and body and were more static. Drum dancing plays a part in all traditional gatherings and celebrations, such as birth, marriages, seasonal festivals, hunting celebrations, ceremonies for a young hunter's first kill and welcoming ceremonies for visitors. Inuit drums are frame drums like the Irish *bodhran*. Drum dances are performed by individuals. Traditionally, women sit in a circle and men dance first, with women and children joining in later. In recent years, communal dancing, particularly Scottish dancing – which was introduced by Scottish and American whalers – has become popular and people have learned the accordion and other instruments to accompany it. The Inuit have created special dances from the originals to reflect Inuit culture. One dance imitates the movement of harp seals. Each community has a favourite dance, which can last for an hour or more.

Inuit throat singing is gradually becoming more widely known through world-music stars such as Susan Aglukark and the singing duo Tudjaat. Throat singing can be carried out by two women standing opposite one another, or by a single woman using a large bowl or kettle to give resonance. It involves making a sound deep in the throat without making noise from the mouth. The sound is made as the singer exhales. The sounds represent the sounds made by different birds and animals. Like Sami *yoik* singing, every Inuit adult had his or her personal song. There were also songs of contest, and humourous, satirical and bawdy songs. There were songs about hardship, happiness, loneliness, love and hatred. There were also songs that

told traditional legends. Some songs were rivalry songs, where two enemies would mock one another. People might give one another their personal songs as a sign of gratitude for help given. No one would sing a song without introducing it properly by crediting it to its creator. Traditional Inuit songs are both powerful and entertaining. Drum dancers beat their drums to accompany songs. A song that describes events often accompanies story telling and helps explain the purpose of the story

Games were for entertainment, but they also had a purpose in that they helped develop the strength and agility needed for the demanding Inuit lifestyle. Men and women competed in tests of strength similar to arm wrestling. Kicking games involve kicking suspended objects, using a single kick or the more demanding two-feet kick, where both feet must be kept together. Games need winners, but small societies need to maintain social cohesion and it was important not to encourage rivalries. Players might boast about their skill, but not that their skills were greater than others'. Losers should concede gracefully and winners must thank losers for being allowed to win on this occasion.

Warmer weather was the time for outdoor team games, including tug of war, *aksaq*, a type of soccer and *aattaujak*, which is more like rugby or American football, where teams try to keep possession of the ball. Teams were usually based on an important division in Inuit society: the winter born and the summer born. The winter born are known as *aqiggiit*, meaning ptarmigan *(lagopus mutus)*, because ptarmigan remain in the Arctic throughout the winter. The summer born are *aggiarjuit*, old squaw ducks *(langula hyemal)*, which return to the Arctic with warmer weather. Some of these games can be seen in the annual Northern Games and the biennial Arctic Winter Games.

INUIT AND CHRISTIANITY

Although there had been earlier contact with Europeans, it was not until the 1820s, when Europeans and Americans began commercial whaling, that western culture began to

The mighty nanuk, the polar bear, is the Inuit's most feared prey. Nanuk hunting was highly dangerous.

Inuit from the Chukotskiy Peninsula on Russia's northeastern coast in summer festival.

impact seriously on Inuit life. Around 1000 CE, during a period of warmer weather, the Thule Inuit of West-coast Greenland began bowhead whaling and walrus hunting from large *umiaq*, skin-covered boats made by Inuit women. This was sustainable, but the new commercial whalers introduced whaling and walrus hunting on a completely different scale. The European whalers had a disastrous effect on walrus and whale stocks and for the Inuit contact with Europeans brought disease, as well as the benefits of new goods and technology. The destruction of the bowhead whale stocks and the walrus population left the Inuit more dependent on caribou, which in turn had a drastic effect on caribou stocks. Inuit traditional life began to disintegrate. Families found themselves travelling further and further in search of ever-decreasing food supplies.

Contact with western culture began to undermine the Inuit in other ways. People are unlikely to question their beliefs and traditions when they live in isolated communities. There are always those who radically question what is around them, but most people only begin to question their tradition cultural when they encounter other peoples or when technological change means that the old ways no longer work. This is what happened to the Inuit. A shamanic world view, although attractive in many ways, tends to be surrounded by complex taboos designed to avoid offending the multitude of spirits. Some taboos, such as those surrounding hunting, were useful; others less so. It was taboo, for instance, for women to sew clothing when they moved their camps to sea ice for late spring hunting. If clothes were sewn, the hunters would not catch any seal. It was also taboo to play the popular string figure games other than in the period of the Great Darkness, as the string was thought to lacerate the Sun. In some but not all areas, it was taboo for boys to play the games in case their

A whale hunt using small boats. Small scale whale hunting had little environmental impact.

harpoon lines tangled. Although the Inuit observed westerners breaking their taboos, the logical conclusion was that different taboos applied to different races, rather than that the taboos themselves were unreliable.

The time was ripe for a change of spiritual tradition. New prophecies often arise as a result of social disintegration. Faced with the loss of the old way of life, people hope for a better future. Somehow, something will happen to make the world a better place. The gods or a god will return and everything will be better than before. Around 1830, in the Kobuk River area of Alaska, a *sivuniqsraaq*, or prophet, named Maniilaq was born. Maniilaq was not a Christian, but he was a highly intelligent radical and a force for rational change. He challenged the shamans and ridiculed many of the taboos. People observed that nothing drastic happened to Maniilaq for his impiety and began to listen to Manniilaq's new vision that the time

would come when the shamans' taboos would no longer apply, that the shamans would lose their powers and that "light would come in the form of a word" to bring new beliefs to the Inuit. Another nineteenth-century prophecy was that the *uivaqsaat* would return to the Earth. These were the spirits of the dead. Instead of reincarnating individually as was usual, it was prophesized that the ancestors would return together bringing a time of plenty. These two prophecies could be linked to Christian ideas and provided a fertile ground for missionaries. Maniilaq was the "John the Baptist" of the Alaskan Inuit.

Attempts in the eighteenth and early nineteenth centuries to convert the Inuit to Christianity were relatively unsuccessful. Inuit did not easily understand the missionaries' way of life. Bachelor missionaries were treated with scorn as too poor to trade, too stingy to marry and too effeminate to hunt. Missionaries found that the few who did convert often did so for free hand-outs and that it was difficult to break the traditional power of the *angakkut*, but at the turn of the nineteenth and twentieth centuries, the situation changed. A great deal was due to the work of two Quaker missionaries, Robert and Carrie Samms. As a married couple, the Samms had an advantage over the Catholic priests – they conformed to social expectations. Their denomination also had another advantage over more clerically based churches in that the lack of Quaker hierarchy matched the Inuit's own social structures. Once converted, no priests were needed and the Inuit could hold their own services. Each new convert could become an advocate for the new belief. Other Quaker ideas could be matched to Inuit ideas. The idea that shamans had inner warmth and light that attracted spirits could be equated to the Quaker idea of developing the Inward Light of the Divine in everyone. The Inuit need for public admission of wrongdoing was accommodated by public confession in Quaker services.

Christianity was also helped by the work of an early Inuit convert, Uyaruq. Uyaruq showed that the taboos could be broken by an Inuit and, with a certain showman's flair, he did so while clutching a Bible, which he declared represented a more powerful spirit than those of the shamans. The idea that the other spirits of the Inuit's animist world view did not exist was more difficult to instill than a more creative approach of teaching either that the Christian spirit was a more powerful one among many or – the approach taken by the Samms – that the Christian spirit was a good one and that the others were bad.

The Samms took a similar approach to that of Christian missionaries to Europe many hundreds of years before. Instead of destroying people's previous belief systems, they endeavoured to build on and reinterpret them. The Samms began to create an Inuit Christianity that was influential beyond their own denomination. This is not to say that the Samms' approach was all "sweetness, rationality and light". An Inuit elder, Beatrice Mouse, who knew the Samms, contributed some of her life story to an oral history collection gathered in the Kobuk River villages. She commented how the missionaries started jailing shamans "because they were afraid of them".

INUIT TODAY

In the twentieth century, the Inuit have suffered greatly at the hands of western governments. From 1953 to 1969, for instance, Canada was keen to establish its claim to Arctic territories and wanted to prove that there were substantial numbers of Canadian citizens in the North. Inuit were rounded up to live in communities of prefabricated houses and were prevented from migrating and hunting. Children were removed from their parents at five years of age and flown to residential schools where abuse of all kinds was rife. Some Inuit were forcibly removed to barren parts of the Arctic where many died of starvation. The fate of the High Arctic Exiles remains a sensitive and important issue for Canadian Inuit. In 1996, a government compensation package of 10 million Canadian dollars was given to the surviving exiles, but no official apology was ever offered.

An Alaskan Inuit family poses in traditional dress for a photograph taken in 1905.

Living in their traditional way, the Inuit were healthy. Women are said to have been able to bear children into their 60s and men continued to hunt into their 80s. "Civilization" has damaged the Inuit's health. When in Canada the government forced Inuit to abandon their traditional lifestyle, they were given government food supplies of grains and milk, only for medical anthropologists to discover that Inuit are lactose intolerant. The new diet, enforced leisure, deprivation of a way of life and separation from their children naturally resulted in social disintegration, and some Inuit took refuge in drink and petty crime. The anger and despair felt by many Inuit during this period is conveyed in Inuit art.

Despite the disastrous imposition of western values on Inuit culture, many Inuit are devout Christians. Christianity helped make sense of the difficult life of the Inuit and released them from the fear and superstition that could be the negative side of a traditional world view of a universe inhabited by good and bad spirits. Traditional spirituality was also denigrated and suppressed by Christian missionaries. People were told that the shamans' spirit guides, *tuunngait*, were devils and that shamanism

was "devil worship", an attitude that has coloured the approach of many Inuit to their ancestors' religion. Today, Inuit shamanism is not practised openly as it is in other circumpolar countries such as Russia or in Native American communities. Many Inuit are, however, aware of ancestral spirits who guide them and there is a revived interest in traditional shamanic healing. Today, with a more positive re-evaluation of the effectiveness of traditional healing happening all around the world, the Maniilaq Association of northern Alaska works to bring together traditional and western culture in health and social services. Its hospital, for instance, has three medical doctors using western medicine working in conjunction with three Inuit doctors using traditional medicine. Cultural events are also making a strong comeback. Elders are encouraged to tell stories, which are also broadcast on radio and television and taught in schools.

Cultural revival may increase as the Inuit gain greater political autonomy. In Canada, after a 30-year struggle ending in 1999, the Inuit gained their own federal state called *Nunavut* – Our Land – in what was formerly the eastern Arctic region. The territory covers two million square kilometres – about the same as western Europe.

While the Inuit are keen to promote responsible tourism, they wish to ensure that tourism does not interfere with wildlife harvesting and their way of life. In recent years, concern about environmental damage in the Arctic has resulted in much greater respect being paid to the ecological knowledge of the Inuit, Sami and indigenous peoples of Siberia who have long inhabited the region. The importance of indigenous knowledge has been recognized by the Arctic Environmental Protection Strategy (AEPS), adopted in Finland in 1991 by the eight Arctic nations – the United States, Canada, Iceland, Denmark, Norway, Sweden, Finland and Russia. In 1984, the Inuit Circumpolar Conference (ICC) obtained non-governmental status within the United Nations. On September 19, 1996, the eight Arctic nations signed a declaration creating the Arctic Council to develop a programme of sustainable

Inuit of the Tchoukotka region of Russia with their summer tent.

Inuit elder with frame drum. Drums are used to induce shamanic trance, but also for dance and in festivities.

development in the region and hope for the future.

For contemporary Inuit, environmental issues of are utmost importance. It is essential to protect animal and fish resources if Inuit lifestyle is to be maintained. Environmentalist westerners can frown upon their way of life. In the early days of European, Canadian and American contact with the Inuit, it was their spiritual traditions that most upset the western missionaries who sought to convert the Inuit to their own supposedly superior Christian belief system. Today, Inuit are under pressure from western environmentalists, whose fellow citizens have destroyed their own environment, to stop whaling and sealing. For many western conservationists, whale conservation means not only stopping western commercial organizations from exploiting natural resources, but also preventing indigenous peoples from pursuing their traditional and more environmentally friendly way of life. Inuit and western environmentalists are, however, developing a common viewpoint on important issues such as global warming. On October 21, 1999, Alaskan Inuit and Greenpeace went to court to challenge BP Amoco's plan to drill for oil in the Arctic Ocean off Alaska's North coast, arguing that this would jeopardize marine life and destroy the local people's subsistence culture. "*Sunakkiniagniq Inuuniaqusiqpu*t" (our life is our subsistence), said Charles Edwardsen, Jr, an Inuit resident of Barrow, Alaska. "The Arctic Ocean is our garden, and we cannot afford to have it contaminated by oil spills and industrialization. This lawsuit is about protecting our subsistence resources and culture for our children." Ideally, the Inuit want to be left alone to manage and control their environment without interference from the major nation states. The Inuit, Sami and other indigenous Arctic peoples believe they have traditional ecological knowledge that allows them to manage their environment and to maintain sustainable, renewable resources – if allowed to do so.

NATIVE AMERICANS

The date when human beings first entered North America is hotly disputed. Conservative scientists prefer to date human arrival from around 14,000 years ago, but more complex analyses drawing on linguistics and genetics suggest that humankind first trod the great continent over 30,000 years ago. The route into America was across the Bering Strait land bridge, which joined North America and Asia during the Ice Age. From the northwest people migrated southward, both overland and by sea. Immigration came in three waves from different communities in Siberia and northeast Asia. The first wave passed through Alaska and from this descended the main Native American peoples of the New World. The second wave was Athabaskan speakers, who are found today over large parts of Canada as well as parts of the southwestern and northwest coastal United States. The third wave of settlers into America became the ancestors of the Inuit and the Aleut peoples of Alaska.

PREVIOUS PAGE: Native American petroglyph (rock painting) of flute player, Galisko Basin, New Mexico.

North America is an enormously varied continent in terms of climate and geography and hence food resources. In the eastern woodlands region from the Atlantic coast to the Mississippi River and across the Great Lakes and the St Lawrence River were peoples dependent on hunting woodland game, agriculture and fishing for their livelihood. To the northwest were coastal and woodland people dependent on hunting and fishing. Further South were the Plains Indians, who by the eighteenth century had captured horses brought by the Spanish, and who lived by hunting the American bison or buffalo. In California and the northern desert and to the southwest, people had to contend with the hotter, drier and more arid climates. Irrigation and agricultural skills were important if people were to survive. Rites and ceremonies reverenced the means of life – the animals that were hunted, such as the buffalo or American bison, or staple crops, such as maize or corn. In the southwest, newer incoming nomadic peo-

ples like the Navajo and Apache found themselves in lands occupied by Pueblo dwelling peoples, whose mud towns are some of the earliest permanent dwellings in North America and are still inhabited today, as well as being found in National Parks like the Mesa Verde. Pueblo culture had learned to harvest the crops of a southern climate and rain ceremonies were an important part of communal life.

The first Europeans who arrived on the continent, such as the Scandinavian Vikings, made little impact. It was not until the late fifteenth century onward, with the arrival of Europeans with the technology of warfare such as canons and later guns, that the lives of Native Americans changed irrevocably. The new arrivals decimated Native populations not only with warfare, but also by bringing diseases against which Native peoples had no immunity. Europeans and their missionaries looked upon Native American spirituality as worthless superstition inspired by the Christian

Monument Valley on the Arizona-Utah border is in the Navajo Reservation.

devil, Satan. Those who survived the sickness and deliberate extermination policies of the settlers were often forcibly converted to Christianity. The United States and Canadian governments instituted policies to force Native Americans on to reservations and to encourage them to become assimilated into the majority culture. Children were separated from their parents and sent to boarding schools far away from home with children from different peoples. The only common means of communication was the language they were taught – English – and they were forbidden to speak their own languages. It is only relatively recently that others have recognized the importance and value of Native American ways of life and their beliefs.

SPIRITUAL VISION

The spiritual ways of different Native American peoples have evolved separately and distinctly, but they share many common themes and core beliefs. These spring from people's

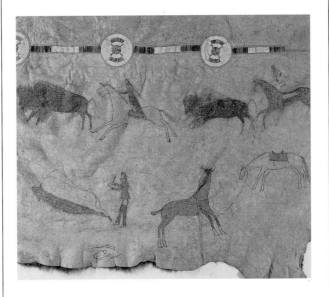

close relationship to the natural world. The landscape features around them – rocks and trees, rivers, lakes, sky and stars – all have special significance and are considered alive. Humans and the spirits of the land can communicate.

The contrast between the typical beliefs of hunting and farming peoples is intriguing. Hunters have animal ceremonies in which they seek spiritual power to help them in the hunt. The spirits of the animals they hunt are acknowledged and appeased so that their kin will sacrifice themselves to the hunters in the future. Often they believe in a Supreme Being who oversees their successes and failures in the hunt. They have an annual ceremony of cosmic rejuvenation but few permanent places of worship, for they move where the animals move. Shamanism and life after death beyond the horizon or in the sky are also central to hunting pattern religions.

On the other hand, horticultural and agricultural peoples develop rain and fertility ceremonies that involve priestly ritual. Goddesses and gods represent forces of fertility and natural phenomena, such as rain, in a yearly round of fertility rites. Horticultural peoples stay in one place and so build permanent shrines and temples. The location of the Otherworld also changes. For hunting peoples, the Otherworld lies in the sky – the starry realms above that travel with a travelling people. For settled peo-

Petroglyph of bison hunters. The destruction of the bison in the nineteenth century by white hunters destroyed the way of life of many Native American peoples.

ples, the Otherworld lies beneath the earth, which is the source of nourishment and therefore of life. Not all peoples believe that after death human beings go to the Otherworld. Some believe in reincarnation and that people's spirits migrate after death to be reborn as humans or animals. Others believe that humans return as ghosts or that people go to another world. Yet others say that what happens when people die is unknowable.

CREATION MYTHS

The origin of the human race is explained by many different creation myths. These myths frequently differ from scientific explanations of the origin of peoples in the North American continent and the differences can be the cause of some controversy. After centuries of exploitation, native peoples are anxious to emphasize their claims to be indigenous peoples rather than incoming migrants – even if the migrations were millennia ago. Each group of people has its own myth, which will be related to, but subtly different from, groups with similar ancestry and language, but there are some common themes.

Some peoples perceive the world as a threefold universe like that of many shamanic peoples, with the natural world being the middle segment. The three levels are linked by the World-Tree, which has its roots in the underworld, a trunk that passes through the natural world, and its top in the sky world or upper world. In the southwest, a different concept is found, whereby the universe is seen as having many underground layers through which human beings climbed to emerge into the present world through a small hole in the ground – the world's navel. Often the world is seen as having degraded in some way. The Apache speak of the time when animals and trees could talk to one another. The coming of fire destroyed this companionship. Humans learned the use of fire from animals that started it accidentally. Trees became resources to exploit and the harmony was broken.

RITES AND CEREMONIES

Although rites and ceremonies differ according to the life style of different peoples, there are some ceremonies that are common to many Native American cultures. Rituals and ceremonies are vitally important in Native American spirituality and are related to sacred myths. It would seem, however, that ceremonies often began as practical actions. They were symbolic enactments of real situations that would provide power to conquer the difficulties in real life. Rites of passage are important in Native American spirituality to mark the transition from one stage to the next in life's journey. One such rite is the Vision Quest. In this, young boys approaching puberty enter a period of fasting, meditation and physical challenge. The boy goes alone to a wilderness area. He will fast and meditate in order to receive a vision that will guide his development and show him his life's path. He will hope to acquire a guardian spirit who will be close and supportive to him throughout his life's journey.

This sweat lodge is constructed around a hole dug in the ground.

OPPOSITE PAGE: Totem pole in Stanley Park, Vancouver.

SWEAT LODGE

Other ceremonies, such as the sweat lodge, are used for rituals of purification, for spiritual renewal and of healing. The sweat lodge is used from as far North as the Inuit down to Mexico. As well as serving the practical purpose of cleaning the body, sweat lodge ritual was important spiritually. Not only the body is cleansed, but also the whole self. Sweating is a prerequisite for other rites and has health benefits in ridding the body of toxins. The principle of sweat lodges is the same as that of the Scandinavian sauna. A sweat lodge can be a small structure made of a frame of saplings, covered with skins, canvas or blankets, or a larger permanent structure accommodating dozens of people. Nomadic hunting peoples used flexible branches, such as willow, arched to form a hemisphere and covered with blankets or skins. Agricultural peoples built substantial lodges of logs and heavy bark, with gaps sealed with mud or clods of earth. Rocks are heated on a fire outside the sweat lodge and then brought in on forked sticks to be placed either by the door or in a specially dug depression in the centre of the lodge. The rocks are then sprinkled with water to create steam, again much like a sauna. In Alaska among the Inuit, in some Pacific Coast peoples and among the Pueblo Indians of the southwest, sweat lodges are larger communal structures built directly over a wood fire. The direct fire method requires participants to be able to endure lung-scorching heat and eye-watering smoke. Some Inuit peoples devel-

Shaman leads a puberty initiation ceremony. In the sky above, animal spirits hover to lend their power to the rite.

oped respirators that worked on the same principle as those used by urban cyclists today. The sweat lodge versions were made of fine wood shavings bound to form of an oblong pad used to cover the mouth and the chin. Among many peoples, sweat lodges were used only by men and became in effect men's clubs. Where women used sweat lodges, then women and men used them separately.

DREAMING AMONG THE IROQUOIS

Iroquois territory is in the eastern woodlands. The Iroquois are the eighth largest Native American nation and currently number around 49,000. In Iroquois creation myth, people are descended from Sky People who inhabit a disk world above the Earth. One of these people, a pregnant woman, descends from the sky and propagates the land below – North America – which is known as Turtle Island. Creation myths among Native American peoples tend to reflect property owning and inheritance. Where inheritance is matrilinear, with family wealth passed from mother to daughter, a woman or goddess is usually the Creatrix of the world. Where property is passed down the male line, then the Creator is male. Among the Iroquois, women owned the homes and held ceremonial precedence.

Dreaming is an important source of vision, guidance and information in traditional cultures. Even if today we do not believe that dreams are messages from the spirit world, we understand that dreams can be an important source of information. In dreaming we are processing information that we have noticed unconsciously but have not consciously registered. This can be information about our own lives, about members of our communities and their interaction with one another, or information about trends in wider society. In traditional and agricultural societies where people live more closely to nature, dreams may also bring information about the natural world. If we spend a long time out of doors, we register subliminally all sorts of information about animal and plant activity and weather conditions that can predict the likely progression of the weather and patterns of animal movements.

Brigadier General E.S. Parker, an Iroquois chief and a member of Ulysses S. Grant's staff in the Civil War.

DREAMING THE FUTURE

Among the Iroquois of central New York State and the Ohio Valley, which consisted of seven nations, including the Seneca, Oneida, and Mohawk, dreams were held to have great significance. The Iroquois confederation of nations was a model of co-operation between peoples that provided inspiration for Thomas Jefferson and Benjamin Franklin in their creation of the United States as a federal nation. The confederation itself was presaged by a dream. At the end of the fourteenth century, an Iroquois woman dreamed that her daughter was about to give birth to a son who would bring good tidings of peace and power to his people from the chief of the sky Gods. The baby was named De-ka-nah-wi-da and in adult life he was inspired to create a league of Iroquois Nations.

Similarly, the life pattern of Iroquois Chief Ely Samuel Parker (1828–95), a Unionist leader in the Civil War, was foretold by his mother's dream, in which she saw a broken rainbow. The rainbow stretched from the home of the

Indian agent Erastus Granger in Buffalo to the reservation. Ely's mother was troubled by this and went to a Seneca dream interpreter for help. She was told that she would bear a son who would be a peacemaker and a white man as well as an Indian. He would become a warrior for the "palefaces", but would never desert his own people. He would win great wisdom and would become renowned and respected throughout the land by both Native and new Americans. The prophecy came true and Ely Parker came to draft the terms of surrender that ended the Civil War. General Lee described him as "one real American". In 1852, in accordance with the custom of his people, he was chosen as a chief by the women – the clan mothers – who had an important role in Iroquois society. Through his lifelong friendship with General Ulysses S. Grant, Chief Ely Parker became Commissioner of the Bureau of Indian Affairs. He was the first Native American to hold federal office

DREAMING THE PRESENT

Dreams could foretell important events or the birth of important people. They could also contain messages about what should be done in the present. Dreams were an important source of guidance about daily life for the Iroquois nations and were used to make decisions about fishing, hunting, war, dancing, marriage and other significant life events. Dreams were especially important prior to war and hunting. A war party would turn back if one of its members dreamed of failure. Ignoring dreams was dangerous and foolhardy; to do so was to ignore the messages of the gods. Iroquois beliefs about dreams were not far removed from those of Jungian analysts today. They believed that people's spirits had desires of which their everyday selves were unaware; in much the same way that we know we have unconscious wishes and urges. Just as we must learn to listen to the voice of the unconscious if we are to know ourselves fully, so the Iroquois taught that individuals must listen and obey the messages in their dreams. Dreams were powerful. They could cure diseases both physical and psychological. Psychological illness was

caused by unconscious desires that dreams could reveal. These desires were believed to come from the secret longings of the soul that might sometimes be at odds with conscious intentions.

ACTING OUT DREAMS

Through dreaming and sharing dreams with others to seek accurate interpretations, the Iroquois contact the sacred power called Orenda. Since dreams come from the sacred spirit world, it is important that they are acted upon. One of the most famous of the Iroquois chiefs is Seneca Chief Cornplanter (c.1732–1836), who fought with the British against George Washington in the American Revolution. In his eighties, he came to regret his co-operation with the whites. In 1819, Chief Cornplanter had a highly significant dream. He walked for three days from home to home describing his dream to people and asking for their interpretations until he heard one that felt right. This was that his dream meant that his time as chief should finish. His name was now Onono, the Iroquois word for cold, associated with winter and endings. Chief Cornplanter had received many gifts from white politicians, such as second United States President John Adams and third President Thomas Jefferson, but the dream seemed to be telling him to remove them all from his home in order to retain the good will of the Great Spirit. Chief Cornplanter followed every stage of the interpretation. He burned the gifts he had received from Adams and Jefferson in Washington. He then chose an old friend as his successor, and sent him a tomahawk and a belt of wampum to announce his resignation and to honour the new chief. Wampum beads are made from different kinds of shell and were highly prized. They could be strung together to form bracelets, necklaces and belts and were highly valuable. They could be used to ransom captives, as payment in reparation for crime or injury, and as gifts to confirm treaties and agreements between peoples. Chief Cornplanter's belt was therefore a valuable and highly symbolic gift. Chief Cornplanter died in Warren County, Pennsylvania, aged 104. In the 1950s, officials ignored Seneca protests against building Kinzua Dam to flood 10,500 acres of former Seneca land. Cornplanter's land and grave now lie beneath a reservoir.

In following the message of his dream, Chief Cornplanter was acting in an appropriate way in accordance with his tradition. Once an accurate interpretation of a dream is identified it is important to follow its guidance as closely as possible. Ignoring these messages would cause all manner of unfortunate and unforeseen consequences. Usually dreaming is spontaneous. The divine spirit world sends messages to humankind in order to help us, or the unconscious brings into consciousness wishes we have suppressed or ignored. At certain important transitions in life, however, the Iroquois would deliberately seek advice from the dream world in a Vision Quest.

IROQUOIS CEREMONIES AND FESTIVALS

Dreams are important aspects of the Iroquois seasonal festival cycle. The peoples of the Iroquois' League of Nations have come together for centuries to celebrate their great festivals. These have significance for both the spiritual and physical life of the peoples. Sacred ceremonies include feather dances, drum dances, the rite of personal chant, the bowl game and Sun ceremonies. Other important festivals celebrated the planting and harvesting cycle of different crops essential to survival – the Green Corn Ceremony, Maple Ceremony, Planting Ceremony, Strawberry Ceremony, Green Bean Ceremony and Harvest Ceremony. Some ceremonies were annual events and others were called when needed. Dreams could reveal that a ceremony should take place. Any member who dreamed that the rite was needed for the welfare of the community could call the Seneca Sun Ceremony of Thanksgiving. The ceremony begins at noon with the firing of three arrows or rifle shots into the sky to

Iroquois and other Native American peoples were skilled craft workers with a strongly developed aesthetic sense that made ordinary objects into works of art. This is a velvet-beaded hat.

inform the Sun of the beginning of the rite. A holy man would then stand by a fire to chant his thanksgiving song while casting handfuls of tobacco from a husk basket upon the flames to carry his words upward to the Sun.

MIDWINTER FESTIVAL

By far the most important Iroquois celebration of renewal is the Midwinter Festival, a six-day festival that takes place around New Year. It is one of the most sacred of Iroquois festivals and begins when the Pleiades are directly overhead at dusk. The Midwinter Festival celebrates the battle between the creative and destructive forces in the Universe. This takes the form of a battle between the Creator and his younger brother. It concludes the old year and begins the New Year, and involves both thankfulness for the blessings of the past and hopes for the future. At this changing point of the turning seasons, as darkness gradually recedes before the light, the focus is on renewal; thanking the Creator for his gifts given in the past year and with a request to continue the fertility of the earth in the year to come.

Then the attention turns to dreams with the first focus on dream renewal. Dream sharing and dream guessing follow this. Although often serious and of spiritual significance, the dream interpretation rituals of the Iroquois are also a time of fun and games, as "dream-guessing" motivates tribal members to challenge one other. Guessing may involve describing the dream, interpreting it, attempting to resolve the key issue of the dream, or otherwise trying to make helpful suggestions. The tradition is that whoever best "guesses" the dream should also help achieve its fulfilment. This is seen as an honour that strengthens communal bonds. Dream interpretation is lead by a special group, the False Face Society, who have "false faces" because they wear masks to help them invoke the spirits and befriend them. The spirits can then assist in combating illness, diseases of the mind and misfortune. Healing is then effected through ritual dances.

Native Americans of the plains who lived in tipis and hunted buffalo. They became perhaps best known through destroying Custer's forces at the Battle of the Little Bighorn in 1876 and through the terrible massacre at Wounded Knee by United States cavalry of their men, women and children on December 29, 1890.

Lakota religion has evolved slightly separately from other Native American groupings with cosmology being particularly important. The Lakota interest in stars and cosmology is reflected in the building of medicine wheels. These are large spoked wheels built with rocks with a large cairn in the centre, which may have been used for astronomical measurement. The most famous one, because it is totally intact, is that found in the Bighorn Mountains of Wyoming. This is aligned to the Sun at Midsummer Solstice and was probably built as recently as 1760. Other medicine wheels on the plains could be up to 10,000 years old.

The Lakota had no means of writing prior to their contact with the European settlers so they had no written history as such. Their method of marking passing time and

Native American drums were often adorned with mythological scenes. On this Pawnee drum, Thunderbird, creator of the Plain's storms, hurls lightning flashes at darting swallows.

DREAM-CATCHERS

We can foster our dream life through dream catchers. These are webs of cotton in a wooden frame, sometimes decorated ornately with beads and feathers. According to peoples of the eastern woodlands, they catch all dreams, both good and bad, and protect the dreamer from nightmares. The beads on the dream-catcher's web guide good dreams through the centre hole so that they may gently drift off the feather below into the life of the dreamer, while bad dreams are trapped in the web. Dream catchers appear to have originated with the Chippewa people, but they have been adopted by some Iroquois and in recent years have become part of New Age culture.

LAKOTA

The Sioux nation is the fourth largest Native American nation, with around 103,000 members divided into three peoples – the Lakota, Dakota and Nakota, each of whom has many tribes. The Lakota were nomadic, equestrian

The plains hunters had portable homes, called tipis, which allowed them to follow bison herds as they migrated. These Sioux tipis were photographed c.1900 beside the Bighorn River.

Shamans frequently took on animal for to travel into the spirit world on behalf of their peoples. This nineteenth-century painting by George Caitlin is of a Blackfoot shaman.

major events was by pictographs the recorded memorable happenings and used a system of counting winters to tie all these events into a chronological sequence. Things that they could not explain were ascribed to the Wakan, the incomprehensible nature of the cosmos. Many pictographs feature significant astronomical events.

SACRED RITES

Lakota religion is structured around Seven Sacred Rites given to the people by White Buffalo Calf Woman around 2,000 years ago. She first appears to two warriors who are hunting buffalo on the sacred Black Hills of Dakota. On sacred ground humans and the spirit world can meet and suddenly out of the North the two warriors find a white buffalo calf walking toward them. White animals are often associated with the supernatural and sure enough the animal does something magical – it turns into a beautiful young girl. Some people know instinctively what to do in such circumstances. One warrior treats the maiden with reverence. He kneels and begins to pray. The warriors are away from home and the sight of the beautiful maiden fills the other warrior with lust: he wants her. The maiden destroys him. A black cloud descends and strips his flesh from his bones, leaving only a skeleton. The maiden tells the pious warrior to go home to his people and to tell them that in four days she will bring a sacred bundle. On the fourth day, when the warrior has gathered the elders and leaders in a circle, White Buffalo Calf Woman descends from a cloud singing a sacred song. She brings the medicine bundle containing a sacred tobacco pipe and spends four days teaching people its meaning. White Buffalo Calf Woman also teaches the people the seven sacred ceremonies: the Sweat Lodge, the Vision Quest, Ghost Keeping, the Sun Dance,

A nineteenth-century Assiniboin or Yanktoni Sioux hand drum showing a horned figure from the spirit world.

Making Relatives, the Puberty Ceremony and Throwing the Ball. The birth in 1994 of a white buffalo calf named Miracle has been interpreted by some Lakota as a sign of spiritual renewal.

The Sun Dance endured even though, in the late nineteenth century, it was strongly suppressed by government authorities. Participants were threatened with withdrawal of food rations or imprisonment. Startling images from films have made the Sun Dance the best-known Lakota ceremony of all. Sun Dance is a mistranslation of Sun-Gazing Dance and other peoples use different names for what is essentially the same ritual. The Sun Dance is not a Sun worshipping ceremony, nor is it purely an ordeal in the commonly understood sense – although the use of hooks being driven into the flesh of the dancers, or that they dance themselves to exhaustion, might suggest this. The dancer volunteers for the dance, which is seen as a way of putting himself and his people into greater harmony with the cosmos. It involves renewal and this includes not only the spiritual renewal of participants and their relatives but also the renewal of the living earth and all its parts. The festival also provides an opportunity for people to socialize and renew friendships.

The circle-cross, a circle guarded by the four quarters, appears in the symbolism of many indigenous peoples, from Native Americans to Celts. The famous Oglala Lakota holy man and visionary Black Elk described in his memoirs the importance of the symbol of the circle. The "Power of the World", the indwelling Divine Immanence, works in circles. When the Lakota were strong and happy people, the flowering tree was the living centre and the four quarters nourished it. The East brings peace and light, the South warmth, the West rain and the North the cold and mighty wind. Black Elk points out that everything important in the Universe is a circle – the Earth, Moon and the stars. The strongest wind whirls in circles, birds build their nests in circles and the cycle of the seasons is circular. For the Sun Dance, which is held in July or August, a large cottonwood tree is erected at the centre of a circle. This is adorned with six colours representing the four directions plus above and below. At the height of the dance, the dancers pierce themselves with pegs through their chest muscles. A rope attaches these to the centre tree. The dancer runs from the edge of the circle and back three times and then runs with such force that the pegs are ripped out of his chest, just as he was torn from the womb in the great mystery at birth.

Through the Sun Dance, the participants seek to obtain supernatural aid and personal power or enlightenment through their sacrifice. This is done not only to assure the achievement of desired outcomes, but also to reaffirm or improve their place in their society, as the sacrifice will ensure the people as a whole will prosper for another year. The whole Sun Dance is a ritual re-enactment of the relationship between the people of the plains and Wakan Tanka, their Creator as made manifest in the form of the Sun, the life-giver. Through all the stages of the ritual – the purification, participation, sacrifice and supplication – the participant is acting as the instrument of Wakan Tanka's power and becomes a conduit through which it can be brought to the people.

THE TINDE (APACHE)

Like the names of many indigenous peoples, the name by which the Tinde or Inde are known is not their own name for themselves but the name given to them by those who

Tinde (Apache) men in ceremonial dance.

acted as guides and interpreters for the white people who first encountered them. The Tinde (the people) are generally known as the Apaches, from the word "enemy" among the Zuni Pueblo peoples whose territory they entered around 1000 CE. The Apaches are renowned for being fierce warriors.

Most Apache, or Tinde, lived primarily through hunting, some livestock and a little horticulture with seed and fruit gathering. The men lived and worked for the families of their wives. Today, there are over 50,000 Tinde, who live mainly on reservations totalling three million acres in Arizona and New Mexico. The Tinde are also found in Texas and adjacent Mexican states and one isolated group, known as the Kiowa Apache, is found in southern Oklahoma as well as the Texan pan-handle. Kiowa Apaches had medicine bundles – collections of sacred power objects. They participated in the annual Kiowa sun dance and held similar beliefs about the afterlife – that the spirit passes into the Otherworld. They kept their own language and customs, however, and may have been Plains Apaches who were separated from their kinsmen when the Comanche swept on to the southern plains.

The Tinde revere animals, elements, the solar system and natural phenomena. That which lies beyond their understanding, that which still has to be explained, is ascribed to the supernatural. Their religion is based on the belief in a supernatural power that manifested itself in almost every facet of their world. Their rituals work to develop a healthy and co-operative relationship with this power, which is believed to offer its services to the Apache through visionary experiences. Apache have solo shamanistic ceremonies, in which individuals interact with their own particular personal power sources. Other rituals require a priest or holy man to officiate. Rites of passage are important within the community; for example a rite for a child who takes his first steps and a girl's first menses or puberty. Both shamanistic and priestly rituals are strongly patterned, with the number four having special signifi-

cance. As in many other Native American traditions, four is seen as the sacred number, relating to the four directions. Songs and prayers occur in quartets. The ceremonial circuit moves clockwise and rites typically last four successive nights.

TINDE CREATION MYTH

The Tinde creation myth reveals the importance of "fourness". The myth is complex and the version below is a simplification of the complete legend. The significance of the number four, the four cardinal points, is clearly established however, as is the fact that, though the Creator was male, it is to a female, "Girl-Without-Parents", that he entrusts the care of the world. The Tinde myth is one of the many Native American creation myths that place the origin of the human race in the skies above. It is easy to see how UFO enthusiasts have taken Native American legends as evidence of our descent from the stars. Interestingly, the Tinde Creator is described as "small and bearded", but the Apache are beardless. We can only speculate as to where this image came from. Like many Native American myths and like shamans in other cultures, the Creator sings the world into being. By naming things we create them and bring them to birth.

Before the beginning of time, when nothing existed:
no Sun or Moon, no Earth or sky – just darkness,
out of the blackness appears a thin disc;
one side yellow and the other white.
In the disc is a small bearded figure:
this is the Creator, the One-who-lives-Above.
Looking into the darkness, he creates light:
looking up and light appears above;
looking down he creates a sea of light;
in the East he creates yellow streaks of dawn;
in the West, tints of many colours and he creates clouds of many hues.
Wiping his sweating face and rubbing his hands together,
thrusting them downward, a shining cloud appears.
On it sits a little girl: the Girl-Without-Parents is formed.

Rock engraving, McKee Springs, Colorado.

He sings about what he should create next;

he sings four times, the magic number;

he creates Sun-God and then Small-Boy,

and there then are four – the four Gods.

He creates Tarantula, Big Dipper, Wind, Lightning-Maker,

and some western clouds to house Lightning-Rumbler.

The Gods continue their work –

between them they create the stars and the Earth,

a ball that through kicking and stretching grows to

immeasurable size.

To four giant posts by cords woven by Tarantula,

they secure it, coloured according to the four directions

– white, blue, yellow and black.

The Earth secured, he creates the sky,

and all the living creatures of land, sea and sky:

it is time for him to leave.

He entrusts the world to those he has created:

Lightning-Rumbler to guard the clouds and water,

Sky-Boy to care for the Sky-people,

Earth-daughter to take charge of all crops and Earth-people,

and Pollen-Girl to care for their health and to guide them.

Over all, he leaves Girl-Without-Parents,

and, as a parting gesture,

he gives them the gift of fire.

NAVAJO (DINÉ)

After the Cherokee nation, the Navajo are the second largest Native American nation, with about 220,000 people. In Navajo, they are known as the Diné, meaning "the People". The Navajo live mainly in the Navajo Nation, a reservation in northern Arizona that is larger that some European countries. They believe that the natural and supernatural are closely interconnected and work to achieve harmonious relationships with the spirit world of the Holy People. In Navajo cosmology, the Earth is a land mass floating in a vast ocean beneath a dome. The sacred mountains – Blanca Peak in the East, Mount Taylor in the South, the San Francisco Peaks in the West and Hesperus Peak in the North – are the four corner posts of the Navajo universe, which support the sky, the roof of this world. In the centre is Huerfano Mountain representing the round roofed home, or hooghan, often known as the female hooghan, and Gobernador Knob, to the East of centre, represents the conical type of hooghan often known as male hooghan. The Navaho creation myth describes the evolution of life through four different underworlds, until in the fourth world human beings emerge. We are now in the fifth world.

CHANGING WOMAN (ESTSÁNATLEHI)

There is no Supreme Being in Navaho mythology, but one of the most important deities is Estsánatlehi, or Changing Woman, who created human beings. Changing Woman is a representation of nature and of the Earth. She represents the ever-changing circle of the seasons. She is birth (spring), fertility (summer), ageing and wisdom (autumn or fall), and dying (winter). She is then reborn again in the spring. First Man and First Woman plan the birth of Changing Woman. At dawn First Man repeatedly holds up his medicine bundle toward the sacred mountain of Gobernador Knob. A medicine bundle contains symbolic power objects and is sacred. From this powerful act, Changing Woman is born and is found lying on top of the mountain by Talking God. First Man then presents her to the Holy People saying she is the child of those who formed the Earth. First Man raises and teaches Changing Woman. She grows to puberty in four days, hence her name. This occasions the first Puberty Ceremony. Talking God officiates and the Holy People attend. Changing Woman is dressed in jewels and blessed with pollen collected at dawn and at twilight. She is bathed in dew and then instructed to run toward the dawn as far as she can and then return. As she does so her dress of jewels shines and jingles. This she does for four nights. During the days, she plans the future of the Earth. The songs sung for Changing Woman as she ran are those that are sung today for young women at their puberty ceremonies. Another ceremony is held for Changing Woman at her next menstruation. This is similar to the first, but it is decreed that no menstruating woman may be present at any ceremonial. The order of the Blessing Way is in this way established.

Changing Woman then sets off on a trail where she meets a stranger who was so dazzling she had to look away. This happens three times and Changing Woman has sex with the mysterious stranger, who is the Sun's inner core. She bathes and after nine days gives birth to twins. These twins become Monster Slayer and Born For Water. They grow in four days to adulthood. At this point she asks First Man for his medicine bundle. She conducts a ceremony over the mating of the corn – the first marriage – and follows the Sun to the West. Here she grows lonely and creates the Navajo people from pieces of skin rubbed off from different parts of her body. She creates four couples – the ancestors of the Navajo nation. She also creates teachings for the people. She teaches the Blessing Way ceremony to two children of Rock Crystal Talking God, who are brought to her by means of a rainbow and a sunbeam. They in turn teach it to all. When the ceremony has been learned the two children and the Holy People leave the ceremony. The Holy People say that they will never be seen again, but promise that their presence will always be there in those aspects of nature that are dear to the people who dwell on the surface of the Earth.

LEFT: Navajo man in ceremonial dress.

Navajo shaman
calling the spirits.

child becomes whole. Ní ch'i surrounds the growing child; it is breathed in at all times. Growth and development are governed by the Ní ch'i.

CEREMONIES

There are many Navajo chant ceremonies – some sources give a figure of 24 and others as many as 58. Ceremonies are conducted by specially trained holy men, or singers. Navaho ceremonies are complex and lengthy, involving special placing of symbols and equipment, the singing of the chants, dances and the construction of sand-paintings. In one ceremony, for instance, 576 songs have been identified and there are between 600 and 1,000 different paintings. Most singers will specialize in two or three of the ceremonies. Singers train by apprenticing themselves to a older man – a privilege for which they must pay – and training can take up to seven years.

Seven of the ceremonies are performed regularly, the best-known being the Blessingway. This chant is one of the central ceremonies of the Navajo way of life, which is known as the beautiful rainbow. The Blessingway recounts the Navajo creation myth after their emergence from the underworlds. Another chant, Enemyway, is a protection following contact with non-Navajos and serves to exorcize ghosts, violence and ugliness. It is derived from ceremonies used to protect warriors from the spirits of those they had killed. Chantways are a form of ceremony that focus on healing. They can be performed according to one of three rituals: Holyway, Evilway or Lifeway. The Holyway rituals work to restore health to the "one sung over" by attracting good. The Evilway chants exorcize evil and the Lifeway chants are used to treat injuries caused by accidents. The Blessingway is the core structure of all Navajo rituals. Every Chantway ends with at least one song from the Blessingway to seal its intent. When sickness occurs, a diviner may be called upon to enter a trance and identify the source of the problem. The diviner determines the correct ritual for the cure and may recommend a singer to perform it.

HOLY WIND (NÍ CH'I)

Ní ch'i is another important Navajo concept. It is frequently translated as Holy Wind, although it is more than this. The Holy Wind refers to the air, the atmosphere in its entirety, when still and in motion. It has a power and a sanctity that have no precise equivalent in European-based cultures. Some people translate Ní ch'i as Holy Spirit. It is breath, it is spirit and it is life force; it is carried by, and it is, the wind. Ní ch'i suffuses all of Nature; it is responsible for giving life, thought, speech and the power of motion to all living things. It is the quickening that is life. Ní ch'i is also the means of communication between all elements of the living world and with our protectors, the Holy People. Ní ch'i reports to the Holy People on people's behaviour and so they act as moral guardians.

Ní ch'i lives in the four cardinal directions and the four stages of the day – dawn, midday sky, twilight and darkness. It was Ní ch'i that entered Changing Woman to give her life. For the Navajo, Ní ch'i is believed to enter at the very moment of conception. When a child is born, the Ní ch'i within combines with the surrounding Ní ch'i and the

Prior to the ceremony, the *hooghan* – the family home – is emptied and swept. Materials are prepared – firewood, plants, sand, sandstone, baskets, buckskins and calico, as well as food for the family and guests. Some ceremonies can last nine days and on the last day of a chant more than a hundred people might attend. For the family the ceremonies can be expensive: the fee paid the singer of a substantial ceremony will be high. In the case of healing ceremonies, the emotional support given by the presence of relatives and friends, and the medicinal plants used by the singer, will all help in the healing process. The healing power of such ceremonies is recognized increasingly by conventional Western medicine. Singers now perform ceremonies in reservation hospitals.

BLESSINGWAY

The Blessingway is the most important of all the chants, as it was the first one to be given to the people after their emergence into this world. The term Blessingway covers everything that is good, including concepts such as beauty, harmony and success. The Blessingway is performed by the singer or holy man in the *hooghan* on a regular basis and is a way of creating hope and good fortune. One family member may be the focus of the ceremony, the one who is "sung over", and the ceremony will be performed on important occasions in someone's life, such as when a woman is to give birth or when a young man is to go away on a quest, journey, to attend university or to enter the armed forces.

Every Blessingway ceremony emphasizes that the *hooghan* is a microcosm of the Universe. If the *hooghan* is well ordered, it will reflect outward into the wider world. The first night of the ceremony involves the singing of special chants. On the second day, there is purification by means of a ritual bath in yucca suds and the making of sand-paintings with cornmeal, pollen and crushed flower petals such as larkspur. The special connection of Changing Woman with the Blessingway is emphasized. This is the only ceremony in which she is depicted in sand-paintings. The songs continue all night each night of the Blessingway. There are different sand-paintings connected with each individual chant and the paintings used on a particular occasion will be those deemed most suitable for the person being "sung over". The ceremony ends with a twelve-word song to please the Holy People and to remind everyone of the goals and ideals of Navajo culture, while also correcting any errors in the ceremony. The final act in the Blessingway is to stand up and breathe in the air – Ní ch'i – at dawn to re-infuse the individual with this holy and spiritual source of life and strength – the life force.

SAND-PAINTINGS

Sand-painting are more correctly known as dry-painting, but the term sand-painting is now more widely known. Sand-paintings are used both to attract good and to dispel

Sandpainting of a deity from the Navajo Reservation.

evil. They are a part of all Holyway and most Evilway ceremonies but are not used in the Lifeway ceremonies. Sand-paintings are created to restore health and harmony in the life of the one "sung over". While most ceremonies create images on the *hooghan* floor by applying mineral materials on to a base of sand, the paintings in the Blessingway ceremony are created on buckskin. Sand-paintings range in size from being relatively small to up to 20 feet in diameter. These larger ones may require 10–15 people to work for most of a day to complete.

Most sand-paintings are made during the daytime but a few are created after dark. They are built up on a base of fine sand laid down in a layer one to three inches deep upon the floor. The colours of the four directions – white for the dawn and the East, blue for the midday sky and the South, yellow for the evening twilight and the West, and black for the night sky and the North – are always used. Making the paintings is technically demanding. Dimensions and the balance between certain figures must be exact in order for the ceremony to work. The top of the sand painting is oriented toward the East and is surrounded by a guardian on the other three sides. This is to protect the sand-painting from evil on those sides and allows strength and all good things that come from the East with the dawn to enter at the top.

The sand-painting derives its power to heal from the coexistence within the image of multiple layers of time, space and meaning. Creating the sand-painting in the right way contributes to the healing process as much the ritual that follows. The act of drawing the symmetrical, orderly images focuses the thoughts of everyone present on the principles of balance and order. The presence of the Holy People, both in their images and thus their implied actual presence, creates power. Layers of meaning come from the myths and stories portrayed, which are specially chosen for their relevance to the situation. The patient sits on the sand-painting in direct contact with the images of the Holy People during the ceremony. This connection transmits healing power.

HOPI

When the Navajo and Apache entered the southwest, they encountered other peoples with a different way of life, such as the Hopi. Their name comes from Hopita, meaning "peaceful one" in Hopi. The Hopi are Pueblo Indians and descendants of the Anasazi culture, one of the oldest known cultures North of Mexico. They occupy seven communal pueblo towns situated in a reservation within the Navaho nation in north-east Arizona at the southern end of the Black Mesa near the Grand Canyon. The Hopi are agriculturalists, growing corn, beans, squash, tobacco, melons and other fruit. Hopi numbers have diminished through wars and epidemics, so now only around 2,200 remain.

Being agricultural, they built communities and developed the land in one place. Their building techniques were sophisticated. Houses are square, flat roofed structures of stone or adobe – baked mud – often several stories high or built into cliffs, with enough rooms to accommodate several hundred people. In case of attack, their storerooms could hold sufficient provisions for a year. To protect themselves further, most of the outer walls are without doors, the entrance being through a hole in the roof by means of a ladder that can be hauled up behind them if they were attacked. In Hopi society, women own the land and houses. Hopi women cook and weave baskets. Men plant and harvest, weave cloth and perform ceremonies.

Corn, the staple foodstuff, plays a special part in rites of passage. When a child is born, he or she is presented with a special blanket and a perfect ear of corn. After twenty days, the child is taken to an eastern facing cliff of the Mesa and held aloft to the rising Sun. When the rays of the sun reach the new-born, it is given its name. A Hopi bride would grind corn for three days at her future husband's house. In return the future husband and his male relatives would weave her wedding dress. When both were finished, she would walk home in her wedding clothes. When she died she would be buried in her wedding dress, so when she entered the spirit world she would be appropriately dressed.

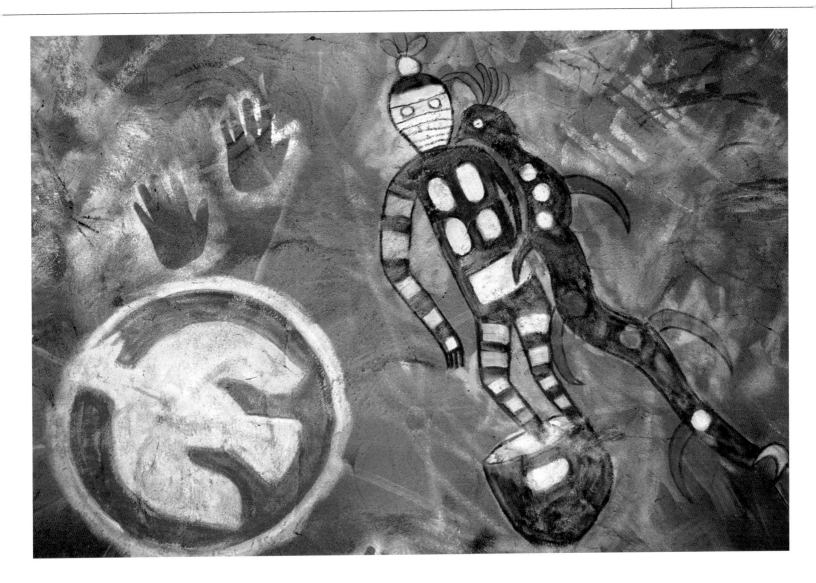

Hopi spiritual ceremonies take place in secret, in large underground chambers known as *kivas*. These are typically circular in shape with a fire pit in the centre and a timbered roof. An opening in the floor represents the entrance to the lower world, from which the Hopi believe they emerged. Being dependent on agriculture, rain has a special significance. Much prayer and ritual is directed toward the Rain Gods. Snakes are the messengers of the Rain Gods and the Hopi hold an elaborate Snake Dance every two years to venerate the Rain Gods and to bring rain to the crops. The Snake Dance is conducted by the initiates of the Snake Society, masked dancers who are trained to dance with live venomous snakes in their mouths.

HOPI CREATION MYTH

Native American creation myths are not only a spiritual rationale to explain the cosmos in which people find themselves. They are also an oral history. Within the myths are hints of ecological change and of interactions with different peoples. The Hopi myth, like the myth of the Apaches of the southwest, speaks of a time when the world was flooded. Millions of years ago Arizona was covered by sea, and shells are still found there. The myths may be a way of explaining regional geology, or the flood may have been something that occurred in the early history of peoples in the region.

In the Hopi myth, people do not descend from the sky. They emerged from the Earth at the Grand Canyon in

Hopi painting of fertility god with principle crops.

Kachina dolls were carved among the Hopi by the maternal uncles of young girls for religious teaching. Kachinas are spirit beings responsible for many of the forces of nature.

Arizona. There are four levels in the Hopi universe – the surface world and three cave worlds, one below each other. Life started in the lowest cave world, which became over-crowded and unpleasant. Two brothers find a way through to the next world and start anew. The successive cave worlds are reached and lived in until they also become too crowded and unpleasant. At each level the people who arrive first fear the place is too small for them all and through various devices leave some people below on the lower levels. The over-riding motivation is to move on and up. Eventually they reach this world, the surface, but this is still in dark-ness. In Native American myth, people, with the aid of animals, create the world as we know it. In Hopi myth, with the assistance of Spider, Vulture, Swallow, Coyote and Locust, who have ascended with them, people create light. This shows them how small the world is – it is surrounded by waters. With the aid of Vulture, two brothers create channels to drain the water, and rivers and streams are made. As the land dries out, they see tracks. These are the tracks of Death. The people follow the tracks eastward and overtake Death, who conspires to have his first victim. Another young girl, who is jealous of her, kills the beauti-ful young daughter of a great priest. The people put the girl on trial and decide to kill her, but she persuades them to look into the hole in the ground that leads back to the Lowerworld from which they came. They see plains of beautiful flow-ers in a land of everlasting summer and fruitfulness. The beautiful girl is seen wandering happily among the flowers. She has no desire to return to the surface world. The people now know they will have life after death.

The young murderess is spared but continues to bring trouble. Her children become powerful wizards and witch-es with wonderful and dreadful powers. They stir up other peoples who had come out of the caves before the Hopi and they make war on the Hopi. To protect themselves, the Hopi must build houses on high mountains reached by only one trail, or in caves with only one path leading to them, or in the sides of deep canyons. Only in this way can they live in the peace to which they aspire.

NATIVE AMERICAN SPIRITUALITY TODAY

Despite the destructiveness of its encounter with Western culture, Native American spirituality retains its rich diversity. Many Native Americans, especially in the southwest, have retained their original traditions more or less intact. Some Native American families have been Christians for several generations. Others combine both traditional and Christian elements. The Native American Church incorporates generic Native American cere-monies. Instead of the bread and communion wine used by other Christian denominations, the Church uses the traditional sacred sub-stance of the peoples of the southwest – the peyote cactus, which has been used for spiritual vision for about 10,000 years. The modern peyote ritual consists of four parts: praying, singing, eating peyote and quietly medi-tating. Pan-Indianism is a recent and growing movement that encourages a return to traditional beliefs, and seeks to create a common Native religion. Summer festivals and gatherings – known as pow wows – have become increasingly popular and keep people in contact with one another and with traditional practices.

Native American spirituality is closely connected with the land and so sacred sites are of great importance. Some have connections with creation myths. Other sites relate to historical events of religious significance. Others are burial sites, areas where sacred plants or other natural materials are available, or places where structures, carvings or paintings with symbolic significance made by tribal ancestors were placed. For many peoples, the continued celebration of sacred rites at these sites is essential to the continuity of their tradition. Unfortunately, the demands of a materialist society conflict with those of traditional spiritual practice. Many sites are in areas with rich mineral and logging resources. According to testimony put before a United States' House of Representatives sub-committee, there are currently 44 sacred sites known to be the subject of disputes concerning land management or development. This is likely to be less than the true total, as traditional religious practitioners keep many of the sites secret. Retaining and regaining control of these sacred sites requires ongoing campaigning by Native peoples and those who share their concerns.

Pow wows in the summer months have become important in the revival of Native American culture. Dance competitions are a popular part of pow wows.

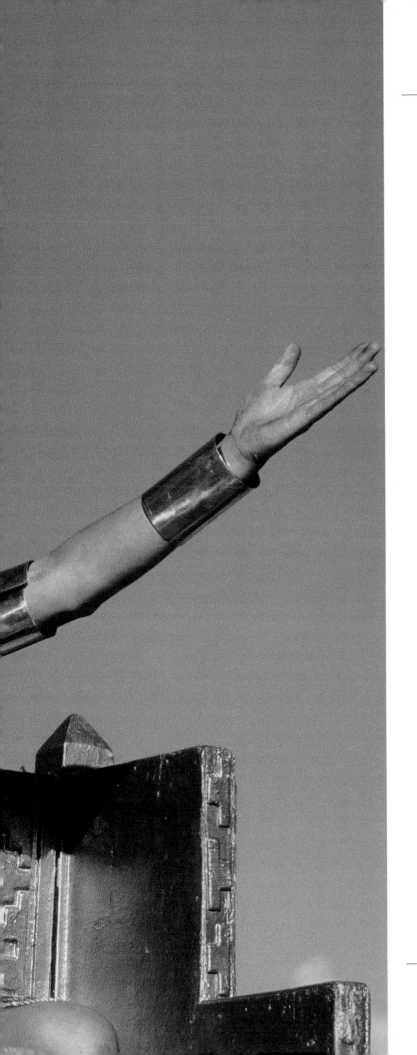

CENTRAL AND SOUTH AMERICA

Hanging as though suspended from North America by the Isthmus of Panama is South America. On the East is the Atlantic Ocean, to the West the Pacific. Northward are the Central American countries of Panama, Costa Rica, Nicaragua, El Salvador, Honduras, Guatemala, Belize and Mexico. To the northeast is the Caribbean Sea where, in past centuries, many European countries staked their colonial claims, leaving a Spanish heritage in Cuba, a French heritage in Haiti and a British heritage in the West Indies.

Down the West of South America runs its spine – the Andes mountain range, which stretches 5,000 miles (8,000 kilometres) from Venezuela to Chile. On South America's eastern side are the great drainage systems of the Rivers Amazon, Orinoco and Paraná. Around the Amazon is dense tropical rain forest, one of the last great lungs of our planet. The North of the continent lies in the hot Tropics, but to the South Tierra del Fuego, at the tip of Chile, extends to the Antarctic Circle.

Central and South America were originally settled by migrants from the North. Some migration was by land, possibly following migrating animal herds. Other migra-

tion is likely to have been by boat. Currently, there are archaeological disputes as to when the first human societies developed in South America, but knowledge advances each year as the earth gives up hidden artefacts. Some of the earliest evidence of human habitation is in coastal regions. Two campsites, each around 13,000 years old, have been found at Quebrada Jaguay (Jaguay Canyon) and Quebrada Tacahuay (Tacahuay Canyon) on the South coast of Peru. At Jaguay Canyon, a team of archaeologists found the remains of fishing nets. At Tacahuay Canyon, researchers found a hearth, tools and obsidian flakes, as well as the bones of small anchovy that could only have been fished by nets rather than hook and line. There is a 12,500-year-old site at Monte Verde in Chile, as well as sites in eastern Brazil and Colombia.

Today, the peoples of the region are a complex mix of ethnicity and cultures brought about by the conquest of different native peoples by Spanish, Portuguese and other European colonists and, in some parts of the region, the subsequent transportation of millions of slaves from Africa to work the land. There was a large native population in South America before the arrival of the Europeans at the beginning of the sixteenth century. Peoples such as the Incas and Aztecs, and earlier the Mayans, had developed elaborate civilizations. In other regions, people lived a simple hunter-gatherer lifestyle or cleared forest for agriculture using slash-and-burn techniques. The arrival of Europeans was disastrous for indigenous peoples. Within a century, as the result of disease and warfare, the population had declined from around 14 million to under five million people.

A small number of African slaves arrived in South America with the first Spanish conquistadors, but the large-scale transportation of slaves was more a feature of Portuguese Brazil, where sugar plantations needed vast amounts of labour that could not be supplied by the conquered indigenous population. With its position on South America's East coast, directly across from the slave ports of West Africa, Brazil was ideally placed to participate in this degrading trade. Anything from between four and ten million people were forcibly transported. In northeastern Brazil, most people today have African ancestry. In Colombia, Ecuador, Venezuela and Peru, Africans have arrived more recently, descended from construction workers on the Panama Canal and from immigrants from the Caribbean islands. Apart from Africans and Europeans, the twentieth century has seen the arrival of Asian immigrants. Brazil has the largest Japanese population outside Japan and in Peru in the 1990s someone of Japanese descent became President.

European settlers in the sixteenth century were mainly men and there was extensive intermarriage with the indigenous population, which has resulted in a large mixed-blood mestizo population. Waves of immigrants from the mid-nineteenth century onward brought large influxes of Europeans into Brazil and Argentina. Germans settled in Chile, Argentina and Brazil. Argentina, Uruguay and Brazil attracted large numbers of Italians. Spaniards went to the Spanish-speaking country of Argentina, and Portuguese to Brazil. German activity in Europe and the Second World War brought Central European refugees, including many Jews fleeing Nazi persecution; ironically to be followed post-war by their former persecutors, the defeated Nazis.

RELIGION

At the time of the arrival of the Spanish conquistadors, indigenous spirituality in Central and South America varied from the animism of the Amazonian Indians to the priestly ceremonies and complex temples of Aztec and Inca civilisations. The conquistadors brought with them their Catholic faith, which was a useful flag of convenience. Conquest of native peoples, destruction of their culture and enslavement could all be justified in the name of saving their souls. Catholicism remains the dominant official religion of South and Central America, but has many pre-Christian features. Many people continue to practise the religions of their ancestors. Others combine

An Aztec pilgrim honours the Virgin Mary at Candlemas.

Catholicism with other faiths to produce traditions that now see themselves as religions in their own right. The best-known is the synthesis of West African spirituality, indigenous Amerindian traditions and Christianity that is known in French-speaking Haiti as Voudon, in Spanish-speaking Cuba and Latin America as Santeria and in Portuguese-speaking Brazil as Candomblé or Umbanda. There are also groups such as the Native American Church in the United States that have woven Christianity into native tradition. Whereas peyote is the sacramental substance of the Native American Church, the *ayahuasca* vine is the sacrament of churches further South.

MEXICAN CATHOLICISM

Mexico is named after the Mexica, whom we know as the Aztecs. Some of today's indigenous Mexicans are descen-

For the reforming Protestants of Europe this was a sign of the Catholic Church's degeneration from "pure" Christianity. For Native peoples, however, it has often allowed important elements of traditional culture to survive.

In southern Mexico, Guatemala and Belize, there are around six million people of Mayan descent, speaking 20 different Mayan languages. Among the Tzeltal Mayans, for instance, God is seen as a remote figure removed from day-to-day life, in much the way that an absentee landlord is titular owner of his fields, but has no direct impact on what occurs. Much more important in people's lives are "Our Holy Mother Saint Mary" and the saints. Christ is considered the leader of the saints, but Mary is the more powerful, and patron saints' festivities are celebrated with more enthusiasm and complexity than those of Christ. Mary is also the Lady of the Crops, and patron of the staple foodstuff – corn or maize. Unripe corn is Mary's "green blouses" and "green garments". Another throwback to earlier beliefs is that statues of the saints are considered to be alive. The blessing of the priest gives them life and they are therefore important power objects. Also important in day-to-day life are the "Holy Angel" – a spirit who lives in caves and guards plant and animal life – and the Earth Lord, who is capricious and must be appeased. When the foundations of houses are laid, four chickens must be sacrificed to the Earth. All mountains are alive, a common belief in Central and South America. The mountains are terraced to provide fields and important beings dwell there, such as Mary and the Holy Angel. Crosses are also believed to inhabit the mountain caves and crosses are placed by sacred springs and at other important features. Crosses are places of devotion where the world of humankind and spirit can communicate. The cross is frequently addressed as though it is a deity in itself and ideas about the Christian cross have been synthesized with the concept of the tree of life in Mayan belief – the Yax-ché, to which petitions are addressed for life-giving water. The Tzotzil Maya make Mary's status even higher. She is "Our Holy Mother The Moon" and "Our Mother In Heaven"

The Mexican Day of the Dead is a fusion of Aztec festival with the Catholic feasts of All Saints and All Souls.

dants of those who created the Aztec Empire that was crushed by the sixteenth-century Spanish invasion. Others are descendants of Mayan peoples whose mighty empire had fallen into decline long before the coming of the Aztecs. Today, Mexico is nominally almost totally Catholic, but Catholicism has shown a remarkable ability to adapt and absorb elements of traditional belief wherever it has spread.

and mother of "Our Father Sun Christ". Other important figures are animal-soul companions, power animals who are associated with the individual's health and feature in shamanic healing rites.

MEXICAN DAY OF THE DEAD

As we have seen in Europe, traditional festivals were incorporated into the Christian calendar and the same process occurred in the Americas. Some of that synthesis can be seen in Mexico in the Mexican *Dia de Muertos*, the Day of the Dead. The Day of the Dead is a continuation of the Aztec feast of the goddess Mictlancihuatl, the Lady of the Dead, who dwells in Mictan, the Place of the Dead. In the Aztec calendar, the festival took place in the month that spanned part of July and August, but it synthesized with the Catholic feasts of All Saints on November 1 and All Souls on November 2. The festival also reflects Mayan beliefs of the region – that the focus of life is about enjoying the here and now. The aim of the Day of the Dead is to release the dead to come back to Earth to do what they most enjoyed in life – eating, drinking, smoking and dancing.

Dia de Muertos hits public consciousness in Mexico from mid-October onward. Shop windows are full of all manner of decorations, flowers and foods that act as *ofrenda de muertos*, offerings to the dead. Decorations include skeletons, *papel picado* – elaborate wreaths and crosses decorated with paper or silk flowers – candles and votive lights and fresh seasonal flowers. Brightly coloured marigolds are popular. Sweets are made into skulls or coffins and bakeries produce *pan de muertos* – sugary sweet rolls topped with bone-shaped pieces of dough on the outside and plastic toy skeletons hidden inside – and soul breads, which are dark breads moulded into human figures called *animas*, or souls.

Preparations are made to welcome the dead back to their homes for the feast day. Altars are created by covering a table or crates with a clean white cloth. The altar is decorated with flowers, photographs of the deceased, candy skulls with their names inscribed on them, a selection of their favourite foods, such as rice, beans, chicken, meat, candied pumpkin, sweet potatoes and breads, and favourite drinks, such as beer, tequila, *atole* or corn gruel, coffee or fresh water. Incense is burned in honour of the dead and candles are lit to help them find their way home. Other traditions to make the dead welcome are the setting out of a wash basin and towel so they can wash before the feast and offerings of cigarettes for adults, or toys and extra sweets for deceased children.

At burial grounds, families gather to weed and repair graves and to hold a sumptuous picnic to commemorate their ancestors. Graves are decorated with marigold crosses and wreaths and children's graves are adorned with coloured streamers. November 1 is the Catholic feast of All Saints when children who have died as pure souls are remembered. November 2 is for adults who may be undergoing suffering in purgatory before entering heaven. As the whole local community is at the cemetery, the Day of the Dead is a festive and community celebration.

OUR LADY OF GUADELOUPE

Like Brittany and other parts of Catholic Europe, Spain in the Medieval period and immediately afterward had its share of miraculous apparitions of female saints who appeared to peasants telling them to go to the church authorities and insist that shrines should be set up in their honour. In rural Ireland, these visions continued into the twentieth century with the apparition of Our Lady of Knock. All sixteenth-century Mexico needed to become a properly Catholic country was its own *bona fide* apparition. This arrived shortly after the Spanish conquest in the form of Our Lady of Guadeloupe. The original Guadeloupe in Spain was also the site of a miraculous apparition of the Virgin Mary. She

A representation of the Virgin of Guadeloupe appearing to indigenous Mexicans.

appeared in 1326 to the cowherd Gil Cordovero to tell him the location of a statue of her donated by Pope Gregory the Great to the Bishop of Seville and hidden 600 years earlier during the conquest of Spain by Muslims from North Africa.

A new miracle manifested to Mexican Indian peasant Juan Diego in 1531. He was on his way to church when he came to a hill called Tepeyacac. Suddenly he heard the most extraordinarily beautiful birdsong and then a voice calling him to come to the top of the hill. At the top, reputed to be the site of an Aztec shrine, he saw a beautiful noble dark-skinned lady. Her garments shone with the radiance of the Sun and the ground on which she trod glittered like precious stones with rainbow colours. It seemed to Juan Diego that he was seeing the "Flower Land", the "Sunshine Land" or Otherworld of his Aztec ancestors. For the Aztecs, the Otherworld is a garden of beautiful flowers, brightly coloured tropical birds, precious stones such as jade and turquoise, light, heat and scents. The cacti and other plants on this barren hilltop shone with jewel-like colours. Their foliage was turquoise and their thorns glistened with gold. How much this was due to Divine intervention, and how much it was facilitated by mescaline-laden tequila or peyote cactus, we shall never know.

Ayamara people of the Bolivian Andes collect a llamato offer at a shrine to the Earth Mother Pachamama.

The colour description sounds, however, like a classic mild hallucinogenic experience and much of the imagery draws directly on Aztec symbolism. After a number of attempts, Juan Diego managed to convince the sceptical local bishop of the truth of his vision and a new cult sprang up in Mexico – that of Our Lady of Guadeloupe.

Papal decree has declared the Virgin of Guadeloupe to be Queen and patron saint of Mexico and Empress of the Americas. Her basilica on the outskirts of Mexico City is a major world pilgrimage site and shrines to her are found all over Mexico, from homes to churches to the front of buses.

THE ANDES

South America's western coast is an area of climatic and geographical extremes, from the world's driest coastal desert to its longest mountain chain and its densest tropical jungles. The Andean mountain area covering modern Peru, spreading eastward into Bolivia and southward and northward into Chile and Ecuador is the birthplace of some of the oldest and most complex civilizations of South America, whose descendants inhabit the same regions today. The best-known civilization is the Inca Empire, which was destroyed by the conquistadors, but this was a relatively short-lived culture and many civilizations had preceded it. Today, the region has many different Amerindian peoples with related but different languages and overlapping belief systems that vary slightly from valley to valley.

The heart of the Inca Empire was in what is now Peru, but the sacred site of origin of the Inca people was believed to be the Island of the Sun in Lake Titicaca, which borders Bolivia. Lake Titicaca is South America's largest lake and the world's highest navigable body of water. The Island of the Sun has an evocative rock formation shaped like a mountain cat, which gives the lake its name. *Titi* is mountain cat and *caca* is rock. From the Island of the Sun, the Incas could contemplate the sacred mountain of Illampu. Illampu, with another local mountain Illimani, is considered by local people to be an eternal deity and owner of the Earth.

Bolivia has archaeological sites dating back 3,500 years that were in use until the Spanish conquest and the area has been farmed for around 6,000 years. It was the people's skill at farming that allowed complex civilizations to develop. With good crop yields, societies do not need all their adult members to engage in agriculture. Time and community resources can be devoted to artistic and religious activities and, in the Andean region, to the building of temples and cities. Most of the region's artefacts are in fact pre-Inca, as the Inca Empire did not begin its phenomenal expansion until 1430. A hundred years later, it lay in ruins.

Cuzco in Peru was the Inca capital and the centre of religious and administrative life. The Church of Santo Domingo now covers much of the site of the Inca Empire's richest temple, Koricahcha, but three side chambers dedicated to thunder, Moon and rainbow are still preserved. Puma were important symbols in the Andes, where they were believed to be the king of other animals and the cats of the mountain gods. This was due to their habit of roaring, which was associated with thunder, and hunting by night – when the gods were believed to be most active. The Incas believed that their birthplace, the Island of the Sun, was raised on the body of a puma and Cuzco, which they considered the life-giving navel of the world, was laid out

The Sillustani Necropolis at Lake Titicaca, Peru.

The base of a giant tower used for astronomical and water rituals at the Inca temple and fortress of Sacsahuaman, Peru.

One of the most famous tourist attractions of Peru is the Inca Trail in the National Archaeological Park of Machu Picchu, which leads by way of a high altitude trek through breathtakingly beautiful mountains to the city of Machu Picchu, used by the Incas for astronomical observation. The Intihuatana stone, the "hitching post" of Inti, the Sun, indicates the date of Winter Solstice and other significant dates. Machu Pichu was never found by the Spaniards. Invisible from below and completely self-contained, it was surrounded by agricultural terraces watered by natural springs, which could supply enough food to feed the population. Those who could foretell the movement of plants, stars and worrying phenomena such as eclipses and comets had considerable power. By hiding the source of this knowledge, the mystery was enhanced.

Ritual activity in the Andes is focused on ensuring the fruitfulness of the source of life. The blessing of farming was a major part of the Inca religion. Each crop had its own spirit and Inca temples contained gold statutes of deities and gold symbolic representations of major foodstuffs. Shrines to the Earth Mother Goddess Pachamama are venerated, as are deities of the region's most evocative landscape features – the mountains. Animals and people are believed to originate from the mountains at birth and to return to them at death. Mountain deities control the fertility of crops and of animals such as llamas. Veneration of sacred mountains is common to many peoples around the world, but in an area such as the Andes, where the

on a grid thought to resemble a puma. Other important animals associated with the gods were serpents and condor birds. The serpent was the chief animal of the Lowerworld. The giant serpent, the *amaru*, lives beneath the Earth and at the bottom of lakes. It aids the distribution of water for agriculture and it some myths assists with the construction of irrigation canals. The puma guards our Middleworld. The Upperworld is the domain of the huge condor. These three animals have been venerated in the region for over 3,000 years.

The most important deity of the Inca pantheon, the Creator Viracocha, Maker-of-that-which-gives-Life, is still worshipped in the region by Peruvians and the Aymara people of northern Chile. Viracocha is omnipotent. He creates human beings from stone and creates other deities. According to the Aymara, Viracocha rose from Lake Titicaca, created the Earth, the sky and human beings, and then went back under the surface of the waters. Like some North American myths, the first humans live in darkness. Later, Viracocha and a new generation of humans together create the Sun, the Moon and the stars. The Sun was venerated as Inti in temples with images made of the finest gold showing a face surrounded by the rays of the Sun. The Moon was Quilla, wife of the Sun, whose temple was served by virgin priestesses.

Bolivians taking part in a partly Christianized ceremony to Pachamama.

mountains do in effect "control" the weather, the desire to ensure their goodwill is particularly strong. Another common feature of mountain life is the spectacular storms. The brothers of the mountain deities are often thunder and lightning.

Priests are considered embodiments of the mountain gods and have an important function in weather magic. Offerings to avert excess rain, drought, hail or frost that can damage crops are still made on the Island of the Sun to the mountains Illimani and Illampu, who are considered superior to all other mountains and to the Earth Mother Goddess Pachamama. First a priest will go to the ancient ruin of Pilkokaina to perform a divination in a room oriented toward Mount Illampu. He then selects a hill on which to make the offering. One of the most important deities on the southwest shore of Lake Titicaca is the mountain Atoja, bringer of rain and source of the streams that feed the fields beneath. Small stone altars can be found on the summit for rain offerings.

Many local peoples worship their indigenous deities directly. Others have incorporated the idea of rainmaking into the attributes of the Virgin Mary of Copacabana, who is considered a goddess of water and of Lake Titicaca itself.

HEALING

The mountain deities play a special role in endowing the traditional healers of the region, the *yatiris*, with power. In this region of violent storms, surviving being struck by lightning can be interpreted as a message from the gods that one is to become a *yatiri*. For many *yatiris*, Mount Illimani is an especially sacred mountain and completing a pilgrimage to the mountain gives healers special prestige. The

mountains are known as *achachilas* – ancestors – which reflect beliefs that human beings originate in the mountains. Rivers also play a role in healing. Offerings are made to the Wakira (Tiahuanaco) River that flows into Lake Titicaca, which is also considered an *achachila*, with the idea that an illness will be removed. As the waters flow, so sickness will flow away with them. Offerings are also made to the goddess of Lake Titicaca to ensure sufficient reeds for boats, forage for livestock, success in fishing, safe passage on the lake and for good weather.

NAZCA LINES

One of the most famous sites in Peru are the Nazca lines, which were made between 200 and 800 CE. They are marked out in the Peruvian desert, about 200 miles South of Lima, between the Inca and Nazca valleys. The lines cover an area roughly 37 miles long and one mile wide. The lines on the desert floor trace out figures of extraordinary precision. Some are geometric figures – triangles and rectangles. Others are of birds and animals, such as a huge monkey with a spiralling tail and a condor with an enormous wingspan. The figures were forgotten until spotted in the 1930s by an aircraft surveying for water. Given that the lines can be seen properly only from the air, there has been much speculation about whether the Nazca could make hot air balloons. Swiss writer

August 1 is the festival of Pachamama in Peru. Here, Peruvians prepare a *mesa* (table) of food offerings to the goddess.

The Nazca lines of Peru were the subject of much speculation in the twentieth century. The lines are thought to have been used in religious ceremonies.

Erich von Daniken suggested that they are a remnant of UFO activity – an idea prompted perhaps by the resemblance of the lines to airport runways – although the more practical point out that the desert floor of Nazca is soft earth, not tarmac, and would not support the landing of a spacecraft. More prosaically, it is possible that the constructors of the figures also created viewing platforms of the kind recently put up for tourists by the Peruvian government. Others have speculated about the astrological or astronomical significance of the figures, but no significant alignments have been found. A promising line of research has been the Andean tradition, pointed out by British explorer Tony Morrison, of pilgrimages involving prayers and meditation at wayside shrines joined by straight lines. Other have taken up the idea that the lines were used for religious ceremonies and recently archaeologists and anthropologists have demonstrated that the figures are precisely the right size for a community to process around

them in spiritual pilgrimage. They may represent community totems walked on special ceremonial occasions.

FESTIVALS AND DANCE

One of the most important festivals in the region is the *Inti Raymi* or Sun Festival, at winter Solstice. This is a major celebration in Cuzco and Sacsayhuaman and has become a tourist attraction. Like Midsummer festivals in Europe, the date has been moved slightly to coincide with the Catholic feast of St John the Baptist – June 24. The festival lasts most of the day and attracts tens of thousands of people. The ceremony is celebrated in much the same way as the Incas celebrated it centuries ago. It begins at the Qorikancha, the remains of an Inca temple. The festival moves up the steep hill to Sacsayhuaman, where offerings are made to the gods of *chichi*, or corn beer, sacred fires are lit and the sacrifice of a llama is enacted – though not carried out in actuality. The festival concludes with a man dressed to represent the Inca being carried on a litter by his subjects.

Communal dance is an important part of *Inti Raymi*. In the Andean countries along the Pacific coast, traditional dances have been moved to Catholic festivals and dances dedicated to animals such as the puma and the condor, which consist of a solo mime in a large circle, have been "Christianized". The Araucanians of Chile, for instance, have preserved their harvest ceremony, *Ñillatun*, which is a combination of Christian ritual and traditional dance. During interludes two men, using shawls as wings, mime the movements of rheas, which are ostrich-like birds.

Further North in Mexico, masked clown dancers often appear at sacred festivals. These dancers are rather like the mummers of Medieval European villages. Their function is to enact sacred teachings through allegory in a way that people of all ages and levels of intelligence can understand. Masked dancers also have a moral function. Behind the anonymity of their masks, they can exercise social control by poking fun at those who violate social norms. The *hikuli*, or peyote dance, in November, follows pilgrimages for peyote. The dance of the Huichol Mayans is ecstatic. After consuming the peyote, men and women enter a trance and dance in an anti-clockwise circle, leaping jerkily and twisting their bodies.

AMAZON

The denseness of the Amazon rain forest has hidden for millennia peoples whose ways of life as hunter-gatherers are dependent on a close connection between the everyday world and that of the Otherworld. Their spiritual practices are based around shamanism and the ability of trained practitioners to travel into the Otherworld, to diagnose sickness and community problems, to deal with spirits who cause harm to individuals and communities, and to commune with animal spirits. The shaman's role does not end when those he serves leave the body. He is a guide who takes the dead to the Otherworld. The shaman usually has greater power among his people than the chief. Shamans hold the keys to health through their healing rituals, their access to the spirit world and their vast knowledge of medicinal plants, which gown in abundance in the Amazon rain forest.

Shamanism often involves imbibing hallucinogenic

Indigenous Bolivian woman in traditional dress.

plants or fungi that produce altered states of consciousness. These include synaesthesia – experiences of hearing colour and seeing sound – flying out of the body, speaking with plants and animals and visions of intensely beautiful colour. Amazonian shamans frequently encounter jaguars – one of the most important power animals of Amazonian spirituality – in their Otherworld journeys. Snakes are also common. This may explain the frequent veneration of sacred serpents. Quetzalcoatl, the plumed serpent of the Aztecs and patron of learning and art is the most well known form.

Yagua shaman collecting medicinal plants. The Yagua believe that the material world is an illusion.

AYAHUASCA – THE SACRED VINE

Twentieth-century Brazil, with its complex multi-ethnic communities, became the source of many new synthesized religions. One of the most thriving involves the use of the sacred vine of South America – *ayahuasca*, or *Banisteriopsis Caapi*, which is also known as *hoasca* or *yage*. *Ayahuasca* grows in the jungles of Brazil, Peru, Colombia, and throughout the Amazon. It contains a mild hallucinogenic, harmaline, and is usually taken as tea with added leaves of *Psychotria Viridis*, a more powerful hallucinogen that contains the active ingredient N-N-dimethyltryptamine (DMT). The unwary Westerner who partakes in an *ayahuasca* ceremony may have an unpleasant surprise. Amerindian tradition frequently welcomes purgation as a means to purification and the first stages of ayahuasca lead to violent vomiting. Fasting is also necessary beforehand because the active ingredients can become lethal when combined with meat or cheese.

One of the main religions that features *ayahuasca* was founded in the 1920s by Raimundo Irineu Serra, a black Brazilian rubber tapper. He was working in the Amazonian forest when he met Amerindians, probably of the Turkano people. The Turkano use *ayahuasca* for healing and for contacting the spirit world. *Ayahuasca* means literally "vine of the dead" or "vine of souls". Its visions can provide communication with the dead and the spirit world, the world of the ancestors. In Turkano tradition, *ayahuasca* is used to climb the stars of the Milky Way, which is also known as the "white road" or the "road to the dead".

Raimundo Irineu Serra, who became known as Master Irineu, tried *ayahuasca* for himself and was rewarded with a vision. A beautiful white woman appeared to him and told him she was the Queen of the Forest. Serra felt that she was also the Virgin Mary. The Queen of the Forest instructed him to found a new religion using *ayahuasca* as its sacrament. Master Irineu created a liturgy for the new religion, which was named Santo Daime, meaning "Give unto me the sacred". Initially, the new religion spread among black Brazilians, but it has now attracted Brazil's white population. Its beliefs include reincarnation and the importance of saving the rain forest. The Brazilian Federal Drug Council investigated Santo Daime, but ruled that its worship has a positive impact and promotes social integration.

Santo Daime played a prominent role at the 1992 Earth Summit held in Brazil, which included an *ayahuasca* service with what would be an unusual sight in other countries – the participation of the head of the country's Federal Drug Council. Brazilian *ayahuasca* groups arrived in Europe in the 1980s, but European governments have been reluctant to authorize the use of *ayahuasca*, which is a prohibited drug. Santo Daime is particularly strong in the Netherlands, which has liberal drug laws, and in Portugal, which has colonial connections and which shares a common official language with Brazil.

AFRICAN TRADITIONS

The African-based traditions – Voudon, Santeria Candomblé and Umbanda – that came to the Caribbean and to Central and South America with the slave trade are sometimes referred to as African Diaspora religions. Their believers were the unwilling victims of the slave trade and were primarily from West and Central Africa. Practice varies both between and within the different traditions. Some groups emphasize their Catholic links while others are keen to return more directly to their African roots. An essential part of their ceremonies is possession – followers are taken over by their gods and so speak with their voices, heal with their touch and give advice that comes from the world of spirit.

For those dispossessed from their homelands and disempowered by the horrors of slavery, this direct relationship with the Divine was a blessing that could make bearable the worldly reality of their lives. To their descendants and to others who have been drawn to these traditions today, they offer much valued experience of the Divine.

VOUDON

Voudon is found in Haiti and other French-speaking islands of the Caribbean, in the New Orleans French-speaking area of the United States and in areas where there are large concentrations of Haitian immigrants. Voudon is also found in large French cities, where France's colonial links with West Africa as well as Haiti have provided a route for immigration. The word *voudon*, or *voodoo*, means spirit. It derives from the language of the Dahomey people of the area that lies West of the Yoruba area of southwestern Nigeria and is now within Benin and parts of Togo. Voudon, indeed all Africa traditional religion, was suppressed in its homeland of Africa during the colonial era, but has been freely practised in Benin since a democratic government was installed in 1989. In 1996, the Benin government gave it formal recognition. In the Caribbean, fears that Voudon inspired those seeking to overthrow slavery led it to be vilified by colonial authorities. Books spread myths about zombies, human sacrifice and cannibalism. These myths were perpetuated by Hollywood in the 1930s during the United States' 1915–34 occupation of

Devotees appearing in the guise of orishas in a Voudon festival.

Haiti. The stories blur the important distinction between Voudon priests and priestesses and *caplatas* or *bokors* who engage in sorcery.

Voudon, like Santeria, Umbanda and Candomblé, has many groups who worship slightly different pantheons of *loa*. The word means "mystery" in Yoruba and denotes deities or spirits. *Loa* are also known by the French names of *les mystères* or *les invisibles*. The *loa* live en *bas de l'eau*, at the bottom of the ocean, in a place called Guinée or Guinea, which represents the exiles' longing for the land of their birth – Africa. There they share their homeland with les morts, the ancestral dead. When the *loas* comes to visit their worshippers, they come by way of the *chemin de l'eau*, the water road. There are hundreds of minor spirits among the *loa*. Those that originated in Dahomey are called *rada*. People can be deified, and *petro* are *loa* who include deceased leaders in the New World. Voudon has women leaders called *mambo*, and male leaders called h*oungan*. They have the power to initiate new members into the tradition. *Hounsi* are the "spouses" of the gods, those who are possessed or "ridden" by them. The congregation of participants are called *konesans*. This pattern of different levels of knowledge, spiritual skills and participation is similar to that found in Santeria, Umbanda and Candomblé. In all four traditions, deities have been fused with Catholic saints. This was partly expediency and partly the natural coming together and rationalization of two different traditions – the Catholic one, to which the slaves were required to pay lip service, and their own. Catholic teachings

were given through pictorial representations of saints and the various symbols associated with them, such as St George and his dragon. The likelihood that tired illiterate slaves would grasp the subtle difference in Catholicism between veneration paid to a saint and worship paid to a deity was slim. The peasants and serfs of Europe had never done so; something which inspired the Protestant reformation to banish saints. The likelihood is that the slaves simply accepted the images of the saints as the white version of their own gods and happily paid homage to beings who seemed at least vaguely familiar and possibly well disposed toward them. In Voudon, the beautiful water goddess

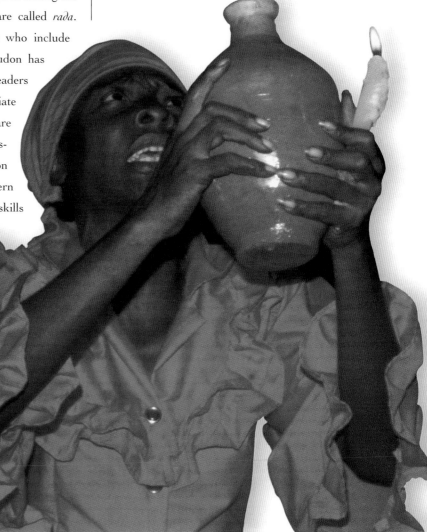

Priestess making offering to a Voudon deity.

Erzulie, Goddess of Love, who was Whydah to the Dahomey people and Oshun to Nigerians, became the Virgin Mary. The serpent god of the Dahomey, Dambala, became St Patrick; the idea of St Patrick being a banisher of snakes being more elusive than the lithographs which showed him with them. Legba, Guardian of the Underworld, became St Peter, keeper of the Gates of Heaven.

RITES

Rites take place in a temple called a *hounfort*. This has a central dwelling room or rooms surrounded by a large area called a peristyle or tonnelle. At the centre is a *poteau-mitan*, a central pole where gods and spirits communicate with their worshippers. The pole is reminiscent of the World-Tree of shamanic cultures, through which the shaman can communicate with the Upperworld and Lowerworld. Some *hounfort* have a special room, a *caye-mystère* or temple, to welcome the *loa*. *Loa* are treated as honoured guests who have journeyed far. Each deity has an altar with candles, pictures and images of the deity, flowers, food and drink, cruches – pots belonging to the dead – and *pots-de-tête*, containing hair or nail clippings of initiates.

Rituals in Voudon are focused on the here and now. They are performed in order to contact a deity and to obtain his or her favour through making offerings and animal sacrifice. The focus of a ritual will be to deal with the practical problems of life – health, food, money. The ritual is a transaction between the deity and his or her worshipper. The implicit contract is that, in return for offerings, the deity will grant worshippers their wishes. Rituals are also held in thanksgiving, to avert a run of bad luck, to celebrate the deity's festival day and at important times of family transition – birth, marriage and death. Animals are sacrificed by clean butchery – cutting the throat. A mistreated animal is unlikely to be a pleasing sacrifice. The animal's blood is collected and the hunger and thirst of the *loa* is satisfied. The worshipper may drink some of the blood and the rest of the carcass is cooked and eaten. Other important aspects of ritual are feasting prior to the

main ceremony and the making of a *veve*, a symbol of flour or cornmeal to invoke the *loa*. Drumming and rattling with cleansed and purified instruments, chanting, and dancing by the *houngan* and/or *mambo* and the *hounsis* are other important parts of the ritual. The dancing builds in intensity, until one of the *hounsis* is possessed by the *loa* and collapses. The dancer's spirit, *ti bon ange*, has left his or her body and the deity is in control. The dancer then behaves as the *loa* and is treated with respect.

CANDOMBLÉ AND UMBANDA

In Portuguese-speaking Brazil, a similar synthesis of African and Catholic belief produced Candomblé, which draws on Angolan, Efan, Fon, Ijesa and Ketu tribal tradition. It uses the term *orixá* in Portuguese to mean the same as the Spanish term *orisha*, which is used in Santeria to describe deities. From the sixteenth century onward, Portuguese colonists began transporting slaves from West Africa to work on their plantations. Africans found that their own beliefs were similar to those of the Amerindian peoples they encountered and over the years a synthesis of their original faith, new ideas they encountered from Amerindians and the Catholicism of their owners began to

Candomblé priestesses perform a washing ceremony. Ritual purity is important in African-based traditions.

form. Originally the rites were lead by men, but on the plantations, where men were sent away for long hours in the fields, women began to take over. Today, Candomblé is led by women known as High Priestesses. Umbanda developed around 1904 from the same influences as Candomblé. Umbandistas generally communicate with Catholic saints through the intercession of their ancestors, but some reformists have removed Catholic influences to return to their African roots. Candomblé and Umbanda are sometimes known as Macumba, but this term is associated with sorcery and it not usually used by followers of Umbanda or Candomblé.

The festivals of Candomblé and Umbanda are important in Brazilian culture. On January 1, the Candomblé festival of the water goddess Yemanji, who is associated with the Virgin Mary, takes place in most communities around the country. The major celebration in Brazil's largest city, Rio de Janeiro, is broadcast on television.

The Rio festival is particularly spectacular, with over a million white-clad celebrants wading into the ocean at sunset. Worshippers float small boats containing statutes of the saint on the waves. If the boats sink, then the petitioners' offerings, together with their requests, have been accepted by Yemanji, who will favour them in the coming year. It is an important spiritual time, as well as a celebration. High priestesses initiate new members of the priesthood. In Umbanda, Yemanji's festival has been incorporated with the Catholic festival of the Purification of the Virgin Mary on February 2. Offering to deities form an important part of the tradition and Yemanji is pleased by sweet foods – white custard, coconut milk and sweet rice – as well as flowers and white or clear blue precious stones. Umbanda also celebrates Yemanji on the Catholic feast of August 15, the Assumption of the Blessed Virgin Mary.

Another important goddess is Nanã or Nanan, the Great Mother. Like great mother goddesses in other parts of the world, she has been absorbed into the imagery of St Anne, Mother of Mary. Nanã is the oldest of the *Cindas*,

or "Mothers of the Waters". She is the midwife who prepares us for birth into "spiritual life" that is death. Vegetables such as aubergine, cassava and purple cabbage are offered to her.

An important role in Umbanda is given to the Old Black Fathers, ancestors who are considered spiritual entities of great power. They are associated with the Orisha Omulu, the Master of the Health, and their festival is celebrated on May 13. Like ancestor spirits elsewhere, they are thought to live in the fields and also in cemeteries. They like to be offered *capitão-de-feijão*, black bean stew, and *rapadura*, a cane broth. Like other elderly relatives on feast days, they also appreciate a glass of port. Ogum, the deity of heat, energy and war is often syncretized with Saint George, who appears in Catholic imagery as a knight in armour slaying a fearsome dragon, and has his feast on April 23, Saint George's Day. His home is the forest and he enjoys beer.

RITUALS

Followers of Candomblé and Umbanda believe that human beings have both physical and spiritual bodies. The human realm is in close contact with the spiritual realm and we can learn to contact deities, spirits and ancestors to help us with healing and with our spiritual growth. Through trance possession, deities can enter the bodies of their worshippers to speak and make manifest their power through them. The ability to allow oneself to be possessed by a deity is greatly prized. Rituals are similar to those of Voudon, with drumming and communal dancing.

Candomblé and Umbanda are entered through rites of initiation that require the aspirant to be pure and dedicated. Aspirants must abstain from food and sex prior to the rite and prove their devotion through long hours of ritual chants and dancing. Although Candomblé and Umbanda accept the existence of many different types of spirits, these are not divided into the good and evil spirits, or angels and demons, found in many dualistic systems of

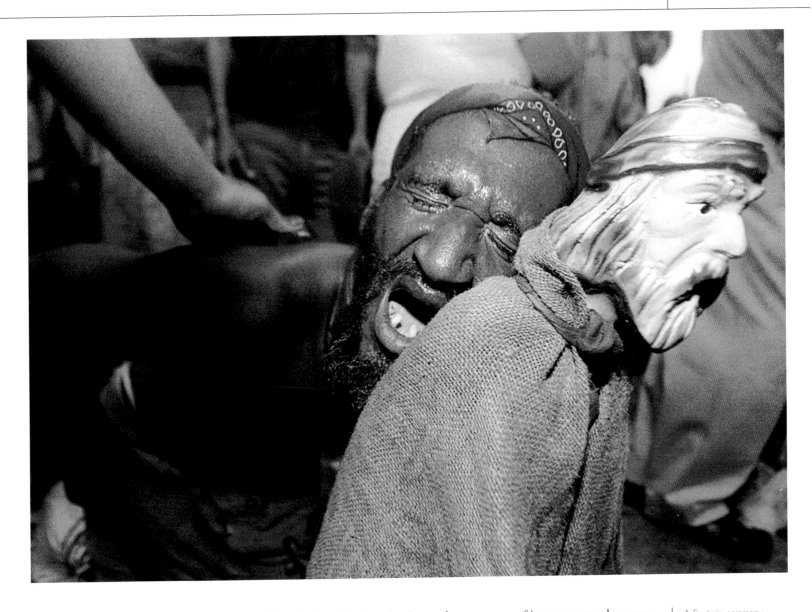

thought. Instead, some spirits are seen as unruly and mischief making and need to be educated by experienced practitioners. Sorcery involves deliberately using unruly spirits for malicious purposes, a practice that is disapproved of by Candomblé and Umbanda.

SANTERIA

Santeria can be translated as the "Way of the Saints". Santeria is a syncretistic religion that has travelled from its homeland in Cuba into the United States and Mexico. During the more extreme Communist period in Cuba in the 1960s, Santeria was suppressed, but since the 1990s

there has been a huge upsurge of interest, not only among native Cubans, but also among immigrants and exiles in North American cities. Santeria incorporates the worship of the *orishas*, West African deities of the Yoruba and Bantu peoples of southern Nigeria, Senegal and the Guinea Coast, with veneration of Catholic saints. Many practitioners prefer to call their religion La Regla Lucumi, Lukumi, or La Regla de Ocha rather than Santeria. Santeria was originally a pejorative term used by the ruling classes to describe the religious practices of their slaves, which to their masters seemed to include an inordinate emphasis on saints rather than on the more

A Santeria ceremony. Catholic saints are fused with African deities to create a synthesis that joins older and newer cultures.

In trance initiates of Santeria become at one with their deity to give prophesy and healing.

remote creator God. Finding that the overall political authorities had no interest in their welfare, the slaves thought logically that Heaven would reflect Earth and that their petitions were better addressed to the saints, who might be more inclined to listen to them.

In Santeria, the supreme deity and creator of the Universe is Olorun, the "owner of heaven" and leader of the lesser guardians or demi-gods, the *orisha*. In Santeria, the *orisha* were adapted to Christian saints with the same ease that we have seen in other indigenous traditions. Babalz Ayi became St Lazarus, patron of the sick. Shango, a male fire god and spirit of thunder and storms, became associated with St Barbara, patron saint of those "acts of god" that today are taken care of by insurance policies – thunder, lightning, fire, shipwreck, etc. Eleggua or Elegba

became St Anthony, controller of roads and gates and finder of lost property. Obatala became Our Lady of Las Mercedes and the resurrected Christ. Oggzn became St Peter and patron of war. Oshzn became Our Lady of Charity and controller of both money and sensuality. The ancestors are important in Santeria and are known as *Ara Orun*, or People of Heaven. They give moral guidance and their names are recited at family ceremonies. There are national variations in Santeria practice. Mexicans tend to emphasize the Catholic saints and the Virgin of Guadeloupe more than African *orishas*.

Santeria has a priesthood of women and men. Women are *santeras* and men are *santeros*. Training takes a number of years and is by oral teaching. It involves learning dance, songs and healing techniques. Traditionally, a *santera* or *santeros* would undergo a period of isolation before being initiated, but this is less easy to arrange in modern times. Other practices have evolved to meet modern realities. In the past, the *santera* or *santeros* would have gathered herbs used in medicines and potions from his or her garden and the surrounding area. Today, many rely on botanicas, specialist stores selling herbs, potions, charms, musical instruments and other materials. Typically, a Santeria ritual begins with drumming and an invocation to the supreme deity, Olurun. The *oru* or drum rhythm varies according to the *orisha* who is being invoked. Dancing begins and continues until someone is possessed by or "ridden" by an *orisha*.

Animal sacrifice, usually a chicken, is an integral part of Santeria and other African-based traditions. *Orishas* are believed to need humans to sacrifice to them in order to maintain their power or energy. The animal's blood is collected and offered to the appropriate orisha. Sacrifices are offered for good fortune, to avert ill luck, for purification and for the forgiveness of sins. Santeria and similar traditions' emphasis on sacrifice can cause tensions with vegetarian and animal rights groups. Santeria practitioners point out that the animals are killed humanely and are not sacrificed simply for the sake of it. The animal is later eaten. While vegetarians may have legitimate objections, for meat eaters the practice may be less cruel than commercial slaughtering.

Family relationships are important in Santeria. Entrance into the tradition means initiation into a spiritual family by the High Priestess and High Priest – the Madrina and the Padrino. Initiation is only a gateway into the tradition. To become a true *santera* or *santero* requires lifelong dedication to a particular *orisha* or deity. The process of acquiring an *orisha* to venerate is not a one-way process. The deity must choose the initiate. Following initiation, there are two paths to spiritual progress – that of the *camino de santo*, the Way of the Spirit, and that of *camino de orula*, the Way of Knowledge or Enlightenment. A priest, *babalocha*, or priestess, *iyalocha*, guides the initiate's development.

SPIRITUALITY IN CENTRAL AND SOUTH AMERICA TODAY

Amerindians remain a significant part of the population of Ecuador, Peru, and Bolivia, where around half of the population live indigenous lifestyles. In the Amazon Basin, indigenous culture is largely unchanged and a few groups survive with little contact with other peoples. The destruction of the rain forest by commercial logging is, however, rapidly destroying these peoples' ways of life. Central and South American Amazonian Indians have begun in recent years to experience the same exploitation by academics, commercial companies and tourism as their Native American cousins further North. In July 1999, shamans from over 50 peoples formed a council and set up an agenda for conserving their cultures and environment. They denounced charlatans who exploit their traditions and the gene patenting of sacred plants by multinational corporations who are attempting to hijack native medicinal healing techniques. All this has drawn attention to the plight of the rain forest, but it will require large governments to act if the Amazon and all it can offer our planet are not to be destroyed.

While the changing environment threatens some indigenous traditions in South and Central America, other traditions have successfully adapted to the needs of multicultural urban populations and show every signs of thriving, bringing their followers joy and meaning in the twenty-first century.

Mayan pyramid of Kukulkan Chichen Itzat.

AFRICA

Africa is the "Cradle of Civilization", the place where humankind first developed. Most of Africa is covered by savannah or grassland that varies from arid shrubs to lush grass. About 15 per cent of Africa is covered by rain forest, with dense foliage and heavy cloud cover. The only jungle areas are near riverbanks. Each region is enormously varied. In eastern Africa, for instance, arid Sudan and Somalia are separated by the Ethiopian Plateau. In the centre are the fertile areas around the East African lakes of Victoria, Albert, Tanganyika and Nyasa, with highlands around Mount Kenya and Mount Kilimanjaro. The remainder consists of savannah, with the depression of the East African Rift Valley running from North to South. The areas of densest population are the more fertile highlands. Central and southern Africa consists mainly of open and dry savannah grasslands. To the northwest are the Congo forests and coasts of South Africa and Mozambique, which are more fertile, with subtropical or Mediterranean climates.

Around 661 million people inhabit the African continent, around 435 million of whom live South of the Sahara desert. Among these are around 1.5 million people whose ancestors were some of the earliest inhabitants of the continent – Bushmen or San, Pygmies and Watusi. There are also around six million later arrivals – white Africans. In total, there are about three thousand different peoples in Africa. Due to invasions by Western powers, the country boundaries of Africa do not necessarily reflect the distribution of peoples. Many peoples find themselves split between two or more nations and others find themselves an ethnic minority in a country that is hostile to them. This has caused many recent tragedies in the continent. North of the Sahara are peoples who speak Afro-Asiatic languages, including the Berbers of Morocco, Algeria and Tunisia, and Arabs who migrated into northern Africa from the seventh century CE onward.

Western Africa's savannah region has three main clusters of peoples: the Mande of Senegal and Mali; the Voltaic peoples of the eastern savannah, such as the Dogon and Mossi; and other non-Muslim peoples who inhabit the plateau and highland areas of northern Nigeria, Niger and Cameroon. Along the coast are the Igbo or Ibo and Ibibio of Nigeria as well as the Yoruba and the Fon of Benin. Ghana has the Akan confederacy, which includes the Ashanti and Ewe. Sierra Leone is home to the Mende and Temne. In Liberia are the Kru and in Senegal, the Wolof, the Serer and Dyula. There are also Creoles in Sierra Leone and Liberia, descendants of freed slaves from the New World. West-central Africa has Arabs in the North, Pygmies in Congo (Brazzaville) and Gabon, and Sudanese and Bantu-speaking peoples in southern areas.

In the Nile Valley are pastoralists, such as the Shilluk and Dinka. The central plains are home to the famous cattle-herding Masai. Near the East African lakes are several once powerful Bantu kingdoms. In the Kenya highlands are the Kikuyu. Other eastern peoples include the Watusi. On the coast are Swahili-speakers, while Tanzania has Bantu-speakers. The Central and Southern region of Africa was once the home of the San or Bushmen and Khoikhoi or Hottentots, but invasions over the centuries have meant that the San are found only in arid southwestern Africa and Botswana. The Khoikhoi have been assimilated into the racially mixed coloured people of the south African Cape. Other peoples of southern Africa who spread across the region around 2,000 years ago are Bantus, such as the Zulus.

TRADITIONAL RELIGIONS

Around 30–40 per cent of the population of contemporary Africa are followers of traditional spirituality, but another 35 per cent or more incorporate traditional practices with their Christian or Muslim beliefs. The main religious divisions in Africa can be mapped out along geographical lines. Islam is found in North Africa and extends as far down as the Yoruba of Nigeria and the Temne of Sierra Leone in the West, and the northern Sudanese in the East. Little traditional religion is found in the Mediterranean countries of Egypt, Libya, Tunisia, Algeria and Morocco, but further South Islam often co-exists with traditional practices. Ethiopia in central eastern Africa is home to one of the oldest branches of Christianity – the Ethiopian Coptic Church. The Coptic Church has also long been established in Egypt, although Christians are now a minority. Traditional religions and Christianity are both found in the rest of southern to central Africa.

PREVIOUS PAGE: Women dancers of Mozambique. Ceremonial dance is an important part of African life and religion.

DEITIES AND SPIRITS

Many African traditional religions have the concept of a "Creator God", who is author of life. This god does not often, however, concern himself – or itself – with everyday living. This is left to a whole host of other deities or spirits that preside over every aspect of life. Western colonialists denigrated Africans as polytheists, believing that their own monotheism was superior, and the Arabs who brought Islam emphasized that "there is no God but Allah". Contemporary Africans are often keen to emphasize that they are not true polytheists and that the various deities they worship do not have independent existence but derive from a Supreme Being – the Hidden-God-Who-Is-Ever-Yet-Revealed, the Discerner of Hearts. The view of African Traditional Religion as "qualified monotheism" is the one taught in schools and as part of the syllabus of school matriculation courses.

A central tenet of belief among all practitioners of African religions is a belief in the spirit world. Whether or not Africa traditional religion is truly monotheist, the hidden god of Africa is much further removed from people's minds than is, say, Christ to a Christian. The focus of people's religious practice is a host of other deities and beings that the hidden god has created. Spirits and deities are found everywhere in everyday life. They inhabit all living things; they reside in people, in the trees, animals, rocks and rivers. They can also inhabit manufactured items, such as cars and machinery, and can reside in individuals' personal effects. They can also be represented by symbols such as carved objects, shrines and sacred altars. The spirits are moral guardians. Their all-seeing presence helps monitor people's behaviour, rather like an externalized conscience. The close connection between the material and spirit worlds means that religion enfolds the whole of life. Religion is not seen as a separate activity divorced from ordinary life; there is no dichotomy between the two.

ANCESTORS

Other important spirits are the ancestors. They are benevolent and powerful representatives of the community. Their symbols, such as the carved ancestral stools of the Akan of Ghana, and ancestor shrines are common features among most traditional African peoples. The presence and influence of the ancestral spirits and their deeds, valour and exploits define the community. The ancestors are perceived to be ever present in the consciousness of those living today.

Spirits and ancestors take an active role in everyday life. They have wishes, intentions and messages to communicate. Care must be taken to identify the will of the spirits in any event or action and to follow it. Ancestors are an integral part of religious rituals. They are a cumulative storehouse of wisdom and can be approached to act as intermediaries with the spirits and the gods. The invocation of their presence strengthens the connection between the people of the present and the past. The feeling is conveyed that the living belong to a continuous, seamless whole. The spirits communicate their wishes, demands and interpretations of events to their priests, who will translate these through to the wider community usually by means of ritual. Prayer is believed to have a powerful intercessory role in these situations: the spirits will listen.

In African societies the individual is not a "self" who is separate and distinct from others in his or her community. It is said that the individual does not and cannot exist alone but only corporately. Each

LEFT, AND OPPOSITE PAGE:
Ancestor figures carved by the Senufo of the Ivory Coast.

person owes his or her existence to others, and in African society this extends not only to contemporaries – the people of his or her close community – but also to past generations, the ancestors. The individual is an integral part of, and inseparable from, the community – present, future and past. Africans in general share life intensely. There are communal farmlands, communal shrines, communal ritual objects and communal festivals for social, economic or religious purposes. Closeness to nature, the experience of life in hazardous and dangerous environments, and the crucial need for security and better performance in developing the means to live are all relevant factors that combine to deepen the natural impulse for gregariousness and sense of community among different African peoples. Family is thus all-important and has a much wider and deeper meaning for an African than for most Westerners, and the invisible members of family, the ancestors, are powerful, more so than living beings. Their reality and presence in the community are acknowledged and honoured, for their neglect could spell disaster for the entire community. Their memory may also be continued in personal names given to children, especially where particular spirits are felt to have reincarnated in individual children.

The reality and presence of spiritual members is acknowledged through a number of taboos found in many communities. The traditional Igbo for example, enforce several such prohibitions on women of childbearing age. It is believed that these women run a serious risk of remaining childless if these taboos are ignored since this could result in scaring away the souls of unborn babies that are believed to hover around homesteads and families while waiting to incarnate.

RITUAL

African traditional religions, like the traditions to which they have given birth in the New World – Voudon, Santeria, Candomblé and Umbanda – are practical religions that aim to help their followers in everyday life. These religions celebrate life and the joy of being alive. Music, dance and festivity are an essential part of their worship. Worship is concerned not so much with the life to come, but with health and well being in the here and now. This does not mean that African religions are not mystical. Common to African traditions is a shared sense of the sacred and a sense of mystery. There is a reverence for sacred places that extends to include holy people and sacred objects. Sacred times are also celebrated, both seasonal festivals and special historical events. Belief in an afterlife is widely held and it is described in myth and incorporated into rituals and rites, particularly funeral ceremonies. Although having a diversity of different beliefs and practices, North Africa, West Africa and Central Africa share characteristics that distinguish them from the religions of East and Southern African. Eastern and southern traditions are less likely to have a professional priesthood.

In addition to priests with ritual functions, there are other religious specialists such as diviners, prophets and rainmakers. The role of diviners is important because the diviner can communicate with the spirit world. In Zulu religion, for instance, the Creator is Nkulunkulu, but is too far distant to interact in day-to-day human affairs. It is possible, however, to appeal to the spirit world by invoking the ancestors through divination. In Zulu society, the diviner is usually a woman and she plays an important part in daily life. All bad things, including death, are the result

Dogon ancestor image.

of evil sorcery or offended spirits. No misfortune is ever thought to be a result of natural causes. The diviner is thus in constant demand to discern the causes of misfortune and to show how they can be put right or avoided.

African tradition has a strong respect for life and the continuity of life. Close family, extended family and spirit family – the ancestors – have tremendous significance. Children are treasured as the hope for the future and old people are held in high esteem for their wisdom, which is often seen to have prophetic qualities. Society is held together by this framework and enriched by the rites and festivities where the progression of the seasons and the stages in the life of the individual are noted and celebrated with appropriate ritual.

Rites of passage and other rites form an essential part of social life. The seasonal cycle – the year-round cycle of fertility, of birth, growth, harvest and death – is echoed and perpetuated in ritual actions. Crises may also occasion specific rites to help deal with these. Similarly rites of passage, of initiation into new social and spiritual roles, are wide-

A San, or Bushman, of Namibia. The San are decendents of some of the earliest African peoples.

Ugandan boys prepare for a puberty circumcision ritual. This ritual marks an important transition from boyhood to manhood.

spread. As there is no real separation between life and religion, so is there no gap between sacred and the secular. Every major event has its own ritual, a ritual that is never overlooked and which is celebrated through song, dance, music and drumming, making offerings and in art. Despite the growth of other religions such as Islam and Christianity on the continent, these rituals survive. Even those who have migrated to cities to work will return to their communities for rites of passage and other important celebrations. As with Native American ceremonies, in African tradition purification and proper preparation before rituals is vital. Some rituals are specifically for the ritual purification of individuals and communities. Purification is also especially important prior to healing rites, which may include not only the sick individual, but also his or her family and wider community. In Africa the individual and community are strongly connected. Sin or wrongdoing committed by an individual harms the collective psyche of the community as

a whole. Periodic purification rites are used to promote public welfare and the public good.

Symbols figure prominently in African beliefs. They are connected powerfully with the spirits and create a strong link between the unseen spirits and the living. It is common to see them on the walls of shrines and other religious places, and on the clothes worn by the traditional priests or ritual practitioners, who will use particular symbols when they wish to express a certain mood, feeling or intent.

MUSIC AND THE DRUM

Music is an important feature of African ritual and the most important instrument is the drum. We now know from physiological research that drumming has a strong effect on the body. Certain drumbeats induce trance, affect heart rate and cause strong mood swings. In more modern religions we have lost the psycho-technology that creates effective ritual, but in African and Native American traditions, among others, these skills have not been lost. Music plays a pivotal role in religious ceremonies invoking, as it does, possession and trance. This is when the possessed individual loses ego-consciousness and becomes the vehicle of a deity. He or she becomes the mouthpiece of that deity and as such is consulted for advice, healing, prophecy and to provide magical power. Possession is a doorway to religious experience, but it is not seen to be sufficient in itself. The moral requirements are also important; to conduct one's life in a way that is pleasing to the deity. The key law of this is the sacredness of all life. Through the experience of dance, song and music the law is conveyed and received both collectively and by each individual. In some traditions, such as the Dogon, the drums themselves are thought to be divine intermediaries. The drum is the "ear" of the god and, through the drum, the drummer is address-

ing the Creator on behalf of his community. The drummers beat their drums with great force, but also with respect. In the words of a song of the Ewe people of Ghana, which is addressed to the deity Blekete, "A feeble effort will not fulfil the self".

African music is participatory. Among those living a traditional lifestyle, songs are present throughout the day to accompany daily tasks and chores. In any special event or ceremony music and dance play a significant part. Almost everyone involved will be taking part in different ways; whether playing instruments, dancing, singing, clapping, observing, commenting or being commented upon. Communication is also accomplished with the drums. All participants can understand the language of the drums to varying degrees. It may be that the subtle messages can only be understood by drumming initiates, but everyone

Detail from sacred artwork at a Yoruba shrine and sacred grove in Nigeria.

will understand something from the drums even if only at a basic level. This is the source of the concept of the talking drum. It tells of the people's history, of their myths and of their legends. It praises dignitaries and comments on topical issues. It can also be used to send messages, sometimes over incredibly long distances.

Singing and drumming play an important part in the work of traditional diviners, who must enter ecstatic trances to do their work. Diviners are usually women and are known all over Africa as is*angoma*, from *ngoma*, meaning the type of music expressed in the singing and dancing of the diviners, which is accompanied by drumming. The dances are performed by the individual diviner alone or at special assemblies of diviners, to which non-initiates are not invited. In Southern Africa, drums were originally used solely for the music of diviners. The music expresses the spiritual link between the diviners and their ancestors, who reveal to the diviners the special sacred songs that help them in their work.

Several peoples place even greater importance on the drum. There are styles of drumming closely associated with the leadership of the people. Among the Watusi, for example, the king himself is the master drummer among master drummers. Wider spread is the notion that each craft or occupational tradition – weavers, hunters, blacksmiths, warriors, farmers, etc. – has its own music and musicians who play throughout special activities, celebrations and festivals.

With the importance placed on music it is not surprising that a musician has considerable status. Among some peoples, the musician is accorded the powers and responsibilities of healer, historian and magic-maker that go well beyond musical accomplishment. The historian role is equivalent to the western bardic tradition. African musicians can memorize vast repertoires of songs and narratives that commemorate past glories and the genealogies of the important members of the community.

To select someone who can take on the responsibility of becoming a master musician takes much thought and is followed by long years of training. Training starts young, not only to produce technical excellence, but also to train people in the wisdom needed for their influential position. The training of musicians is a complex matter and varies according to people. Some are apprenticed for training and have a mentor to guide them. Others go through an initiatory process and only those initiates of a certain grade may play certain pieces of music in rituals and rites. Others go further afield to acquire their skills. There is a pan-African exchange among culturally related groups, which helps to enrich both the skills of the individual and the musical diversity of the communities involved.

EARLY AFRICANS – BUSHMEN OF THE KALAHARI

Life in Africa has evolved with the development of agriculture and herding. Few peoples have retained the hunter-gatherer lifestyle that would have been typical of early Africa. Some of those who have endeavoured to retain their traditional lifestyle include some of the oldest people of Africa, the Bushmen or San of southern Africa who became famous throughout the world through Sir Laurens van der Post's book *The Bushmen Of The Kalahari*. The San appeared as a separate group over 20,000 years ago, but there is now a danger that they will disappear as a distinctive race. There are only two thousand traditional San remaining.

Traditionally, the San were hunter-gatherers, using bows and arrows and eating edible roots and berries. They also employed small-scale subsistence farming using centuries old methods. The San did not develop complex settlements. They lived in the open, in rock shelters or in temporary shelters of twigs, grass and animal skins. They

Gitega drummers of Burundi. African drum rhythms are complex and can convey the whole range of human emotion.

make no pottery, instead using ostrich egg shells for holding and storing liquids. The San once roamed all the Natal region of South Africa, except for thickly forested areas. Gradually, they were forced back by newcomers with a more competitive approach. These were Iron Age people and precursors of the Bantu. Initially, there was interaction between the two groups – the San's ability to make rain being of considerable interest to the agricultural Bantu. However, as the Bantu developed extensive farming, both arable and pastoral, this brought them into conflict with the San, whose traditional territory they were occupying. As the numbers of Bantu increased, so the San were pushed further back. The enforced retreat was inexorable and was probably completed by the seventeenth century. Subsequently, the San have suffered greatly from interaction with cattle farmers. The San had no concept of

Kalahari San, or Bushmen, hunting with traditional bow and arrow.

The San were skilled artists whose images have a wonderful vibrancy. This cave painting is from the Eastern Cape of South Africa.

animal ownership in their hunting culture. They saw cattle as "fair game" and as a result both black and white cattle farmers hunted the San to the edge of extinction.

ROCK ART

The San believe that all things in nature are equal, including humans. They hunt, but only for what they need to survive. The San believe that over-indulgence will cause the gods to become angry, causing them to show their displeasure by delivering drought, famine and sickness across the land. The San's survival depends on the ingrained knowledge they have of the land; knowledge passed down through generations and enhanced by acute observation. San survival depends on this knowledge. They know where every fruit tree will grow and when it will fruit. They know where the water will be found even in periods of drought and, once found, how best to conserve it. They know the habits of birds and animals and how to catch or snare them. And it is said that they even know when and

how to chase a lion from its kill in order to steal the meat. They are famous for the tale of outwitting the monkey. The San gather nuts and place them in a gourd hung from a tree. The opening of the gourd is just wide enough for the monkey to squeeze its hand through. The clenched fist full of nuts cannot, however, be removed and the monkey will not let go…

The San have no written language as such; all knowledge is discovered through experience and transmitted through retelling. They will spend many hours telling and retelling stories and legends from their past and from their history. They also have pictorial records in the form of rock paintings that tell of their lives and history, some of which are ancient. One of the main sites of the paintings is Maqongo near Rourke's Drift in the eastern Biggarsberg area of South Africa. This occupies a special place in early San society. The site was occupied continuously for over 5,000 years and was abandoned around 4,000 years ago. These are, however, recent paintings. The earliest have been dated to over 27,000 years ago. Rock paintings are usually found on the flat rock walls of exposed horizontal strata of yellowish sandstone rock weathered to form overhangs or shelters that protect the paintings from the elements.

The paintings are exquisitely executed and there is still controversy over the precise materials used to make them. How, especially as some are in exposed places, did they produce colours that have endured for so long? Red has proved to be the most durable colour, which is probably produced from either red ochre or from an iron oxide. Various shades can be produced from the latter by heating it in a fire. White, probably produced from a range of substances including silica, white clay and gypsum, has less permanence. Black was produced from charcoal, soot and minerals such as manganese. These substances were made into paint by mixing them with a liquid rather than being applied dry. What precisely was used to dilute the pigments is more difficult to ascertain as generally only the pigment remains. Suggestions include antelope blood, fat, urine, egg white, plant sap and water. The paint was applied using fingers, quills, feathers or very thin bones.

But what was the real significance of these paintings? The paintings can be viewed as a pictorial history of San life, but they also played a key part in their religious beliefs, rituals and practice. Complex rituals and practices are all depicted from their art and from study of these rock paintings an understanding of their belief systems and practice can be gained. It is clear from these that their ritual was shaped by their attitudes toward the supernatural and the spirits. They feared the spirits because they thought they brought disease, sickness and death. Perhaps because of this the paintings are concerned with rituals involving healing. In particular they illustrate the activities of San shamans at medicine dance rituals. At the centre of their religion is the shaman, who has the ability to enter a trance in order to heal, to protect against evil spirits and sickness, foretell the future, control or interpret the weather, ensure good hunting and generally to look after the general well-being of his clan or group. Shamans had

tremendous importance for the welfare of kin and were held in high esteem.

Within a ritual, women generally sit around a central fire and clap the rhythm of special songs relevant to the purpose of that particular trance dance. The men then dance around the women in a circle in a formalized dance, inspired by the movements and behaviour of a particular animal. They believe that the rhythmic power that builds up – the thud of the dancing steps combining and reinforcing the insistent rhythm of the women's clapping – activates a supernatural potency that resides both in the shamans and in the very songs themselves. This, plus intense concentration and hyperventilation, creates an entry into the state of trance. During their trances, shamans assume the potency of various animals so that they may communicate and plead with the spirits. It is during the trance that their tasks are performed. This will seek healing for the sick, which can include curing the individual of both known and unperceived ailments. This is done by laying hands on the patient, drawing the sickness into the shaman's own body and then expelling it.

Other tasks carried out during these ceremonies, which are all vividly portrayed in San art, include rain-making, visiting the camps of other clans by means of out-of-body travel and controlling animals in order to hunt them. During trance, shamans sometimes see spirit animals attracted by the dance standing in the darkness. Contact is

San shamans dance and drum themselves into trance.

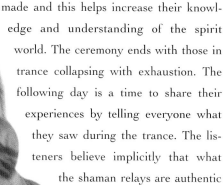

made and this helps increase their knowledge and understanding of the spirit world. The ceremony ends with those in trance collapsing with exhaustion. The following day is a time to share their experiences by telling everyone what they saw during the trance. The listeners believe implicitly that what the shaman relays are authentic revelations into the mysteries of the spirit world, a world separate from and beyond human understanding.

It is likely that those responsible for the rock paintings are the shamans themselves, using this medium to try and convey their experiences while in trance. It appears that they will often experience "after-images" that may recur for many months after the trance. These provide the inspiration for the painting. When viewing San rock paintings, we must remember that they are bridges between two worlds; incredibly complex and intricate bridges that come from the very centre of Sa understanding and being, the heart of their religious experience. The places of the painted rock faces develop their own power and become storehouses that facilitate and help the continuing and developing contact between humankind and the spirit world.

SHILLUK OF THE WHITE NILE

As one might expect, in common with all humanity, African traditional religions have sought to understand where they came from and why. There are three common explanations of the origin of human beings. Some myths describe humans as being fashioned out of clay. These ideas also reflect magical thinking – life can be breathed into an inanimate object. Other myths speak of humans being brought into being by a word spoken by a Creator. This reflects the ancient magical idea that a word spoken by a person with magical powers is the same as the thing itself. Other myths speak of a cosmic egg from which the Universe is hatched.

The Shilluk of southern Sudan in the northeast of Africa came originally from somewhere East of the African Great Lakes. As both their population and herds increased, they migrated northward, reaching their present territory in the late fifteenth century. Today, they live along the banks of the White Nile. Bracelets of ivory or wood and tribal markings of dots or scars on their foreheads indicate their tribal identity.

The Shilluk are now sedentary farmers who raise crops as well as cattle, sheep and goats. Men hunt hippopotami, antelope, buffalo and giraffes. They also herd, milk livestock and fish with spears. Women tend the gardens, prepare food and make cooking utensils. Cattle are a valuable commodity and are treated with the utmost care. At night they are tethered near fires so that the smoke will deter insects from biting them. The Shilluk creator deity is named Juok. Juok is everywhere. He gave the Shilluk their staple foodstuffs – cattle, millet and fish. He also heals the sick. The Shilluk communicate with Juok through sacrifices and through the person of their king, the *reth*, who was a descendant of the first king and cultural hero, Nyikang or Nyikango. The king represented the land and the people. His physical health and well being ensured the prosperity of the land.

Like many other African peoples, the Shilluk believe in the power of the "evil eye". This belief represents human

guilt and fear. Envy of or anger against another person may bring the evil eye upon them. This can be averted through magic, and prayers and sacrifice directed toward Juok. Although slave traders set up slave stations in the area, the Shilluk were well-organized warriors who fought off the raiders. Their traditional way of life has not therefore suffered the disruption that the slave traders brought to others.

The creation myth of the Shilluk explains something that must have perplexed their earlier ancestors, especially as they migrated northward in the fifteenth century encountering new peoples: why are people different colours? The Shilluk creation myth is one in which people are created from earth. In many Africa creation myths, humans are superior to other creatures and are created first to play a central role in the unfolding of creation. The Shilluk see the world as two divine loaves, or *opunne*, which represent Heaven and Earth and are divided by the great river Nile. In Shilluk belief, humans were created last. Juok has already created animals when he decides to create human beings. Juok creates everyone by moulding bodies from clay and gives them life through his breath. During his wanderings around the Earth, as he comes to different soils, Juok finds different colour clays. Red or brown people are created from the mud of the Egyptian Nile. White people are created from white sand, which Juok finds in the land of the white people. Black people are created from the black earth found in the land of the Shilluk. Juok has a practical turn of mind. Each part of the human body is created because it can fulfil a particular function. Juok gave us arms in order to work.

FIRST WOMAN IN CREATION MYTHS

In the Shilluk myth, having created the first perfect man, Juok sends him out into the world and the story ends. We are not told about the creation of women. Other myths describe woman as the first created being, the mother of humankind from whom everyone else originated. The Akposso of Togo, for instance, say that when their Creator Uwolowu made human beings, he first made a woman. He mated with her to create the first human child, who is descended from both human and god. In the creation myth of the Ibibio of Nigeria, human beings are not the children of the original Creator, but his grandchildren. Human beings come from the divinity Obumo, who was the son of the Mother Goddess Eka-Abassi. In eastern Africa, people tell the story of a virgin woman called Ekao. She falls to Earth from the sky and bears a son. The son marries another woman and founds human society. These myths connect human life with the ultimate divine through the feminine principle. It is first woman who passes on life.

This is illustrated in a myth of the Tutsi from Rwanda. This tells of the original pair of humans. They live in paradise but both are sterile. They begged their god to help them. He mixes clay with saliva and forms a small human shape. The woman must keep this figure in a pot for nine months. She must also pour milk into the pot each morn-

LEFT: Shilluk woman with traditional tribal markings.

OPPOSITE: A young man of the Shilluk tribe of southern Sudan with typical tribal markings.

ing and evening and is not to remove the figure until it has grown limbs. She does as instructed and after nine months she pulls out a fully formed human being. Here the pot represents the womb and after nine months, the normal term of pregnancy, the child is born. In this way the first woman shares directly with the god the secrets of life and birth. Some tribes accredit women with the discovery of how to make fire, obviously something of great value and of vital significance to the well being of the community. Thus the cooking skills of the woman are attributed to her from mythological times. Women are also credited with inventing or discovering foodstuffs and how to prepare them, a reflection of the role of women in many peoples as gatherers of roots and berries, and in settled societies as horticulturalists and agriculturalists.

In many other myths women are given less of a starring role. The Kwotto of Nigeria, for instance, say that the Creator made the first human beings out of earth. First he made the husband and then, though tired, he carried on to make the woman. As he was tired when he made her, she turned out to be weaker than the man.

Women of the Nimba tribe in northwest Namibia perform a traditional dance.

BOSHONGO

In many African myths creation occurs through the mouth, or the spoken word accompanies the act of creation. The importance of "the Word" and the ability to speak well are valued across many African peoples. In the creation myth of the Boshongo, who are Bantus of Central Africa, Bumba the creator brings forth everything through first vomiting up the Sun. The world is covered by water, but the Sun spreads light over everything and dries up all the water until the black edges of the world begin to show. Light can now be separated from darkness, and sea from land. Bumba then vomits up the Moon and then the first nine living creatures. All things first pass through his mouth before coming into existence. Then the nine go forth and create more creatures in their specific image – the creatures themselves create the creatures. The small fish, Yo, brings forth the world's fish, while the beetle creates all the insects. Heron creates all the birds of the air. Crocodile makes the serpents and iguana. Goat produces all horned animals. Although the beetle created most insects, the serpents make grasshoppers. Iguana makes the creatures without horns, until all the world's creatures appear.

There is a moral message in this creation myth, the underlying inference being that everyone should do his or her fair share of work in the community; each person has a role to play. Bumba also makes clear that those who do not fit in with the community will not be tolerated. Tsetse, who is lightning, is chased away for being a troublemaker. Ants are praised for not only are they industrious, but in working to bring black earth up from the depths of the world to cover the barren sands they are both burying and honouring their Creator.

An excerpt from the Boshongo creation myth, as a representative of African tradition, features in minimalist composer Philip Glass' new *Symphony no. 5, A Bridge Between The Past, The Present And The Future*, which was commissioned as a Millennium work for the Salzburg Festival in Austria

YORUBA

There are about 24 million Yoruba, who live in coastal West Africa in southwestern Nigeria, Benin and northern Togo. Their beliefs were exported to the New World with the slave trade and flourish today in many of the African based traditions. Most Yoruba men are farmers. As well as growing foodstuffs, cocoa is a major cash crop. They are, however, much more famed for their craftsmanship in blacksmithing, weaving, leatherwork, glassmaking, ivory-carving and woodcarving. Women are independent traders and control the complex market system. They also spin cotton, dye cloth and make basketwork. The Yoruba developed what is known as the lost-wax bronze casting technique and beautiful brass and pottery sculpture was produced at the city of Ife from around 1100 to 1450 CE. Through their craft skills, the Yoruba developed a complex society with some of the most important urban centres of pre-colonial Africa, which are the origins of many contemporary cities. The women's markets have given rise to economic institutions that give women commercial power, such

Carved figures of women deities of the Yoruba god Shango, god of thunder.

as the *esusu*, a credit union whose members contribute a fixed sum of money, from which they can receive loans.

Shango (also spelled Sango and Sagoe) is one of the most popular deities among the Yoruba, but he is not the chief deity. As in Norse tradition and ancient Egypt, the chief deity is remote in traditional cultures and the concern of the royal family rather than ordinary people. Shango may originally have been a deified king and one legend describes him as the fourth king of Oyo, the ancient Yoruba capital. The need to venerate Shango may stem from the problems that storms can cause in an agricultural society. People frequently venerate that which they need to appease. For instance, Shokpona, god of smallpox, was once worshipped and so feared that people were reluctant to speak his name. Instead, he was known as Elegbana, Hot-Earth, or A-soro-pelerum, One-not-propitious-to-name-during-dry-season. The cult declined with the decline in smallpox.

Shango creates thunder and lightning by casting "thunderstones" down to Earth. The Yoruba believe thunderstones have special powers, so when lightning strikes, priests will search the surrounding area for the thunderstone. Thunderstones are kept in temples dedicated to Shango. Shango is married to four major Nigerian rivers. His chief wife is Oya, the River Niger. Different cults have their own symbols. Shango, for instance, is associated with the symbol of the staff with a double axe. Carved mortars are placed on Shango's altars because pounding food in a mortar sounds like thunder.

The Yoruba have an extensive oral literature of poetry, stories, myths and proverbs. Religious ideas have much overlap but they vary between regions. This is typical of oral traditions. It is only when religious ideas are committed to writing that they become standardized. Among the Yoruba, a deity may be male in one village and female in the next. Sometimes two deities merge into one and sometimes the same deity is worshipped under a number of different names, in the same way that in a Catholic country Mary the Mother of Jesus might be Blessed Virgin Mary, Our Lady of Lourdes and St Mary. Different names do not necessarily imply different personages.

The Yoruba creation myth talks of people being created from earth by Olurun, Owner-of-the-Sky, the Yoruba Creator who is sometimes known as Olodumare, meaning "Almighty". Olorun, like Brahma in Hindu tradition, is rarely actively worshipped. While Shango shrines are numerous, Olorun has neither priests nor shrine. In his work of creation, Olorun is often assisted by the lesser god, Obatala (also known as Orishanla or Orisa-nla) and his wife Odudua. Olurun, Obatala and Odudua pre-date the creation of the world as we know it. They live at the beginning when there is only water and chaos. Olurun sends Obatala down from the sky to form land out of the chaos. Obatala descends on a long chain, which could represent the umbilical cord, bringing with him a rooster, some iron and a palm kernel. He puts the metal on the ground and on top of this he places the rooster. The rooster scratches at the metal and spreads it out to create land. Then Obatala plants the palm seed and from this grows all the vegetation of the Earth. Olurun names the Earth Ife, and the first town is Ile-Ife. Orishanla creates humans from the soil and then Olurun blows into them to give them the breath of life.

Oduduwa, the founding ancestor of Ife, was said to have been the first king of the Oyo kingdom of the Yoruba. He was deified after his death and virtually every traditional Yoruba community can trace its lineage back to him. Kingdoms developed, ruled by hereditary kings called *oba*.

Traditionally, the king was the centre of community and religious life and his palace was at the centre of the towns. The town of Ile-Ife has important religious significance as the place where the Earth was created. In addition to these early deities, there are traditionally either 401 or 601 lesser deities and spirits, each of whom has his or her own cult and priesthood.

MANDE OF SOUTHERN MALI

The Mande live on Africa's western coast in southern Mali, Burkina Faso, Senegal, The Gambia, Guinea, Sierra Leone, Liberia, Ivory Coast and Ghana. The Mande social system is an unusual one, with two main groups, the Horonw and the Nyamakalaw. The Horonw take care of the material side of society. They are the aristocracy, warriors and commoners. The Nyamakalaw are separated from the Horonw and can marry only within their own group. They are religious specialists who possess and control nyama, the spiritual energy of nature. A strange symbiosis exists between the two groups, who often dislike each other. The Horonw need the Nyamakalaw to carve ritual masks and head-dresses. The Nyamakalaw depend on the Horonw for food. The two groups live separately. The Horonw live at the centre of villages. The Nyamakalaw live on the outskirts beyond the fields. The separation of the two groups is based on cosmogony – the Mande creation myth.

In the beginning was Mangala. Mangala is the Creator deity, but Mangala is not personified in human form. Instead, Mangala is a round energetic presence. This sphere of energy divides into four. The number four, as in indigenous traditions on other continents, is important and symbolic. The four divisions signify, among other things, the four days of the Mande week, the four elements of matter and the four directions. From the fourness Mangala now has two sets of male and female sex organs. Mangala grows tired of holding all this energy inside itself and so uses its male and femaleness to create a seed. From the seed Mangala creates the world. This first attempt does not hold together well. It disintegrates violently and Mangala begins again. This time Mangala begins with two sets of twin seeds, which it plants in an egg-shaped womb. These gestate. Mangala continues with this process until there are eight sets of seeds that then transform themselves into fish, a Mande symbol of fertility. This time creation is a success.

Mangala tries to maintain this state of perfection but inevitably chaos creeps in. One of the male twins grows ambitious and tries to escape the egg. He is called Pemba and is symbolic of human mischief, the "trickster". His first trick is to steal his placenta. This becomes the Earth. He fertilizes it in order to create a new being in his image, but this is incest and is not permitted. Mangala reacts by sacrificing Pemba's brother Farro, in order to raise him again from the dead. He takes what is left of the placenta and with this makes the Sun. This leaves Pemba associated only with the darkness. Farro is made into human form and is taught the language of creation by Mangala. Farro and his female twins come to Earth and get married to other beings they find there and become known as the Horonw, who ever after practise the custom of exogamy, whereby a man must marry outside his own kin group.

African traditional dances and songs are today an important part of political campaign rallies.

The origin of the Nyamakalaw lies in Sourakata, the first shaman, a figure we have found in other myths around the world. Sourakata arrives from the sky bringing the first sacred drum, a hammer and the skull of Farro's first body that was sacrificed. Sourakata begins to drum and sings for the first rains to come. Sourakata teaches Farro and his followers how to control nature. From Sourakata comes the Nyamakalaw.

THE DOGON

The Dogon number around 600,000 and live principally in southeast Mali and Burkino Faso. Dogon oral history tells of a migration from Western Sudan on the West bank of the Niger River, where they lived from the tenth to the thirteenth centuries CE. They emigrated first to northern Burkino Faso, but around 1490 they were forced to flee an invasion of Mossi horsemen. They found refuge in the Bandiagara Cliffs, safe from the approaching invaders. The Bandiagara plateau is one of the most impressive geological and landscape features of West Africa. The Cliff of Bandiagara is the heart of Dogon culture. Its beautiful architectural structures – houses, granaries, altars, sanctuaries and *toguna*, or meeting places – have recently been declared a UNESCO World Heritage site. The Dogon are well known for their extensive and sophisticated carvings, which include ornate masks and wooden figures. The colours they use are predominately red, black and white in recurring patterns, including spirals and black and white checkerboard motifs. These themes can be traced to their origin or creation myths. They are also well known in recent years for the myths themselves, which have captured New Age and UFO enthusiasts' imaginations. The Dogon believe that their Creator deity came from Sirius.

Dogon religion gives thanks for the bounty and fruitfulness of the soil and is primarily concerned with ensuring renewal and the continuing fertility of the land. Dogon altars contain soil to connect with and encourage this fertility. They venerate their ancestors and the spirits they encountered as they undertook their forced migration across the Western

Sudan to what is now their home. Their rituals are concerned with rites of passage, to mark the phases and changes in their lives. Their priesthood, the Awa Society, carries these out. All the rites are masked and are the exclusive preserve of males who have been initiated and have learned the techniques required to emulate the supernatural beings, the gods. The leader of the Awa is the Olaburu. It is he who understands the language and symbolism of the bush country in which they dwell. Funerary rites, *bago bundo*, allow the souls of the deceased to leave the world of the living and a special ritual, the Dama ceremony, is carried out to signify the end of the period of mourning. The Awa are also responsible for the planning of special Sigui ceremonies that occur every sixty years. Their purpose is to pass on the function and practice of those in the Awa who have died to new recruits who will replace them. This sixty-year cycle also has a relevance to their creation myth.

Dogon dancers of Mali. Dogon star myths have given rise to speculation that they had early contact with extraterrestrials.

DOGON CREATION

The Dogon have a remarkable legend to explain their origins. It combines myth with a scientific understanding of astronomy and the stars; a knowledge that only comparatively recently has been verified by Western scientists. The Dogon myth speaks of the Nommo, terrible looking beings who arrived in a vessel accompanied by much fire and thunder. Dogon drawings of the Nommo show them as amphibious humanoid beings with feet and fish scales. They could not live entirely on land and on their arrival they made a reservoir of water and dived into it. *Nommo* means "To make one drink" and the Nommo are also called Masters of the Water, Monitors and Teachers. Although ugly to look at, they are the saviours and spiritual guardians of the Dogon. A Nommo divided his body among the people to feed them; for as the Universe had drunk of his body, the Nommo would make men drink. He gave his life principles to human beings.

The mystery behind the myth deepens when we learn that the Dogon believed that the Nommo came from the star, Sirius, or rather an invisible companion star around Sirius. Sirius is called Sigi tolo by the Dogon, who say it has a tiny unseen companion called Po tolo. *Tolo* means "star" and *po* is the name of the smallest seed known to the Dogon. Po tolo, they say, is the smallest thing there is. They also claim it is the heaviest star and it is coloured white and that it orbits Sigi tolo, or Sirius, every 50 years. The Dogon myth dates back at least to the thirteenth century, but it was not until the nineteenth century that astronomers found that there was indeed such a star. Further investigation showed that the Dogon were right. The white dwarf star Sirius B does orbit Sirius every 50 years. Sirius B also has the characteristics described by the Dogon: it is small, heavy and white.

Not all the Dogon myth fits the astronomical facts. The Dogon also speak of a third star called Emme ya tolo. This is larger and four times brighter than Sirius B. It was from a planet orbiting around this star that the Nommo visited Earth. No such star has yet been sighted. Perhaps we will

know the source of the Dogons' knowledge if other parts of the myth are confirmed.

Masked Dogon dancers.

PARADISE LOST

Creation myths explain many things – the cosmos, the gods, the relationships of humans with their deities and the history of a people. They often attempt also to explain the problems that beset everyday life and the great causes of human suffering – sickness and death. A common theme among African creation myths is that of a lost time of peace

Young Mozambique men perform traditional dance.

and plenty when all was well, a Golden Age or Garden of Eden. The first humans lived with their creator in peace and harmony and he provided for them. At this stage they could enjoy one of three important gifts: immortality, resurrection if they died or rejuvenation if they grew old.

Somehow Earth and Heaven become separated and these gifts are lost. In their place there come disease, suffering and death. Sometimes this is because humans fail a test that the creator puts to them. Others talk of population explosion: there are quarrels among growing numbers of families

196

of her pounding *fufu*, the national food. She builds a tower to reach him and the further he retreats in the sky the higher she builds. The tower almost reaches him and she needs one more brick. This she pulls from the bottom of the tower causing it to collapse, destroying many people.

One Pygmy myth is remarkably like the Old Testament myth of Adam and Eve. People have been forbidden to eat the fruit of a particular tree, but the woman persuades her husband to get it for her. He sneaks out at night, but the Moon sees this and reports it to the Creator who punishes them by sending death to the people.

Ancient African myths brought meaning to their people's lives. But can they help today and will they come to represent a "Paradise Lost", a phase of African culture that cannot survive in the modern world?

AFRICAN RELIGION TODAY

In Africa today traditional religion, Islam and Christianity are all thriving. The future of traditional religion will depend on whether it can adapt to meet changing conditions and the urbanization of many Africans in conditions of extreme hardship. As on other continents, Christianity is synthesizing with indigenous beliefs to create new forms of spirituality that may meet the needs of urban Africa. While South of the Sahara, Catholic and Protestant churches have had their successes in Africa, new independent or separatist churches are springing up that have no colonial legacy to contend with. They are African churches run by Africans for Africans and incorporating elements of African tradition, culture and religious participation in ways that are not always possible for traditional churches with stronger doctrinal constraints.

In northern Africa Islam is likely to continue to grow. It can accommodate many traditional African practices and has an attraction for those who see their own traditions as backward or archaic. Traditional African spirituality will therefore thrive in original forms, though evolving to meet the needs of people today, and will grow in new syntheses with the world traditions that make them truly African.

that cause the split. Others blame animals, for example the hyena which, being ever hungry, chews through the leather rope that connects Heaven and Earth. Many legends and myths blame women. The Ashanti myth is one where the woman drives the Creator further away through the noise

ABORIGINES
OF
AUSTRALIA

Australia is the smallest of the Earth's seven

continents and the most sparsely populated. It lies

between the Indian and Pacific Oceans, southeast

of Asia, a unique landmass about 2,500 miles wide

(East to West) and about 2,300 miles long (North

to South). It has evolved its own distinctive flora and

fauna. Species, such as the enchanting koala,

the duckbilled platypus and members of the

marsupial family, which include kangaroos and

wallabies, exist only here in this land, separated

from other continents millions of years ago.

Around fifty million years ago it is thought to have

taken on its current shape when Antarctica split

away and drifted southward.

PREVIOUS PAGE: Young Aboriginal boy on top of an escapement in Arnhemland. Since the 1970s, large tracts of Arnhemland have been returned to their original Aboriginal owners.

The original people of this land, whose society dates back at least 60,000 years with all but the last 200 years or so spent in total isolation from the rest of the world, have also evolved their own unique culture, with a way of life and ways of spirit that are in tune with this separate land.

ABORIGINES

The indigenous people of Australia, the Aborigines and the Torres Straits Islanders – a seafaring people of the small islands of the Torres Strait, which separates Australia from Papua New Guinea – now account for little more than two per cent of the population. A 1996 census gave Aborigines' numbers as around 314,000. Once Aborigines inhabited the whole continent but now many who remain live in the towns and cities in generally disadvantaged circumstances. Only a few maintain their nomadic way of life, living mostly in isolated pockets in the northern territory, the northern part of Western Australia and Northern Queensland. The first Europeans came and settled from the late eighteenth century onward. Lack of resistance to the diseases brought by the Europeans, disruption of their traditional way of life and a hostile approach by the new-

Cave painting from Arnhemland, which has a priceless heritage of Aboriginal art.

comers combined to cause a decline of their numbers, thought to be at that time upward of a million. Nowadays, there is evidence to show that this decline has been halted. Aborigines have a much younger profile than the rest of the population. The 1996 census gave their median age as 20 compared with 34 for the rest of the population; 40 per cent of Aborigines are under 15 years of age. Their life expectancy is short, however, 20 years less than the rest of the population.

No one quite knows for sure the origins of Aborigines. There is no connection with any other living race. Some ethnologists suggest they come from an archaic Caucasoid type, perhaps migrants from the Asian mainland in prehistoric times. Their language, Walpiri, gives no clues; linguistically they are related to no other people. Within their small and reducing numbers there is, however, a multiplicity of different dialects.

Traditionally, Aborigines were nomadic hunters and fishers with little or no knowledge of agriculture. They did not domesticate animals, apart from dogs, and their homes were only temporary shelters against the elements. They wear little or no clothing and hunt by using the boomerang, the throwing stick (a device for throwing a spear) and the waddy, a type of war club. These weapons are lethally effective and so they had no need to invent other weapons, such as the bow and arrow.

They base their social structure on language groups. Each has its own language or separate dialect but communication between groups is possible, as most Aborigines would be bilingual if not multi-lingual. There may have been as many as 500 of these groups and, though nomadic, these would live in defined territories. Australian Aborigines have strong attachments to sites and areas within this home territory where most of their hunting and gathering would be done. The environment can, however, be harsh and offer limited resources. People survived better if they dispersed into smaller family food-gathering units, but several times a year, when circumstances were propitious enough, much larger gatherings would be organized. Much social and religious business would be carried out at this time, a time of intense social activity. This rhythm of coming together and then, through necessity, dispersing for food gathering and hunting is the base rhythm behind all Aboriginal life. Aboriginal society, which has had to adapt to a climate inhospitable due to extreme heat, has some similarities with that of the Inuit, who adapted to extreme cold. As no large permanent groupings formed, there was no need for hierarchies or chiefs. Aborigine society is egalitarian. All are perceived equal as everyone is placed firmly under the laws of the Ancestors rather than under laws imposed by other people. An individual's autonomy is valued highly and anyone who tries to deny or diminish it is likely to be met with fierce resistance. Having said that, however, men enjoy superior rights over women and those who are younger show deference to older men.

DREAMING AND DREAMTIME

Aboriginal beliefs centre on the concept of Dreamtime. This is a complex and all-embracing concept that includes virtually every aspect of life and all that surrounds current existence. It is all that is, in both this life, in what has gone before and what will come in the future. It began in the dawn of time when all things were created; when mythic beings shaped the land and set the rules for earthly existence. In a sense they were spiritual ancestors and many stories survive about beings such as the Fertility Mother and the Great Rainbow Serpent, who carved the hills, valleys, gorges, cliffs and rivers through the writhing of its body. The Great Rainbow Serpent gave birth to many babies. Some became men and women. Others became the first of the animals, birds, fish and reptiles. The rainbow in the sky is the mirrored reflection of this legendary Dreaming Being. In addition to Fertility Mother and the Great Rainbow Serpent, there are many human and animal totemic spirits – even Sky heroes – who all have their part to play in this first great act of creation. After this creation, the original dreaming time, the creators died on a physical level but, being indestructible,

they were transformed into heavenly or earthly bodies. They thus withdrew to dwell forever in the spiritual realm.

The Dreaming Beings retain control of all power and

Snake Dreaming – dreaming images are an important feature of Aboriginal art.

Dreamtime ritual on a
Northern Territory beach.
Rituals maintain harmony
between humans and
the Dreamtime Beings,
ensuring human
society will flourish.

Dreamtime ritual on a Northern Territory beach. Rituals maintain harmony between humans and the Dreamtime Beings, ensuring human society will flourish.

fertility. As long as people followed their plan then these qualities would be released into the human realm. The rules include regular performance of rituals to ensure the continuous flow of their life-giving power. Many rituals celebrate the Dreaming Time. In these age-old ceremonies, Aboriginal men enact the roles of the creators of the physical world. The rules that the Dreaming Beings passed down are not, however, a one-off set of instructions, more an initial blueprint from which more could evolve and flow. Contact can always be made with the Dreaming Beings through dreams and altered states of consciousness. Spirit beings can be used as messengers to act as a communicative link between humans and the Dreaming Beings in order to introduce new knowledge to the living.

Through these means the living could contact the spiritual realm and gain strength from it. Various features of the landscape took on a special significance and proved the reality and world-creating powers of these Dreaming

Beings. A rich complexity of myths, rituals, dances and special objects help bind and connect the human, spiritual and physical realms together into a single cosmic order. People therefore have a religious confidence and strongly defined sense of self, which in turn leads to confidence in coping with their physical and social worlds, despite the toughness and uncertainty of their lives. For them, the natural landscape has its own beauty and its own spirit that will never change. In Dreamtime they become at one with the spirit of the land.

SONGLINES

On one level, Songlines, or *Yiri*, are tracks across the landscape created by the Aborigines' Divine Ancestors. When the Dreaming Beings rose up from the dark earth and travelled across the land creating mountains, waterholes, valleys and cliffs, all the physical features of the land, these were the tracks they left. Songlines are the ceremonial songs that celebrate and acknowledge the work of Divine

Ancestors who created them, but they also serve more practical purposes. As the Ancestors undertook their adventures, the laws for living in this environment were established and the techniques and skills for successful hunting were imparted. The songs and the stories are inextricably intertwined; each adds to the other creating a sung history of the land. It is in this way, it is said, that the land is sung into existence.

Beyond all this, there is a more practical reason for the songs. Aboriginal society had no writing or maps, relying instead on a strongly oral tradition. As Aborigines travelled, they named each place, either informally or more ceremonially, and sang of its creation, the role the Ancestors played in this and the place's special significance for them. This practice serves at least three functions: it strengthens and reinforces people's knowledge of local geography, it serves a social function in that it can bring people together by following the song and it serves religious and ritual functions. The first of these is key to the Aborigines' survival. The song can plot food routes and the location of water and hidden water holes. It can tell of places to avoid, places of danger and places of safety, apart from describing the general terrain. Songlines are a verbal map, but a map in which factual and survival information intertwines with mythic stories and a profoundly religious celebration of the land.

Singing is telling a story, but it is also a performance. As such it is a key part of rituals and ceremonies. Ceremonies can be religious or secular. Secular ceremonies, *Corroborees*, are large social gatherings where Song Cycles are recited. These are vastly developed and complicated Songlines. They follow the journeys of the Divine Ancestors but, because sometimes these journeys cover vast stretches of land, only a particular group knows a segment of the entire story. These segments are exchanged at meeting points and, though different dialects may be involved, music, visual displays of dancing and acting, repetition, and drawing and sweeping away images in the sand all serve to make the segment clearly identifiable to the listeners. It is

not just a song but a performance to convey the unchanging verities; the unchanging yet continuing relationship between the ancestral past and the present that enables people to find a way of access to their mythic past and to the eternal present of the Dreaming.

WALKABOUT

As nomads, Aborigines wander the plains, deserts and mountains in search of food, hunting animals and gathering fruits and roots as they pass. These wanderings could be called Walkabouts but, over and above this vital search for sustenance and survival, the Walkabout has a far greater spiritual significance. The land itself has a spiritual meaning for Aborigines. When on a Walkabout, the land reflects a sacred geography. The travelling becomes a Dream Journey that connects the traveller to the Dreamtime. Someone on Walkabout sees and connects with the stories of the Songlines; the stories of how the land was created by the Dreaming Beings and how they are represented in the contours of the land. The Dreamtime creators became living features of the landscape, so a sacred dimension is added to the journey. In order to receive a message from the spirit world, whether profoundly spiritual or more practical, people will regularly cross vast areas following the Songlines. While on a Walkabout or Dream Journey, the individual is connected to the eternal moment of creation in the present, which is perhaps a state of mind akin to a trance or highly devel-

Aborigine musician playing didjeridoo, a tree truck hollowed out by insects.

oped meditative state. Through the traveller's inseparability with the land, the Dream Journey becomes a path to spiritual renewal.

RELIGION

Aboriginal culture puts great emphasis on rituals and ceremonies. They are not only ways to create community by bringing kin together – although this social function is very important – but a celebration of the undeniable acts of the Dreaming Beings who created the world and provided the blueprint for ways of being and surviving in that world. Their mission and the purpose of their lives is to live in agreement and accordance with the legacy passed down by their mythic ancestors. This means that there is no need for progress and no reason to question or attack the *status quo*. Everything that now exists was created and fixed by the mythic Ancestors. The sole requirement of those now living was to obey the laws of the Dreaming and to perform the

Aboriginal burial poles, an important feature of death rites. The poles are carved from ironwood.

rituals correctly, following guidance laid down by their spiritual ancestors. Social and physical reproduction was dependent upon this.

This might appear a static view of life, but in practice it is not so rigid. Despite claims of adhering to the original rules, new revelations come through contacts with the Divine Ancestors in dreams and through calling on the intercession of people's own ancestors. Tradition is frequently added to and enlivened by new developments, but Aboriginal belief in their Divine origins has given rise to a more accepting and spiritually based view of the world than is common in other cultures. There is less emphasis on probing and intellectual questioning in order to understand why things occur. A constant and restless desire for progress has no place in traditional Aborigine culture.

TOTEMS

Many of the mythic beings not only exemplified the life force that created a particular species but also, at the end of their wanderings, they were metamorphosed into hills or rocks or turned into a particular creature or plant. Links made to these places or to specific plants, animals or minerals that connect with that place are said to be "totemic" as the symbolism takes on a far greater importance than the object or place itself alone. Totemic beliefs are perhaps more developed in Aboriginal culture than in any other culture. The adoption of a particular totem, which can be an animal or plant, connects the individual to that species, its appearance in the story of the creation, to places associated with it in the landscape and to others from different kin who share the same totem. If the totem is an animal, the individual may not eat it, for this would be cannibalism. These connections give people the ability to access the enormous powers that emanate from the spirit realm, powers that will help them in a life-sustaining way. It also connects people to others in their society or in related groups who share that particular totem. It also means that one's sense of identity is linked to the land. If the land is threatened or destroyed one's sense of identity is diminished.

RITUALS AND CEREMONIES

Rituals and ceremonies are a key part of the Aboriginal yearly rhythm. They will not occur until families and groups reconvene in one place, but particular rituals may be planned or discussed throughout the year, especially by senior initiated men. The main ritual roles in most of the major rites were reserved for men, but women have their own part to play in a range of other religious activities. In some areas, such as the Great Sandy Desert, women have their own secret rites. Children are also present for some rituals.

Great significance is given to rites of passage, particularly those from childhood to adulthood. For women, the transition into adulthood occurred at puberty and led directly into a marriage that would have been arranged

years in advance, sometimes when the girl was still an infant. A marriage might only be considered binding, however, if and when a child was born, even if the couple had been living together. For girls, puberty is marked by either total or partial seclusion and by various food taboos. After this, they are decorated and ritually purified. In a few areas defloration and hymen cutting might be practised.

For boys the transition to manhood is considerably more complex and requires more of an ordeal. From a relatively carefree life, the process toward initiation helps prepare a boy to cope with his new responsibilities as a man. Initiation is a symbolic re-enactment of death. One has to die in order to be reborn again as an adult. As the novice is taken away from the camp, the women wail as if in mourning. Other noises are made that symbolize the voice of a mythic being, one of the creators from the Dreamtime, who will swallow the boy and then vomit him forth as a man. Those who help with the initiation will be relatives who will continue to play a significant role in his future adult life. The initiation rites are concerned with training. They include songs and stories that help to educate the young initiate and ensure that the vast amount of

Uluru, formerly Ayers Rock, is a sacred site. Visitors are asked to honour it as such.

knowledge and experience that has been accumulated over the centuries is passed on to subsequent generations. This is especially important in an oral culture. Initiation and on-going ritual are effective as they provide a continuing basis for accumulating this wisdom throughout the person's life. Rites of ordeal in the initiation ritual involve cutting or blood letting. Blood is taken from the arm or sometimes the penis and is used for anointing or for sipping. Sometimes red ochre is used as a substitute. Circumcision is one of the most important rites and subincision – incisura of the urethra – is important if the person is to go on to greater involvement with secret, sacred ritual. Other rites include tooth pulling and piercing of the nasal septum. Hair removal, cicatrization (scarring) and fire ordeals are also practised.

With the concept of the Dreamtime permeating all their conscious and unconscious feelings and thoughts it is not surprising that the circle of birth, life and death was seen as an ever-continuing, seamless whole. They emerged from the Dreaming; its spiritual and religious power was taught to them through life experience and through initiation and subsequent religious ritual. Finally, in death they were re-absorbed into the Dreaming. They may be reborn again

Boys prepare for initiation into manhood. Circumcision is an important, and painful, part of the rite.

for a child's spirit was held to come from the Dreaming to animate the foetus in the woman's belly. The circle of life continues according to rules set down countless years ago by the mythic ancestors during the Dreamtime when they created the land.

ART

Although Aborigines had no writing and relied almost entirely on song and story to pass their knowledge on to subsequent generations, they also portrayed this information visually in rock paintings, in paintings on bark and in other decorative forms. Each area developed its own distinctive form. These forms include incized patterns on flat stones and boards. Body decoration and elaborate head-dresses were common in Central Australia. In Western Arnhemland, realistic and stylized representations of natural species have been produced. Also common are carved wooden figures of mythic beings and of real individuals; the former being used in sacred ritual, the latter more commonly as memorial posts for the dead. Paintings in ochre on sheets of bark are indigenous to the Arnhemland Aborigines although examples have been found in the Kimberleys and in southeastern Australia. They were commonly used on the initiation ground for the instruction of novices. Sacred ritual was the motivator for creating art. Much of it is impermanent. The making was more important than the finished object.

The paintings on the rocks, which are found mainly in Western Arnhemland and the Northern Territory, have extraordinary vitality. They portray the Divine Ancestors and sky heroes performing Walkabouts and creating land, people, sacred places and totems. Uniquely, Aboriginal artists developed a type of "X-Ray" depiction of animals and humans that depicts their internal organs accurately. Hand shapes are common where the hand has been placed against the wall of the cave and coloured pigments blown around it to create a silhouette. The paintings provide a fascinating insight into an ancient but still living culture, which is now more than 40,000 years old.

THE MAORI

New Zealand consists of two large islands, North
Island and South Island, plus a scattering of
smaller ones of which Stewart Island is the largest.
The narrow Cook Strait separates North Island and
South Island. To the North and East lies the Pacific
Ocean and between New Zealand and Australia is
the Tasman Sea. New Zealand is about the same
size as United Kingdom or the US State of
Colorado. North Island is volcanically active with a
central plateau. South Island has the high snow-
covered mountain peaks and glaciers of the Southern
Alps. The Maori are thought to be the first settlers
of New Zealand. Around a thousand years ago, the
same time as Eric the Red sailed West to North
America, the exceptional Polynesian navigator Kupe
set off by canoe from his Polynesian homeland of
Hawaiki to discover Aotearoa, the Land of the Long
White Cloud, or New Zealand.

During ceremonial rites Maori priests were forbidden to touch food. Here a priest is fed by an assistant dressed in traditional feathered cloak.

The Polynesians were master navigators. Using stars, the direction of sea birds in flight, cloud patterns and by observing changes in the colour of the sea around them, they crossed the Pacific Ocean with canoes built to withstand heavy seas and able to carry people and goods over great distances.

In time, the Maori established an agricultural society, which flourished with little or no interference from outside influences. A complex social structure of families, kin groups and clans, and a stratified society made up of nobility, priestly and slave classes, developed. Genealogy, *whakapapa*, was of considerable importance and defined origins and status. People were either born into chiefly, priestly or commoner families. They became slaves if they were captured in a war. Land was held communally, with each group and clan having a *marae* or meeting house, where the people's ancestral spirits resided, and they often lived in a fortified village or pa. Communal patterns of life in Maori settlements were organized around food growing, food gathering and, in areas of frequent fighting, warfare. Large parties of workers carried out cultivation and searched for food. Maori were also skilled woodcarvers, farmers, seafarers and warriors. Clothing, ornaments and

clubs were fashioned from feathers, dog fur, bone and jade. Objects made from whale, bird, dog and human bones were skillfully and ornately carved.

Warfare was an accepted way of life and great war canoes were the pride of the tribe. Various weapons were made of bone, wood and stone. Men were glorified with tattoos and ornaments. Warfare was carried out to obtain territory with food or other natural resources, to avenge insults – either real or imagined – or to obtain satisfaction from others who had broken the social code. Losers often become slaves or were eaten. Eating of the body of one's enemy was not so much a violation as a mark of respect. It was a way of securing an enemy's power or *mana*. Competition between clans was an accepted basis of the Maori life. Although warriors receive high standing and respect, it was also possible to achieve high standing as an artist or priest.

The whole of life to a Maori was unified – every aspect of life is related to every other. Art, religion, war, food gathering, lovemaking and death were all an integrated pattern of a single fabric, an intricate piece of tapestry. Universal acceptance of concepts like sacredness, spiritual authority, life force, satisfaction and a belief in magic regulated all these aspects of life.

MAORI CULTURE

In traditional Maori society, all human activities were subject to rules laid down by the offspring of the gods. These were issued as edicts through the gods' priests, the *tohunga ahurewa*. It was the priests' duty to memorize the sacred chants and to see that they were passed on to the next generation. They conducted rituals at planting and harvest, communicated with gods when there was drought or other natural disaster and ensured that the burial of chiefs was performed in the proper manner. Prohibitions were also laid on people who behaved badly toward their friends or broke the ruling that certain *tapu* (sacred) places, such as the scene of a recent death, should not be visited for a time. Priests therefore not only interceded with the gods, but encouraged people to behave properly toward others.

Protocol and ceremony were of considerable importance and were correspondingly elaborate and involved. Examples of etiquette are the fierce, eruptive greetings known as the *haka*, meaning war chant, and *wero*, meaning challenge, which involve protruding the tongue and which are still used today. People reading this may well be familiar with these if they have ever watched the New Zealand Rugby Team, better known as the All-Blacks. The rites of *haka* and *wero* are performed before the start of each match they play.

The *marae*, or traditional meeting house, is the focus for ceremony and community identity. Visitors are welcomed to the *marae* but within a strict formal protocol, which must be fully observed. This is to honour the dead, the ancestors who are identified with the meeting house. It is essential to show respect for ancestral spirits at the start of any meeting. Speeches of welcome and ceremonial chants follow. At the end of the welcome, people shake hands, press noses and offer the *haka* (challenge). Oratory is an art in Maori society. Chiefs who were great orators would dance up and down, waving their spear or club and sometimes breaking into songs or chants. The Maori brought with them a Polynesian culture rich in song, dance, carving and weaving, which were intertwined with strong oratory skills as no written language was used. Maori history, as with their Aboriginal neighbours in Australia, was recorded in long stylized songs and chants.

CREATION MYTHS

In Maori mythology, the earliest being was Io, the primal cause of motion, space and moving earth. Then came Rangi or Ranginui, the god of sky and space, and Pahpah or Papatuanuku, the Earth Mother goddess of matter. Ranginui and Papatuanuku give birth to the Forest and bird god Tane Mahuta, the sea god Tangaroa, the wind god Tawhiri Matea and three other children who represent wild food, planted food and humankind. They are remembered through song, dance and ritual. These young deities created the plants and animals on Earth and the heavenly bodies in the sky. Another important goddess in Maori legend is Hinetitama, Dawn Maiden, daughter of Tane Mahuta, god of forest and birds, and Hineahuone, a woman made from earth. Tane Mahuta is proud of his daughter Hinetitama. One day he calls two of his brothers, the wind god and the sea god, to ask their advice about who she should marry. Tane Mahuta's brothers are reluctant to interfere with such a matter, but Tangaroa suggests that Tane Mahuta marry Hinetitama himself. Tane Mahuta changes his form into that of a man. Not knowing that this is her father, Hinetitama falls in love, marries him and bears children. All is well until the other gods begin to interfere. Tane Mahuta's brothers begin to plant seeds of doubt in Hinetitama's mind. Tawhiri Matea sends a breeze to whisper in her ear asking her who her father is. When she is out gathering shellfish, Tangaroa sends a wave that rip-

Eleventh-century breast pendant reproducing in stone the pearl-shell pendants of Polynesia.

211

ples around her ankles asking the same question. Hinetitama goes home to Tane Mahuta and when she asks him this question he tells her the truth, but she flees in horror to the Underworld. Tane Mahuta goes into the Underworld to bring her home, but she will not come. She determines to remain in the Underworld. No longer is she Hinetitama, Dawn Maiden, but Hineuitepo, Goddess Of Death. And there Hineuitepo has stayed, greeting her children, her children's children and so on down the generations, as they enter the kingdom of Death.

VOLCANOES

The Maori have many myths that have been passed down through generations. Some of these explain how the Maori world was formed and how the land took on its shape. Several describe how particular features of the landscape came into existence. All are vividly expressed using vigorous language and colourful imagery. There is, for example, the legend of Ruamoko, which explains an important geographical feature of New Zealand – volcanoes.

Ranginui (Sky Father) and Papatuanuku (Earth Mother) are so inseparable and cling together so tightly that their children complain bitterly. No light can penetrate between the parents and there is little space for a growing family. When the newest baby, Ruamoko, is born life becomes unbearable. He is a troublesome baby – overactive and bad tempered. He is made god of volcanoes. The children cannot bear the commotion and decide there is no other solution but to push their parents apart. Tane

Mahuta, god of the forest and birds, pushes Ranginui into the heavens. Light rushes into the world. Tangaroa spread his waters around their mother, Papatuanuku, while Tawhiri Matea, god of the wind screams across the empty space between his parents. Ruamoko has been left out of all this activity and is furious. He cracks open the ground and throws boiling mud and fire into the air, with huge clouds of foul smelling steam. Papatuanuku eventually stills his anger by folding her arms around him and singing him to sleep.

After a while, Ranginui stops weeping for Papatuanuku and Papatuanuku begins to take an interest in her children's work, especially when they dress her in gowns of many colours. Ruamoko does not, however, cease his temper tantrums. When he wakes up he shakes Papatuanuku and throws mud and hot, foul-smelling steam into the air. When Papatuanuku cannot sing him to sleep, he hurls rivers of red fire into the forests of Tane Mahuta, puts islands of molten rock upon the waters of Tangaroa, and the attention-seeking Ruamoko shouts to his brothers to notice him, saying, "Harken to the rumble of the earthquake god".

TATTOOING

Intricate tattooing was common among the Maori and today it is enjoying a revival among young Maori people, who are seeking to re-root themselves in their cultural identity. In traditional society, the higher the individual's status the more tattoos he had, with men of importance being

heavily tattooed from face to feet. Only priests and Maori from higher ranks were permitted to carry out the tattooing. Men were tattooed all over the face in deep cuts with pigment inserted that looked blue under the skin. Northern warriors often had additional tattoos over their thighs and buttocks. Tattoos are an extension of Maori cultural art. The most common designs are the spiral and the *koru*, a stalk with a bulb at one end. Besides body art, similar designs can be found on house panels, woodcarvings, wooden, whalebone and stone clubs and canoe prow and hull carvings. Animal and human figures were also used. Women were only tattooed around the lips and chin. On women tattoos were to enhance beauty. On men they demonstrated virility and fierceness. The challenge was to bear the tattooing without flinching. The Maori dance and wero challenge, where men leap out with a spear, sticking their tongue out as far as it will go, shows how they will challenge the enemy and scare them away. The tattoos, of course, assist in making them look even more frightening. The human figure with a protruding tongue and enlarged head is a dominant image in Maori art. The head is enlarged to signify that it contains the life spirit.

MAORI ART

Artists had considerable status is Maori society. The Maori were skilled wood carvers and carving is an important art form. The *marae*, meeting house, is beautifully decorated. Intricate carvings record the *whakapapa* (genealogical tree) of the village. Canoes, especially war canoes, were artistic as well as practical creations. Wooden memorial posts to the dead were outstanding and other important monuments to the dead were carved canoes, which were buried vertically in the earth.

Many everyday household objects were transformed under the hands of a skilled woodcarver into evocative objects of great beauty. Houses, even storehouses, fortifications, weapons, food utensils and tools were all intricately carved. Items for personal adornment were also of great

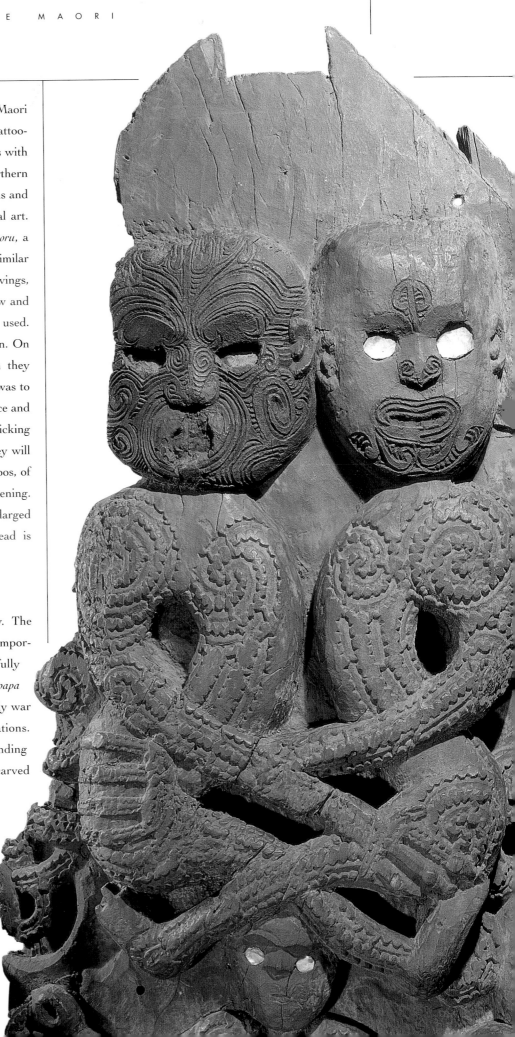

beauty. The Maori took pride in their personal appearance and combs, cloak pins and greenstone jewellery were all exquisitely made. Cloaks made of feathers were highly prized. All created objects as well as natural objects had inner power or force. Those items that were set aside for religious and spiritual use were therefore created with special care.

The *marae* or meeting house has always had a special significance to the Maori. The meeting house is thought of as a living being, with a head, arms, fingers, spine, rib cage and belly. A central mask placed below a carved wooden standing figure represents the head. The ornamental boards that cover the edge of the roof represent the arms. These boards often have fingers carved out at their lower ends. The ridgepole of the meeting house is its spine. The rafters represent the rib cage and the interior of the meeting house is its belly.

Human figures are often carved. As well as the common distorted head and protruding tongue, figures often have slanted eyes and hands with only three fingers. All these departures from the everyday suggest that these are supernatural figures. Another supernatural figure that often appears in artwork in the half-human, half-bird, the Manaia. The Manaia is an ancient mythical being, which acts as messenger between the human and spirit worlds. The Manaia has great spiritual energy and protects against evil. The image of the Manaia is incorporated in many Maori designs although there are subtle differences between tribes.

There are four distinctive eras with distinct features, which indicate the development in their art: Archaic, Classic, Historic and Modern. The Archaic Maori were the earliest settlers, who survived on hunting and fishing. Their artwork includes woodcarvings, bone carvings and stonework. Although their artwork was not as elaborate as that of later centuries, the pure simplicity of line gives their artefacts a remarkable beauty. The Classic period of Maori civilization was a more settled era that reached its culmination in the eighteenth century. Agricultural developments and advances in forestry and fishing techniques created more abundant food supplies. Greater utilization of land – and probably population expansion – created more regulated societies. The tribal system became stricter and more organized and fixed boundaries evolved. Territorial boundaries give scope for territorial disputes that were settled by warfare.

The arrival of European colonists brought new trade goods and technology. The Maori adopted metal tools and began to use Western fabrics and various types of gun. Christian missionaries made inroads into Maori society and a process of Christianization began. The new society was much more utilitarian than the old. Great carved war canoes were less important now that there were weapons that used gunpowder. Beautifully carved storehouses were replaced by functional sheds. The Modern period of Maori

Maori people developed beautiful wood carving techniques to decorate their buildings. This lintel, dating from around 1850 shows the separation of the Sky Father from the Earth Mother..

OPPOSITE: Stone fertility god statue said to have been brought to Mokoia Island, Lake Rotorua from the legendary Maori homeland of Hawaiki.

art has seen an increased interest in Maori culture, which has been inspired be a renewed pride in Maori identity.

CULTURAL AND SACRED SITES

Maori cultural sites divide into two broad categories: everyday secular sites and *wahi tapu* or sacred places. Everyday cultural sites include the *marae* or meeting house and *pa* sites – which are formerly fortified villages – quarries, and *mahinga kai*, specific fishing or other food gathering areas.

The English word "sacred" does not fully convey the essence of *tapu*, and there is further confusion when *tapu* is mistakenly thought of as "taboo". The deep spiritual value of *wahi tapu* transcends mere sacredness. *Urupa* (burial grounds) are the most obvious examples of *wahi tapu* but there is a wide range of sites which may qualify. These include *ana tupapaku* (burial caves), ossuaries, *pa* where battles have occurred, other sites where blood has been spilt, *tauranga waka* (sites where ancestral canoes beached) and some mountains. Intricate and indissoluble bonds link the most important *wahi tapu* sites to their appropriate clans. These sites may be associated with the creation stories of the local people and form one end of a continuum which moves from prehistory to the present and links the people genealogically to their past. Their *whakapapa* (genealogy) and history are identified by reference to land features with names that recall the *tipuna* (ancestors) who preceded them, and the

events that shaped their lives. For example Hikurangi, the sacred mountain of the Ngati Porou, is the resting place of the canoe of Maui, the demi-god who is credited with catching the North Island (Te Ika a Maui – the Fish of Maui) while fishing, and drawing it to the surface.

Only a small proportion of the thousands of *wahi tapu* are located in New Zealand's 12 national parks. Ironically, New Zealand's first national park, Tongariro, was gifted to the nation "for the use of both Maori and the Europeans" by Te Heuheu Tukino IV, Horonuku, paramount chief of the the Ngati Tuwharetoa tribe in 1887. Tongariro is the ancestral mountain of Ngati Tuwharetoa and, at the time of gifting, held the remains of Horonuku's father, Te Heuheu Tukino H, Mananui, a chief of great rank.

Protection of sacred sites is complicated by the fact that many Maori are reluctant to reveal the presence of *wahi tapu* to outsiders. A compromise has been reached between the Pakeha, the Maori name for Europeans, and the Maori by use of "silent files" or registers that can maintain the secrecy of the site. A silent file is kept in confidence by the appropriate clan or family and lists the location of that group's *wahi tapu*. Land titles, which Maori know to contain *wahi tapu*, could be marked in local authorities' plans, to show that some part of the property was recorded in a silent file as having a *wahi tapu*. The precise location need not need to be recorded on the plan. If any development is planned on that title, the local authority has the responsibility of checking with the holders of the silent file to ensure that *wahi tapu* are not threatened before approval is given for development to proceed.

MAORI LIFE TODAY

From the time of the white peoples' settlements two hundred years ago until recent years, the relationship between the two races has varied from uneasy co-existence to open warfare. In 1840, the Treaty of Waitangi ceded Maori sovereignty to the Queen of England in exchange for the Queen's protection in the exercise of their chieftainship over their lands, people, villages and possessions. The

Ngati Porou Maori perform traditional songs at the sacred mountain of Hikurangi on the remote East Cape of North Island on January 1, 2000.

rights, privileges and duties of citizenship and a policy for land sales were also agreed upon. The treaty's promise of benefits for both sides by regulating settlement and land sales proved a chimera. The demand for land by the arriving settlers and reluctance on the part of the Maori to sell land, plus the length of time such a procedure took in a system where land belongs not to an individual but to a clan who must come to a consensus about the decision, sparked a series of skirmishes which escalated into the Maori Wars (1860–1865). Pitted against superior numbers and firepower, the Maori eventually succumbed. The treaty, praised previously as a document of sincerity and

utility, was hastily dumped, paving the way for widespread land confiscation by the Pakeha administration.

At present, there are about 400,000 Maori in New Zealand's population of 3.5 million. Most Maori live in the North Island around North Auckland, which is known as the Waikato-king County. Today, most of the old Maori way of life has disappeared and the Maori live more or less the same lifestyle as the Pakeha. Many speak Maori and English but retain membership of their tribes, even though tribe members may be widely scattered. Maori today want New Zealand society to recognize that both Maori and Pakeha are equally important.

OPPOSITE: Carving from the Cook Islands of Tangaroa, god of the sea and patron of fishermen.

EARTH TRADITIONS
IN THE
TWENTY-FIRST CENTURY

In our journey from Europe to the Americas and from Africa to the Antipodes, we hope that we have shown that those religious traditions that are known as the primal, indigenous or earth traditions have powerful messages for us in the twenty-first century. The Earth traditions challenge us to experience for ourselves the forces and energies of nature and of the wider cosmos that surround us. They challenge us to think about our relationship to the natural world, to the other creatures that share our planet, to its plants and trees and to this small portion of space that is occupied by the Earth. Each of us has a responsibility to leave the planet in a better condition than we found it, so that it can thrive and support the generations of humans that are to come. Many human failings make our planet a less green and beautiful place than it could be. Humans have a tendency to ignore serious problems until the last possible moment. In the West environmental pollution is at last being seen as a serious threat, having been previously derided and dismissed.

Outside the developed world, environmental issues are of utmost importance. Many indigenous peoples are living in environments that are threatened by development and pollution. Sometimes their own governments are the major cause, as they seek to draw their people out of poverty and to share the benefits of technology and the higher standard of living it can bring. The governments of the developing world can challenge objections from Westerners about the destruction of rain forests pointing out the fact that we have wreaked destruction on our own environments. Who are we to tell other countries that they are to live in primitive poverty to make the planet a better place for us? There are no easy answers to these issues, for they require global co-operation. They require a leap of the imagination to understand that the fate of an Amerindian people in a

Brazilian rain forest might be important to us, even if we live far away. It requires unselfishness on the part of the West that could come about through sustained public campaigning. The campaign to wipe out Third World debt to Western countries seemed to be a hopeless cause, but as leading figures from the world of music and other media have lent their support, things are beginning to happen. Economies are being given the chance to regenerate.

What role can the Ancient Wisdom of the Earth traditions play in this? They are important reminders that before we are citizens of our own countries, we are citizens of the planet. These traditions remind us to reverence the forces that give us life, the Earth that nourishes us with food, the rivers that give us water to drink, the sky that gives us clean air to breathe and the Sun that is the source of life. Earth traditions remind us also of the rhythms of life. Too often people are dismayed by illness, ageing and death, but they are part of the rich fabric of existence, of the warp and weft of life itself. In their seasonal rites, indigenous peoples and those who have revived indigenous spirituality today give recognition to summer and winter, to the times of plenty and the times of want, to love and laughter and to pain and death in the knowledge that we will inevitably experience all of life's complexity. The Earth traditions teach that we can transcend all these changes, that life is eternal. Whether life is thought of as continuing after death in the spirit plane, or that it continues through reincarnation, all the Earth traditions teach that life does not just exist in the body. Consciousness is not purely a by-product of the brain but can exist separately from the body. Through their journeys into the spirit world, shamans in all times, cultures and continents have found the same revelation – that our everyday reality is only one layer of consciousness, that there are wide and deeper states of being may be our ultimate destination.

Once, the Earth traditions were denigrated, their wisdom scorned. Today, all over the world people are recognizing the wisdom of these traditions and are returning to them. In the West, traditions such as Druidry, Wicca and goddess worship have revived our spiritual contact with nature. In the past, Native peoples were urged to embrace Western culture in pursuit of technological progress. Now people have realized that their own cultures are equally valuable. This does not mean that people want their lifestyle to remain static. While living close to the land has advantages and joys, people also want the comforts of running water, of television and the access to information and new skills that are the product of the Internet. The latter has become a major tool for many indigenous peoples who can use it to attract tourism and industrial development to their communities and can also inform people about their lives and situation when they have so too often been denied a voice.

The aim of this book has been to show the beauty and strength of the indigenous traditions around the world today. There are many that could not be included – we have not been able to include Asian or Polynesian traditions, for instance, and of the sometimes hundreds or thousands of spiritual traditions different people follow on each continent, we could describe only a few. We hope though that this book has inspired you to know more and that it may help you reflect on how you live your own life and whether there is room in it for a spirituality that reverences the Earth. We hope too that we have conveyed that our global community can be built only through respect and understanding of one another's ways of life. The time is past for one culture or religion to believe itself superior to another. It is a time for mutual learning, for only by mutual learning and communication can we solve the problems that our planet faces today.

The messages of the Earth traditions are that our planet is a beautiful place, that the gift of consciousness and all of life is a wondrous gift and that we must daily remind ourselves of the wonder of it. To be a sentient being on our beautiful Earth is a privilege and a joy and one that each of us must in our daily life strive to be worthy of:

for we are the children of Earth
and of the starry Heavens
and there is no part of us

INDEX

ACKNOWLEDGEMENTS

AKG London 10, 13l, 30t, 31, 46b, 48, 62, 64, 66, 82/83, 90, 93, 96t, 99, 100, ESA 8/9, Herbert Kraft 14, Erich Lessing 21,

Bryan and Cherry Alexander 114

Archive Photos/Jeff Greenberg 72/73

The Art Archive/Archaeological Museum Cividale Friuli/Dagli Orti 43, 49

Jean-Loup Charmet 70, 71, 79

Dee Conway 68

Corbis 139t, 140, AFP 217, Archivo Iconografico,S.A. 20, 65, 106, Tiziana and Gianni Baldizzone 115, Anthony Bannister 15, Dave Bartruff 133, Bass Museum of Art 94, Tom Bean 147, 153, 154t, 155, Nathan Benn 150, Bettmann 36, 47, 130, 139b, Bojan Brecelj 24, Barnabas Bosshart 174, The Bowers Museum of Cultural Art, Santa Ana, California 142,178/9, North Carolina Museum of Art 1, Christiana Carvalho;Frank Lane Picture Agency 107, Ric Ergenbright 58, Robert Estall 34t, Jack Fields 112, Kevin Fleming 148, Owen Franken 23t, Gallo Images; Anthony Bannister 185, ; Hein von Horsten 186, Arvind Garg 52, Raymond Gehman 76, 81b, Farrell Grehan 57b, Lindsay Hebberd 6, E.O.Hoppe 210, Jeremy Horner 165, David G.Houser 110, Wolfgang Kaehler 89t, 129, 195, Catherine Karnow 170, Peter Johnson 190, Danny Lehman 159, Charles &Josette Lenars 18, 46t, 51, 55, 85, 116, 145, 160, 175, 204, Buddy Mays 151, Stephanie Maze 171, Minnesota Historical Society 108, David Muench 134, O'Brien Productions 39, Gianni Dagli Orti 25, Diego Lezama Orezzoli 67b, Christine Osborne 201, PEMCO-Webster& Stevens Collection;Museum of History & Industry, Seattle 131, Caroline Penn 169, Premium Stock 102, Chris Rainier 202, Reuters Newmedia. Inc 61,173, Michael St.Maur Sheil 22, Kevin Schafer 166, Richard Hamilton Smith 89b, Ted Spiegel 67t ,91, Jim Sugar Photography 78t, Tim Thompson 127, Peter Turnley 84b, Penny Tweedie 206,207,218, Nik Wheeler 216, Nevada Wier 3,16, 156, Adam Woolfitt 26, 86, 101, Alison Wright 168,

Mary Evans Picture Library 32, 95

Finnish Literature Society/Timo Setala 1998, 105

Finnish National Theatre/©Leena Klemela 104

Finnish Tourist Board, London 109

Werner Forman Archive 41, 143t, 214, Alaska Gallery of Eskimo Art 118, Auckland Museum and Institute 215, Canterbury Museum Christchurch 211, Dorset Natural History & Archaeological Soc.

30b, Friede Collection, NY 180, P.Goldman Collection,London 2, 192b, Greenland Museum 119, Haffenreffer Museum of Anthropology, Brown University, Rhode Island 23b, Musees de Rennes, France 40, National Museum of Anthropology,Mexico City 5t, 158, Courtesy His Highness Oba Laoye II,Temi of Ede 191, Otago Museum 5b, 213, Peabody Museum, Harvard University, Cambridge M.A.154b, Plains Indian Museum,BBHC,Cody Wyoming 144b, Private Collection, New York 7, H.W.ReadColl.,Plains Indian Museum B.Bill Hist.Center,Cody, Wyoming 136, ©N.J.Saunders 164t, Smithsonian Institution, Washington 121, 122, Statens Historiska Museum, Stockholm 4b, 92 , 96b,97, Tara collection, NY 192, Viking Ship Museum, Bygdov, Norway 88, Museum fur Volkerkunde,Berlin 212

Fortean Picture Library/Janet & Colin Bord 38, 44, 45, Allen Kennedy 33, 42,
Lars Thomas 98

Gettyone Stone 208

Robert Harding Picture Library/Gavin Hellier 78b

Hulton Getty 29,54

Hutchison Library/A.Singer 188,189

The Image Bank/Andy Caulfield 113, The Cousteau Soc. 123, David W.Hamilton 120 , Eric Meola128, 136, Andrea Pistolesi 138, 163, Simon Wilkinson 205,

Peter Newark's American Pictures 143, 144t

Panos Pictures/ Peter Barker 56,57t, Betty Press 183, 193, Brian Goddard 60, Mark Hakkanson 200, Janie Hampton 19, Rhodri Jones 167, Bruce Paton 176, Caroline Penn 59, Giacomo Pirozzi 184, David Reed 194, Paul Smith 161, Penny Tweedie 198, 203, Rui Vieira 196, Paul Weinberg 181, 187, Ray Wood 182

Rex Features Ltd/ Sipa Press/Patrick David 132, Nigel Tisdall 124, 126

Roman Baths Museum, Bath 4t, 28

SCR Library 69, 74, 80

Science Photo Library/Roger Harris 11, Novosti 81t, 4t, John Reader 13r, Sinclair Stammers 12,

South American Pictures/Tony Morrison 162, 164b

The Travel Library/Stuart Black 34b